Cover: Look into the eyes. You could be looking at your ancestor or ancient relative. Regardless of whether a blood of kinship treks through your veins, at least some of your ancestors probably bore a similar demeanor. A firmness of gaze. Eyes that, because of primitive conditions of the time, had seen ample death at a young age and ample work. Except for the train, no transportation then moved faster than the horse – a horse, which often enough you fed, saddled, and cleaned up after. Sufficient income to be well dressed when required, never a dandy. A vest, suit, and a deliberately displayed pocket watch chain. In a studio chair of suitable style, a tasseled one at that, getting one of the few photographs ever taken of you. Properly speaking, not a photograph at all – it was printed on metal and called a tintype. A photographer could prepare and deliver the finished item to the customer in a few minutes. From about 1865 to 1910, the most popular sizes were in the neighborhood of 2.5" x 3.8," as was the one which was enlarged for this cover. Surely an expert can read the clothing and chair to better date the picture and status of the man, but let's pull 1880 out of thin air and out of equally thin air say this man was at the 80th income and wealth percentile. With the spreadsheets and data used in this book, an estimated inflation adjusted annual income for this fellow would have been about $7,300, and his net worth may well have been about $45,700. Whether you wish to look to history or to the present, we wish you the very best in your journey through the following pages. By the way, this fellow is believed to have lived in the Appalachian Mountains of Southwest Virginia – a fortunate person to live in such a nice place.

And on the rear cover there is a couple about whom you may conjecture on your own. Their image too came from a tintype.

The cover shows real people of the kind that have existed throughout time. From this starting point we go on to see how income and wealth distribution now influence us common folk and the economies we live in.

The Condensed

Distribution of Lives

Ike Jeanes

DiLives
Publishing

Published in the USA by
Dilives Inc.
Dilives Publishing
Dilives.com

ISBN-10: 0985665629 (pbk.)
ISBN-13: 978-0-9856656-2-3 (pbk.)

ISBN-10: 0985665637 (hbk.)
ISBN-13: 978-0-9856656-3-0 (hbk.)

Library of Congress Control Number: 2012946969
Library of Congress Subject Headings, Cataloging Data:

1. Equality – United States.
2. Income distribution.
3. United States -- Economic conditions -- 21st century.
4. Income distribution -- United States.
5. Wealth -- United States.

Summary: This work reveals a new method for viewing and understanding income distribution from bottom to top. It illustrates the profound adverse impact of maldistribution on individuals and the economy as a whole.

In Memory of

Frances Jeanes

Contents

What do you mean condensed *Distribution of Lives*? What if I want the whole thing?

This edition is intended for people who are interested in income distribution, but who are not interested of delving into economics and U.S. history as is done in the unabridged *Distribution of Lives*. If at a later date you want more, you can get it. The unabridged version has five chapters which in combination deal with: 1) the explicit reasons an economy needs an equitable income distribution in order to thrive, 2) the story of the Great Depression and the great lessons it provides for us in the present, 3) the history of USA distributions, and 4) reasons the 2008 Calamity occurred and could have so easily been prevented. Except for the five removed chapters, this edition is identical to the original. The unabridged *Distribution of Lives: the income maldistribution plague 2012* (ebook and pbook) contains Chapters 4, 5, 7, 8 and 9 that were removed to create this compact maldistribution story that you now have in your hands.

Ebook Tips

So that you can page through the book easily, each graph has an identification number that corresponds to the print version's page number. For example, graph-15 will occur on page 15 of the printed book. All graphs (subsequent to page 71) have been renumbered and thus are different from the unabridged version. Ebooks (whether condensed or unabridged) use the same page and graph numbering as in the unabridged book.

CH. 1

GETTING STARTED

How am I doing?
How are we doing?
How are they doing?

Whether you are at the highest reaches of society or at the lowest, you will see how income and wealth distributions alter your life. They form the vital meeting point between personal and national economics. Once we see their shape, we can see how people at all times have fared, whether it be in 1776 or in the present. On this topic, the following pages deliver greater precision than has been previously available.

Over coffee, tea, or your liquor of choice, you can speak with greater confidence. Notwithstanding more than a passing interest in this area, I could not fathom the story until the data took form. A form far clearer than I have seen before. A worldview forever changed.

Income-distribution numbers are such a disappointing collection of dubious, obscure, and insufficient data that the high-powered computer that I hear humming in the background has been grinding along for four days and nights without pause just to deliver a basic printout. Such slugging along calls out that the subject matter is not obvious.

The economic language commonly used to describe income distribution has prevented us from arriving at solutions that can be easily calculated. This book shows how you can arrive at solutions. It quickly becomes clear that the first need is to dispense with technical language. The most reliable gauge for income distribution in your nation or in your workplace is highly democratic: the percentage of total income that the bottom 60% (the clear majority) receives, abbreviated as the MAJ. This reference point shows how well corporations and nations treat the majority.

At its extremes, the MAJ *(to repeat it: the percentage of income received by 60% of the population)* can range from about 48% on the high end to about 9% on the low end. Yes, nations have existed under such widely different schemes. The worldwide historical median settles down to about 33% for the MAJ.

MAJ33, 33%MAJ, and 1/3MAJ all mean the same (pronounced $\text{MAJ}_{\text{ority}}$).*

At the time of the American Revolutionary War, the MAJ stood at about 30% in the United States and exceeded 35% in the New England States. In Europe it was stuck in the 18% to 21% range. The greater degree of fairness and liberty in the USA was a potent motivator, intellectually and economically. However, initial U.S. income equality slowly eroded until the era preceding the Great Depression when the MAJ hovered in the neighborhood of 25% in the U.S. and many other nations. The great story is that many nations, including the United States, completely reversed maldistribution by the 1950s and continued to progress toward even greater equality until the 1970s, when a few nations, including the United States, slowly moved back to pre-Great Depression levels.[1]

To change an income distribution is to change the distribution of incentives. When you reduce incentives at the MAJ in order to provide disproportional compensation at the top, the character and culture of 60% of the population changes. This book argues that maldistribution diminishes incentives for more than half of the population. It does the stockholder no good. It does the customer no good. It does the company no good. It does the nation no good.

The data is uncomplicated and straightforward. Using MAJ data is easy enough that you need not wait for governments or economists. On your own, you can easily see how changes in income and wealth distributions influence you, your family, your nation, and your world. Without information at the level of specificity provided in the spreadsheets that come with this book, it would be impossible to competently manage an economy

---

* On a few occasions, when the context implies, the expression MAJ alone without a number refers to the people in the 60% majority rather than the distribution. In this book "the majority" refers to the 60% majority.

for a democracy or to comprehend your economic place within the democracy.

Income distribution is a cultural decision. In all of recent history, highly successful nations, including the United States, have performed well when income distribution was equitable. The market economy does not necessitate maldistribution. The vast majority of high per capita income nations now have distributions roughly equal to or higher than MAJ33. Just as an equitable distribution was attractive to our forefathers, it is attractive for us. However, a 25% MAJ is a threat, and a practice.

There is a cautionary tale here that leftist revolutionaries and rightwing politicians should be well schooled in. Extreme income distributions, left or right, do not work. *The unambiguous position in this book, as will be shown in the data, is that a MAJ significantly exceeding 36% does reduce incentives for highly capable people to such an extent that the wellbeing of 60% of the population is imperiled because of a failure to adequately remunerate some of its most productive citizens. A 25% or lower MAJ is catastrophic. A MAJ in the neighborhood of 33% is reliable and appropriate.*

Albeit the cry "1/3 for the MAJ" or to state it in workaday language – "1/3 of the income for 60% of the population" – may strike you (as it did me) as being grossly unfair, revolutionaries at the right and left would find themselves to be of greatest benefit to their constituents by marching under that single uncompromising and consistent banner. The problem is a dicey one. In either a democracy or an effective market economy, an uncertain balance must be struck between sufficient compensation for the 60% majority (so that they can live productive and fulfilling lives and be rewarded for their essential work), and adequate income for those of exceptionally high ability who need to be compensated for their education, conscientiousness, responsibility, inventiveness, value to society, and sometimes difficult and hard work. Your view may be different. Examine the data. See what you think.

It is inappropriate to focus on redistribution. The focus is on giving people a realistic and honest chance, from birth to death. The primary wrong is that, at all levels, maldistribution distorts the vital relationships between people necessary for an economy to thrive. That is where the damage is done.

The USA does not now suffer from being a "mature economy." It suffers from being a maldistributed one. The market economy suffers greatly at the hands of maldistribution. Maldistribution in any nation has broadly reaching adverse tentacles – the bigger the nation, the more adverse the global impact. More positively, the long throw of United States and global history shows that prudent distributions in market economies cause nations to thrive. Maldistribution anywhere requires sensible attention and correction.

Income distribution fundamentally influences how economies perform. For too long, serious thinkers have viewed the objective of changing income distribution as allowing compassion to interfere with economic process. It has been viewed as a laudable objective to keep the topic confined to malcontents, agitators, and other undesirables outside of mainstream thinking. That view is wrong. Every citizen, every economist, and every businessperson needs to know how income distribution works.

Structure.

This work is in two parts: the words you have in your hands and separate data in spreadsheet form, which you can download and use as you see fit.[2] The spreadsheet data show outcomes produced for individuals across the spectrum: 1) at different rates of economic growth; and 2) under various conditions of income and wealth distribution. To disproportionately emphasize any of these components without taking all of them into consideration is a monstrous wrong and reliably leads to unfortunate outcomes.

When you look closely at real world income distributions, you will see variations about the trend lines. They plainly exist. The variations do not tell the story of maldistribution. The small disputatious points along the way are of little importance. The story is about enormous influences that occur because of changes in the central tendencies as maldistribution progresses or is reversed. Characteristic shapes of the curves, when implemented as they are in the real world, deliver the damages coming from maldistribution. That is the story told here.

Five years ago, I began writing the basic computer program that made this book possible. Time since then has been spent repeatedly improving programs and bringing the work to a point where maldistribution could be adequately discussed.

The spreadsheets include a USA distribution of income and wealth analysis from 1776 to the present. To the extent possible, they also include most nations of the world as far back as there was sufficient data. For nations other than the USA, the spreadsheets mainly include data going back to about 1950. The 235 years of analysis for the USA and the often 60 years for other nations are intended to provide a long-term worldwide scope of the general condition of income distribution and, at a less reliable level, wealth distribution.

It was a great, but not insurmountable, impediment that in many instances important data were unavailable. It was still possible to make inferences and interpolate between known points or mathematically combine data from several sources. I attempted to do this to the best of my ability, honestly, and without bias. There were many judgment calls. In an unknown few I will have been wrong. Those instances can be corrected when new and more complete information becomes available. But, overall, the outcome seems to give a reasonable, broad view of how we and our ancestors fared from the distant reaches of history to the present.

A key spreadsheet accompanying this book contains a sorted lookup table of 400 representative distribution curves based on thousands of income-distribution reports worldwide compiled over the past 50 years. When you hear someone mention a MAJ25 or MAJ33 (or any other specified distribution), attempt to picture in your mind the shape of the distribution curve. You can plot these curves using the lookup-table spreadsheet to see their precise shape. And you will often see these curves throughout this book. From them you can get a clear view of income distribution from bottom to top.

The lookup table shows income distributions for people along the complete percentile-scarcity scale from lowest to highest income earners (as soon will be shown). This is the go-to list for viewing central tendencies throughout all possible income distributions. Graphs in the upcoming chapter were developed from this lookup table. You too can use the table to make graphs and to answer your own questions. In most instances, the table is sufficient to describe principal features of most distribution scenarios. It is especially useful for illustrating the influence of changes in income distribution over time for people of the same ability at high scarcity levels. An abbreviated lookup table is duplicated in the Appendix.

A motivated few may want to use the data to reverse-engineer the income-distribution programs. That's fine and presumably advantageous. If you like, you may copy and publish graphs used in this book. A citation would be appreciated.[3]

A few clarifying remarks and calculations are included within reduced-sized square brackets. When you see square brackets, you can safely ignore them, unless you want to delve deeper than customarily necessary.

Kinds of distribution.

Distributions come in three distinct forms: the static case, the transitional case, and the wealth case.

The Static Case:

The static case shows how a nation is distributing income now. As long as income distribution remains unchanged, the saying "A rising tide floats all boats" applies. This is to say that at all points on the income-distribution curve, people at all strata tend to receive an equal income increase when average per capita income grows, no matter how equitable or adverse the distribution may be. For example, at a real per capita income growth rate of 1.5% (after inflation) substantially everyone's standard of living doubles each 46.6 years [2= (1+1.5%)^46.6].

The Transitional Case:

The transitional income-distribution case (such as going from a 33% to a 25% MAJ), which has been in progress in the USA since the 1970s, presents entirely different conditions. In the USA, it is now the most damaging of the three forms. For the MAJ, the transitional case adds to the insult of receiving less income, the pestilence of reducing or negating income growth. With the maldistribution transition, even when average per capita income grows, "the boats don't float evenly." People at the bottom find their incomes decrease or grow at a slow rate. Those at the high end of the curve often find their incomes growing three or more times faster than the average per capita income. Because of this great range of influence, average economic growth rates reported in the news usually have little to do with how individual families fare, whether they are at the high or low end of the spectrum.

The Wealth Case:

Lastly, there is distribution of wealth. Only when necessary will this book discuss it. The focus of this book is on INCOME distribution, not WEALTH distribution. They are vastly different. Income distribution is about getting out of the starting gate. The wealth data I have developed is not quite ready for prime time, so it is relegated primarily to spreadsheets.

Notwithstanding, a great deal of effort was spent to develop USA wealth curves that approximated known conditions during the past three decades. For earlier dates, the data is as accurate as I am now able to provide. With time, better data is apt to become available.

The Percentile-Scarcity Scale and the X$.

Within income-distribution analysis, there is a subtle and surprising point of transformative impact. There is no zero percentile. There is no 100th percentile. Conventional percentiles are limited to 99 points: 1 to 99. This is perfectly satisfactory in most instances for discussing ranking. But in all income distributions, the total of the parts must sum to 100%. Thus the conventional 99-point percentile system has an unintended adverse consequence. It does not cover the full 100 points (100%).

By using a 100-point system for income distribution instead of a 99 point system, there is a fortunate convergence. Each of the 100 points simultaneously tells two things: First, and most obviously, it tells the percentage of total income received at each point. Second, and presumably more important for most readers, the same number tells the X$ (pronounced "X" "Dollar"), which is the income multiple relative to average income.

For example, if the 95th percentile received **2.7** percent of total income, a person within the 95th percentile would also receive **2.7** times the average income (the X$). That makes the business of understanding incomes and distribution simple – the numbers are the same for the first 100 points. The majority of the data in the spreadsheets are shown in an X$ configuration. Let's look at the first and second features of the X$ in greater detail.

First feature:

With the 100-point method, the income multiples for any size group of interest up to the Top1% can be summed to determine the percentage of income earned in any subsection you want to investigate.* And you can precisely see how anyone's income stands relative to any other person. It becomes abundantly clear that the 100-point system delivers the message: *Income distribution and your income position relative to the average income are precisely the same thing.*

---

* A technical point: Observe that points numbered 100 and higher are ranks within the Top1%, as are the Lower½% and the Upper½%, and cannot be summed. Their sum is already contained within the Top1%.

In conversation, the difference between the 99 and 100-point ranking systems is slight. So, for simplicity, when using the word "percentile," this book will always refer to the 100-point system unless it explicitly states "conventional percentile" (the 99-point system).

You will notice that the 100-point ranking system is a simple percentage system where, for example, the numbers 1, 50, 95 refer respectively to the person at the 1%, 50% and 95% points.

Second feature:

The X$ is similar to the way high income is described in the media, where a CEO may be described, for example, as earning 200 times the income of the average citizen (a 200X$). The principal difference in the spreadsheets and here is that you have X$ for everyone from bottom to top, not just your CEO.

The X$ always indicates the multiple, which when multiplied by the average income, gives the income at that point. This applies whether your income is high or low. Like a balloon, you narrow it in one place; it becomes larger in another. The X$ indicates your relative standing in the economy. When your standing is unjustifiably reduced, you have good reason to be concerned.

To give hypothetical examples: In a country where $50,000 was the average income, an X$ of 10 would indicate that the annual income at this level would be $500,000 [$500,000= $50,000x10]; a 20X$ would be $1,000,000 [$1,000,000= $50,000x20]. A fractional X$ of 0.5 would denote a $25,000 income [$25,000= $50,000x0.5].*

The X$ method makes it easy to convert any currency into whatever currency you are comfortable using, whether it be dollars, yuan, yen, euros, pounds, pesos, et cetera. It also accommodates for changes in income over time. Whether the data is 50 years old or resides 50 years in the future, the same technique applies.

Or, to say it another way: The X$ is just a different form of currency. It cuts across nations and classes. It expresses how many average incomes you are earning a year. Some of those at the top might crudely argue, pay

---

* The hypothetical $50,000 average income will be used for purposes of example when dollar amounts are used in the upcoming chapter.

me a 1,000 people* a year (1,000X$) and I'll be perfectly happy. Such sentiments are not as remote as you might imagine. In the modern USA, about one-in-4-million people are at this income level.[4]

Combining the two:

Throughout this book, the Percentile-Scarcity Scale is used on the horizontal graph axis to show income from lowest to highest rank. It starts with percentages and then at the 100th position, switches to scarcity. To reiterate its construction, the scale shows percentile rankings when the number is less than 100. But when it reaches 100 or higher, it denotes scarcity. To see the Percentile-Scarcity Scale in action, glance at graph-12 (page 12; observe that graph and page numbers will always be the same). In graph-12 a low number like 95 indicates the 95th percentile, but a high number like 125 denotes the income for a person at the one-in-125-income level. Similarly 2,000 indicates a person at the one-in-2,000-scarcity level; and 1,000,000 (had it been on the graph) would have shown a person at the one-in-a-million level.

To differentiate the Top1% from one-in-a-hundred, which is a single point within the Top1% (as are all other numbers greater than 100), this book and its spreadsheets will always state "Top1%," and the simple number "100" will always refer to one-in-a-hundred.

Using MAJ income to evaluate nations.

Knowing these simple relationships illustrates the irrelevancy of average per capita GDP data, as generally reported. When evaluating nations, per capita GDP is reported as if it were the gold standard for measuring the wellbeing of an economy. If your interests are democratic, that would be far from the truth. You need to look at how each individual fares from bottom to top. The X$ puts this information in your hands.

Using MAJ designations to measure income-distribution characteristics makes it easy to perform back-of-the-napkin calculations for how the economic wellbeing of the majority changes when income distribution changes. You do not need reams of data.

Once the MAJ is known, the average income for the 60% majority can be easily calculated. Just use this formula: The average X$ for the majority = MAJ/60. The "60" refers to the 60 points represented by the majority.

---

* Or, "average incomes" if you prefer.

For example, a $45,000 average income at a MAJ25 distribution means an average $18,750 income for the majority [At a MAJ25, $18,750= $45,000*25/60]. And, in case it should cross your mind, at MAJ33 it would have been $25,000 instead of $18,750 [$25,000= $45,000 * 33.333/60].[5]

For evaluating nations, this method is far more useful than GDP per capita for telling how the majority is doing because it takes into account income distribution [Average MAJ income = GDP per capita * MAJ/60]. *Average MAJ income simultaneously measures economic vigor and income distribution.*

This formula plainly drives home the point that when economists and commentators freely talk about average income without adjusting for maldistribution, they are ignoring the wellbeing of the majority of the population. Many governments also do not seem to care much either. They often ambiguously, infrequently, and wrongly report income distribution, even in major nations.

CH. 2

A WORLD OF DIFFERENCE: one third or one fourth

Basic graphs of the 1/3 to 1/4 transition.

Many of us know about the Forbes 400, which gives a focused view of the wealth of individuals at the top in the USA. What is provided in this book and its spreadsheets is a broad estimate of income and wealth for everyone. At current population levels worldwide, I am unable to resist the temptation to glibly say the "MAJ 4 billion" [4.2= 7*60%]. To carry it to the next level, why be more attentive to the Forbes 400 than a MAJ 4 billion?

In this light, the work departs from a history told for and by the victors. Instead it finds its heart in a deliberately balanced view of everyone's position on the income scale. Regardless of the distribution curve or the transition between distribution curves, there are discernible threads. We can see their influence as we move from equitable MAJ distributions to maldistributed MAJs.

To draw focus to the influence of the downward transition toward maldistribution, the move from a 33% to a 25% MAJ over 30 years will be the case illustrated in this chapter. As seen in the next two graphs (#12 & #14), income levels are expressed as a multiple of the average income using an X$ designation.

The differences between MAJ33 and MAJ25 income distributions are so great that they cannot be easily represented on a single graph. In the following graph-12, we start with the upper 5% of income earners comparing earnings on the MAJ25 and MAJ33 distribution curves. The MAJ of 33%

income remains in approximately the same range as at a MAJ of 25% at the low end of this graph.

#12

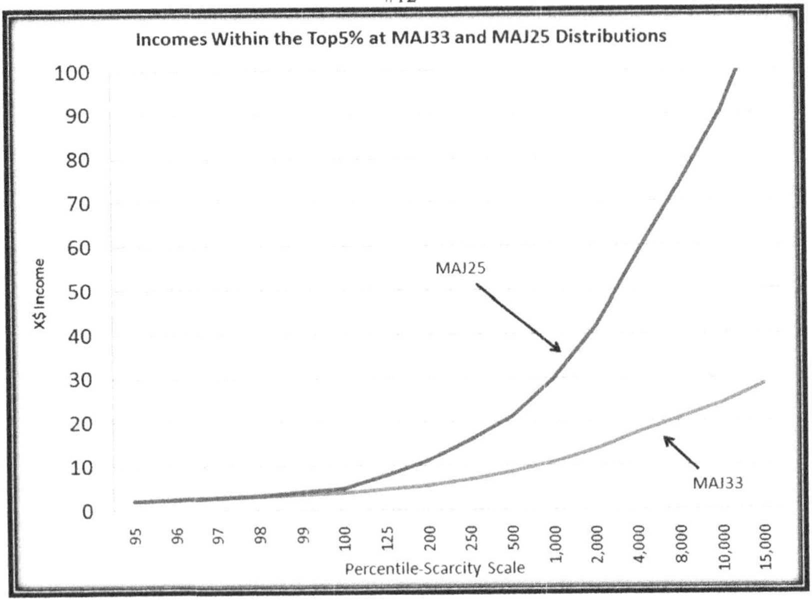

But as scarcity increases, the incomes on the two curves diverge widely. By the time a person reaches the one-in-10,000-income-scarcity level, the income at MAJ33 is a 24.3X$ and the income at MAJ25 is a 90.7X$. To familiarize you with the process, this would mean that a person classified at an ability equivalent to a one-in-a-thousand-scarcity level would tend to earn $1,213,000 at MAJ33 versus $4,537,000 at MAJ25 [$1,213,000= $50,000 x 24.3 and $4,537,000= $50,000 x 90.7]. In short, a person of the same ability earns vastly different amounts based on the prevailing income-distribution culture.*

Keeping the MAJ share of income low has substantial advantages for those at the top. Those advantages progressively increase as scarcity increases. Keep in mind that a person who truly possesses economically desirable abilities that are so rare as to be present in only in one in 10,000 people – presumably by his or her merit – is contributing greatly to how

---

* Using this same method as in the first graph-12 but looking explicitly at U.S. history in the spreadsheets (not in the graphs here), a person at the one-in-a-million level of income ability in the USA would have tended to earn roughly 128 times as much as the "average income person" in 1977, but in 2007, would have tended to earn about 661 times as much.

the economy and society operates. The objective is not to begrudge that person high compensation. However, maldistribution results in overcompensating all of those high scarcity levels, whether they possess economically desirable characteristics or not. This is seen in the above graph-12 by the difference between the lower and upper curve.

Maldistribution gains accrue primarily to the Top1%, most particularly the upper half percent. To continually say "upper half percent" and "lower half of the Top1%" exercises the tongue excessively. To get around it, the two halves of the Top1% are referred to as the "Lower½%" and the "Upper½%," notwithstanding that those in the "Lower½%" usually do quite well.

Whenever you think of the Top1%, keep in mind that the dividing point between the Lower½%, and Upper½% is the one-in-200-scarcity level [scarcity= 1/(1-percent probability); 200= 1/(1-95.5%); Upper½%= 100%-95.5%]. The same number of people within the Top1% exist on each side of this point. The numerous points within the Upper½% displayed in the graphs serve to show the range of income within the Upper½%.

The teeter point.

Now that we have looked at the upper portion of the curves, we will turn our attention to the lower portion. But before doing so let's consider how analyzing income-distribution curves differs from most forms of economic analysis where you need to control for various factors and you usually need to qualify your analysis with a variety of hedging statements.

In a pleasant contrast to ambiguity, the nice point with income-distribution curves is that you do not need to control for other components because the data is already isolated to reflect income distribution alone. Whether you are a labor union member, a CEO, an economist, or an interested citizen, you can easily reference the spreadsheet lookup table and compare different MAJ-defined income-distribution curves.* With simple access to the curves, you can speak with great authority, even when you don't have economic training. Often you can make broad categorical statements when discussing income distribution that are not possible in other forms of economic analysis, as you will see from time to time in the following pages. Graph-14, for example, gives a definitive picture.

---

*My curves and curves based on other studies are included in the spreadsheets. The Congressional Budget Office data (first released in Oct. 2011), in my view, presents the most credible full-range U.S. 1979-2006 data now available, as discussed in greater detail in the Appendix.

In it, the wedge-like separation between the curves at all points lower than the 92nd percentile shows the loss sustained as a direct result of going from a MAJ33 to a MAJ25. The bottom 92% lose so that the top 8% can gain.

#14

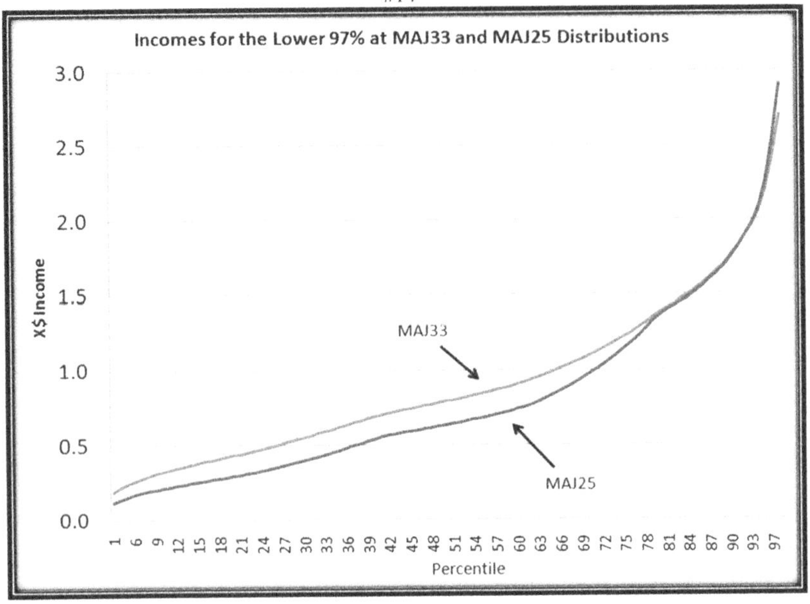

Think of the old seesaw. In income distribution, the teeter point is like a seesaw fulcrum. On one side you have the rich and near-rich. On the other side you have everyone else. The teeter point can occur anywhere between the 82nd and 92nd percentile. Because of its centrality we will often refer to the teeter point when discussing income distributions. The invariant rule is that those beneath the prevailing teeter point are harmed by maldistribution. Those above it benefit.

There is a zone of indifference where income-distribution changes have slight influence. If we take a 6% income change as an arbitrary threshold sufficient to be significant, then those from about the 76th to 96th percentile (1/5th of the population) would be indifferent to changes produced by transitions in income distribution. As you can see in the above graph-14, the two curves are practically indistinguishable within this range. The sum of the incomes for this 1/5th of the nation would remain approximately constant at 34.8% during a move from MAJ33 to MAJ25.

Given that the 34.8% income share for this 1/5th of the population is greater than the income share (33% or 25%) for the 60% majority (either at

MAJ33 or MAJ25), this mid-region can be a political status quo deadweight that can readily align with the highest earners who receive the huge bounty from maldistribution. This midrange mainly comprises highly responsible people. If they extrapolate from their own income conditions, they are apt to be disinclined to take great interest in income-distribution issues.

Notwithstanding that the damage becomes increasingly intense beneath the 72nd percentile, the 60% majority is apt to face daunting opposition at MAJ25 because the zone of indifference is so large (graph-14 and 16). The slim hope for the 60% majority resides in those people within the zone of indifference being concerned about the problem, and those at the top also seeing the impropriety of receiving a disproportionately large share.

A change in income distribution is a society-wide decision to increase incentives for one sector and reduce incentives for another. Explicitly, you cannot increase incentives at any point on the scale without reducing incentives elsewhere because a total income pie must be divided. And it must mathematically sum to 100%.

A maldistribution transition subverts the normally beneficial influence of Adam Smith's "invisible hand" for the narrow purpose of providing advantages for the wealthy alone.*

The following graph-16 shows a large range from those at the bottom up to the one in 200 scarcity point. The MAJ are the first 60 points on the Percentile-Scarcity Scale. As seen in the graph-16, all points in the MAJ (points beneath 61) are having their status reduced at least 18% by moving to MAJ25, and in some instances more than 40%. The influence is not abstract.

Once the MAJ income share plummets to 25 or there about, the 60% majority is no longer a player in the economic system to the degree it once was. The opportunities that allowed it to contribute to the vitality of the nation have been removed. This observation is not overlooked by families. They can see that their parents and grandparents walked with their heads higher and with greater pride – a sense of accomplishment and wellbeing for having been able to contribute a greater share to the nation.

---

* By way of introduction for those of you who are not economists, Adam Smith was one of the great broad-minded figures of the Enlightenment who wrote an influential book, *The Wealth of Nations* (1776). His work illustrated how the market economy, by free interactions of people to buy and sell goods, tended to be of widespread benefit to all. Much economic theory can be traced back to him.

Your income reflects the degree to which you contribute to the economy (GDP), and often by extension to society as a whole – what you build and what you leave behind. The majority in former generations (particularly in the 1950s-1970s in the U.S.) contributed relatively more to society and to the nation than their descendants have had the opportunity to do. The 60% majority experiences it today, as do their children. They have been crushed by a process so tortuously slow that it was barely perceptible, until the damage was done. It was an exercise of poorly performed Bonsai economics – small changes over long periods of time that radically changed the ultimate configuration; an exercise that needs to be reversed.

#16

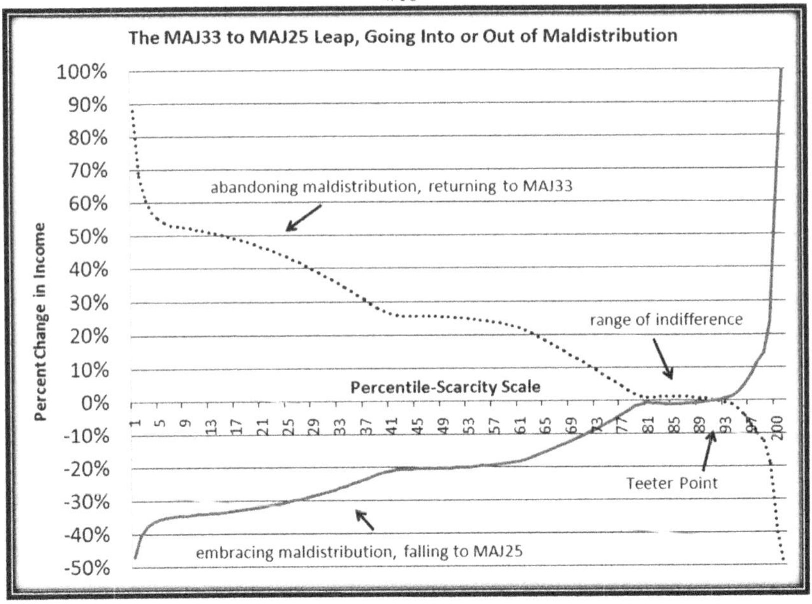

As shown in the graph-16 at all points beneath 60 on the Percentile-Scarcity Scale, abandoning maldistribution would increase the majority's income at least 22%, and for most people in this region, the increase would be considerably greater.

The point should not be lost on the 92% of the population that their income, too, would increase as the conditions at the MAJ improve. The focus on the MAJ carries with it the implicit changes throughout the continuum along the income-distribution curve.

You can DIY (Do It Yourself). To address scenarios of your own, you can develop graphs similar to the above by using the spreadsheet lookup table. The first curve was produced by dividing the MAJ33 curve by the

MAJ25 curve; the second, by dividing the MAJ25 curve by the MAJ33 curve. It's quite easy. No need to wait for governments or economists to do it for you.

Above and beneath the teeter point.

#17

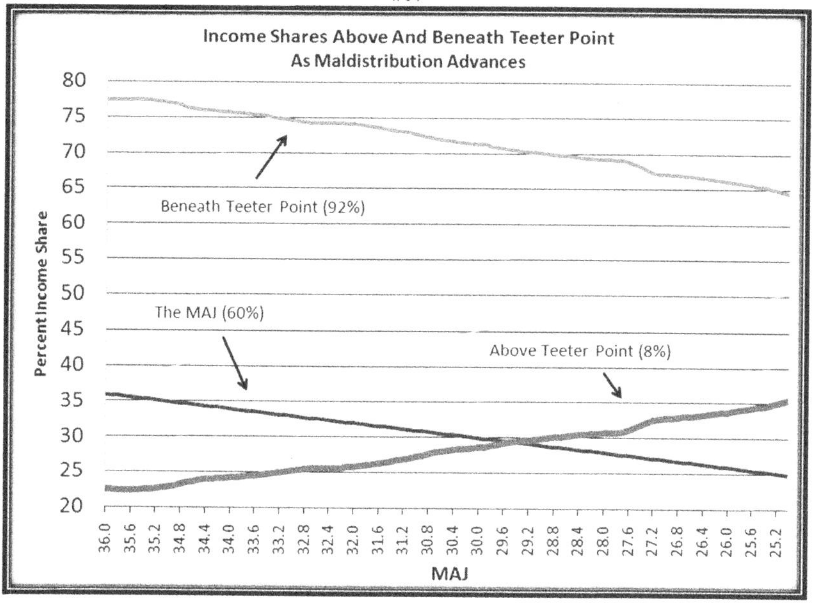

In graph-17, we can see how income shares change above and beneath the teeter point as maldistribution advances. Ninety-two percent of the population lose 10.6% of their income share by going from MAJ33 to MAJ25. At a MAJ 29.5, the upper 8% of the population get the same income share as the bottom 60%. By MAJ25, the upper 8% receive 10.5% more of the income than all of the bottom 60% together.

Unemployment trumped by maldistribution.

There is important work to be done at all levels. The degree to which income is reduced by virtue of moves toward maldistribution results in a loss of status for the 60% majority and all others beneath the teeter point. It reduces the degree to which they are afforded the opportunity to contribute to the economy. Assuming a generation to be about 26 years, the 30-year transition discussed here is slightly longer than a single generation.[6]

Many people living today have never seen a fair distribution. Instead, they are now living with an income distribution that has resulted in their incomes being a fraction of what they should be, as the following graph-18 zooms in to show.

Let's pause and consider the following graph-18 from a different angle. In the news, we hear repeated reports about employment rates. In the 1990s, U.S. unemployment rates looked fine. Yet this era created an economy based on low wages for most workers that sharply contrasted with their formerly better and steadier blue-collar jobs.[7] Often in economic theory and policy, full employment is a guiding mantra; but for the majority, it was maldistribution, not unemployment, that sucked out the lion's share of income.

#18

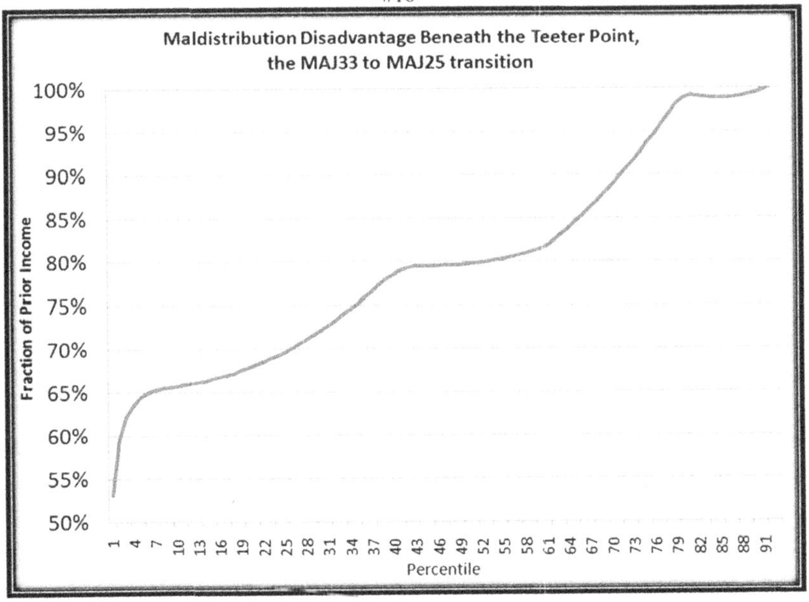

The economics of full employment has taken our eye off the ball. Unemployment rates vary and there is the expectation that difficult periods will be ameliorated in the future. *Not only is maldistribution usually more devastating than common variations in unemployment, it is persistent.* In the transition to a MAJ25, the 60% majority has been hit harder by maldistribution than by the absence of full employment. As seen in graph-18, some members of this class have been trampled.

If we ask ourselves, "Is unemployment the key issue?", perhaps numbers tell a story. A 10% unemployment rate represents a 5.5% increase over customary unemployment [at a structural unemployment* of 4.5%, 10=

---

* Structural unemployment in the formal sense refers to a mismatch between labor demand and worker skills or location. Frictional unemployment relates a normal time lag between a worker searching for a job and finding one. However, for purposes of this book, I refer to structural unemployment

4.5+5.5]. Using back-of-the-napkin techniques, a 5.5% increased unemployment for the MAJ translates into about a 5.5% loss of income for the MAJ. A MAJ25 *unremittingly and in every year and in every future year* takes away 25% of the income they would have received at MAJ33 [-25%= 25/ 33.333-1]. Which do you prefer – a 5.5% transitory loss in income or a 25% permanent loss in income?

If the economy had stayed at a MAJ33, the 60% majority would have had an income, on average, one third higher than it now is (note the gain of ⅓ is greater than the loss of ¼ because the base was reduced to such a small number). In many instances, the ⅓ gain would have been sufficient to have avoided going heavily into debt, or to raise children so that they had greater advantages, and _____ well, you fill in the blank yourself. A one third higher income would have spelled vast advantages for this class. Just think how an instant one third income raise for the rest of your life would influence you [⅓= 33.3%= 33.333/25-1; -¼= (25/33.3333)-1].

#19

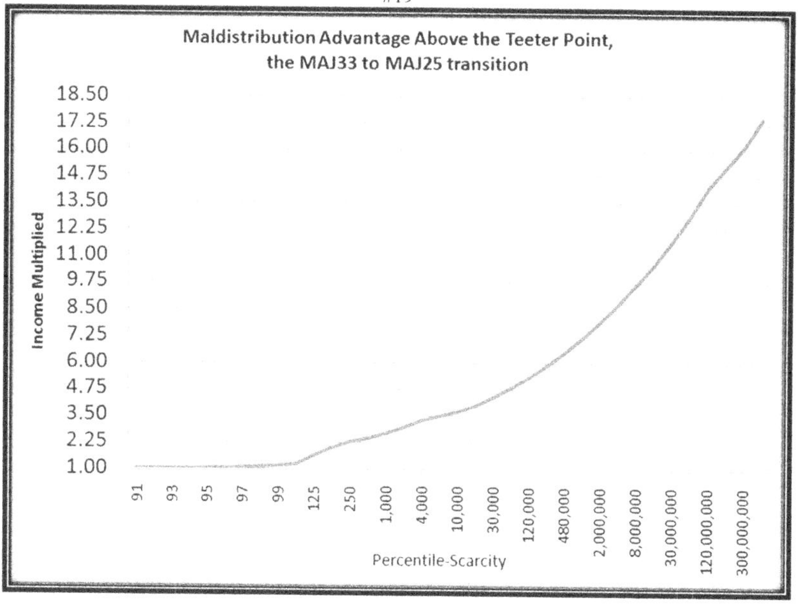

By contrast to circumstances at the MAJ, the income at the one-in-a-million-scarcity level is 7.2 times greater at MAJ25 than at the old and quaint MAJ33. Maldistribution enthusiasts have developed an economy where advantages accrue, as shown in the above graph-19.[8]

(4.5%) as that small remaining group of jobseekers who (for whatever reason – frictional, structural, or otherwise), are customarily unemployed during a thriving "full-employment" economy.

Now that you have seen key maldistribution features, but before you invest more of your time, it seems appropriate that a few remarks about the method should be provided. *But if you detest math and details, please skip the following Technical Remarks and move on to Standard of Living.*

A few technical remarks.

To determine the general characteristic of the distribution in each nation, a 100-point mathematical backbone is constructed. This backbone defines the exact total percentage of income received by the MAJ segment and each of the remaining two groups (quintiles) above it. Only two specially derived technical numbers are required to define the backbone curve for each nation. The backbone always delivers the precise income shares for the above three segments of the curve – in short, the full basic distribution curve. When deviations from the backbone exist, the backbone can be bent. For example, it can be bent at the lowest quintiles (1/5ths) or at the upper reaches of the curve if data from the particular nation or other data in similar distributions warrant it. This is the logic behind the shape of the first 100 points on the income-distribution curves you will see throughout the book.

Methods originating with Pareto are usually used for analyzing the Top1% of income earners.[9] The programs I wrote do not use Pareto numbers.

The income distribution within the Top1% is of such vast range that a separate dedicated method is necessary to uncover the full distribution there. From good and recent works on income distribution within the Top1%, we have data showing income shares received by the upper and lower half of the Top1%. From this we can create a moving average Top/Bottom Ratio [Upper½%/Lower½%] trend line, and where warranted, extend or modify it.

Mathematically, the Top1% method is grounded in the precept that scarcity and income scale at different rates, and that scaling is modulated. The computer program then satisfies three objectives:

1) It anchors the low end of the Top1% curve at the one-in-a-hundred value established by the backbone and its bending.
2) It delivers a distribution curve where the Top/Bottom Ratio is substantially the same as the intended ratio. This ensures that the income allocated for the two halves of the Top1% are appropriately allocated.

3) The method accounts for income by summing the incomes of each hypothetical person in the Top1% of the population to ensure that the total of their incomes indeed exactly sums to the income share allocated to the Top1%.

Any method that cannot deliver on these three minimum requirements is footed in fiction. All the curves shown here have passed the test.

When the Top1% method is used in combination with the backbone, a complete distribution curve from top to bottom can be produced from five numbers alone: two for the backbone and three for the Top1%. If the backbone is to be bent, then the percentage received by any of the lower three quintile, the Top5%, or the Top1% can be also be used. Population size is required. Interpolation is not used within any portion of the method. That is all there is to it.

The 400 case lookup table illustrates median central tendencies – enough to approximately indicate what a distribution usually means for the complete population. The cases are also identified by the Gini index (a technical number widely used in the field to measure inequality), which is calculated for each of the distribution curves.[10] This makes it possible to cross-reference the lookup curves with distributions reported elsewhere. In historical data, there are, of course, deviations from the lookup table.

In instances where the Top1% value deviates from the represented case, a technician can readily employ the values shown at scarcity points of 100 and higher and marry them with previously known distributions to get a first approximation for distribution at high scarcity levels. This technique was never used with any data in this book, but without dedicated income-distribution computer programs, it may provide adequate first approximations. Such cutting and pasting can create distorted representations because the shape of each curve is determined by values within the Top2%. Please keep in mind the focus in this book is on the representative cases that would interest most readers, not the deviations from them.

Now we return to the business at hand.

Standard of living.

To have an intuitive grasp on how the downward transition in income distribution interacts with an average per capita growth rate of 1.5%, the following graph-22 illustrates the years required to double income, and thus presumably, standard of living.

#22

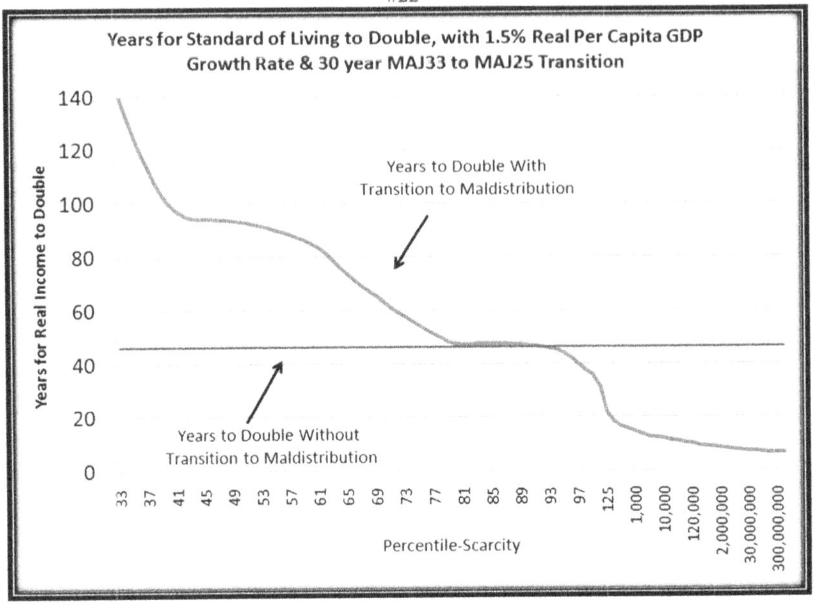

When income distribution is held constant and per capita income grows at a 1.5% rate, all segments on the distribution curve double their income in 44.6 years. However, with the maldistribution transition, the rich are able to double their standard of living much faster. At the one-in-a-thousand-scarcity level, the standard of living doubles every 21.3 years. For those at the one-in-60,000-scarcity level, income doubles every ten years. The maldistribution blessing is bestowed on them.

But for those in the MAJ, it would require a minimum of 70 years to double standard of living. For those at the 40th percentile, doubling standard of living would take a century. For those lower on the scale, the figures are so sad that I cannot bring myself to write them. If the rate of downward movement continued for a century more at the same rate as in the case of a MAJ33 going to a MAJ25 over 30 years, it would ultimately reduce the MAJ to a brutal 9.6% – a figure that a few barbaric nations have attained. Presumably the leadership is raised from its slumber before that point, and the disaster is put to an end [annual reduction in the MAJ equals 0.990459731= (25/33.33)^(1/30); 9.6= 25*(0.990459731 ^100)].

Graph-22 tells the story of how the move to maldistribution, even in the face of economic growth, influences different individuals in the economy. The way one views the future depends on rank – grim at the bottom, bright at the top.

There is a window of opportunity. If the downward transition in the majority's income share is completely halted, then there is an instant remedy, at least in part: The standard of living doubles for everyone each 46.6 years. *Maldistribution alone is evil, but a constantly increasing maldistribution is the nail in the coffin.*

Accelerating or retarding income growth rates via the maldistribution transition.

It is too easy to have inflated expectations about economic growth. Business and economic news often report glorious advances in one index or another. But over the long throw of a generation or more (including booms, busts, inflation, and population growth), the average real growth in per capita Gross Domestic Product now often falls in the neighborhood of 1.5% annually in the United States.

#23

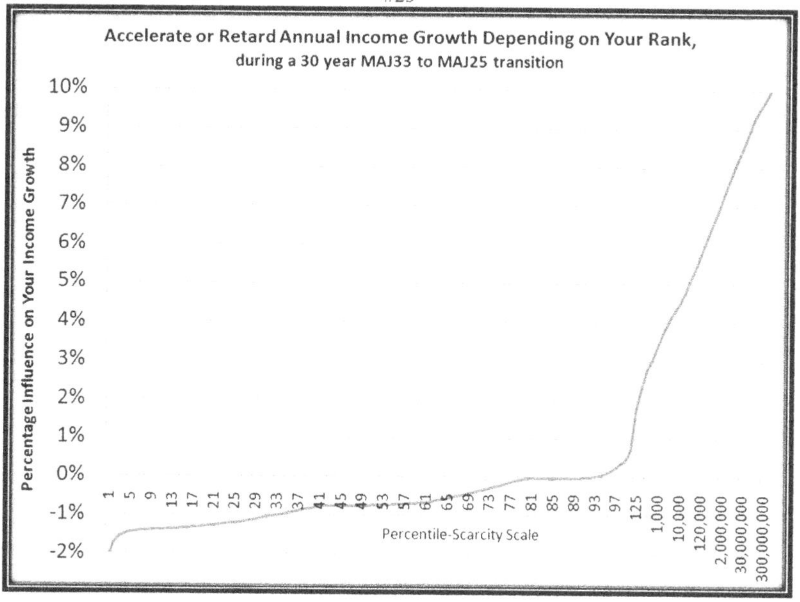

At the high perch of one-in-a-million, you would receive a windfall 6.8%+ income growth produced by the maldistribution transition alone, over and above your ordinary 1.5% GDP per capita growth (graph-23). On the other hand, for two-thirds of the population, the brakes are forcefully applied (graph-24). For them, more than a half a percent of growth is lobbed off the meager 1.5% growth. They are lucky if they can squeeze out a 1% annual growth. Most do worse.

#24

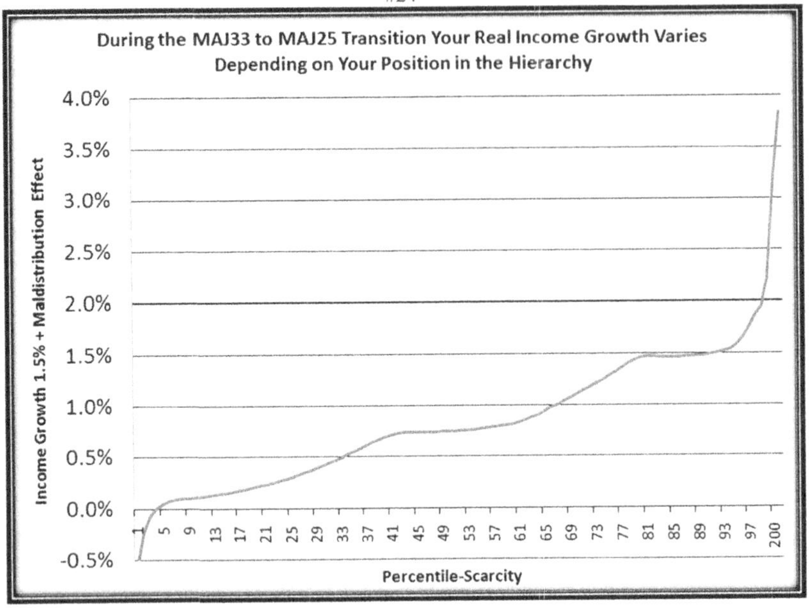

The increased rate of income growth as a consequence of the maldistribution transition is so great for the highest income groups that they receive increased immunity from periods of low economic growth and recessions. A decision-maker who is not sharing the full consequences of his decisions is well recognized as placing the entire system at risk. For example, consider an airplane mechanic who repairs an airplane on which he and his family are frequent passengers. The smart money will bet that he is likely to be particularly attentive and careful on that plane.

The high earners in a market economy are the crowd making key economic decisions. Their airplane has always flown nicely, whether they are attentive to the needs of others or not. To have decisions shaped by the maldistribution incentive – would that be perilous for the rest of us? Let the deep thinkers study it. A quick answer from the rest of us should suffice.

It is no longer exclusively a market economy for the rich. It is a maldistribution economy. Their monetary incentive is to promote it. After a 1.5% normal per capita growth rate is added to the maldistribution transition outcome, income growth across the spectrum looks like the above graph-24. The curve is truncated to focus on the majority of people.

The following graph-25 draws focus to the remarkable story that very few people experience the average growth rates reported in the news or in economic and business literature. To be precise, only one-tenth of us experience the average growth rate as evidenced by the flattening at the 1.0 multiplier.

#25

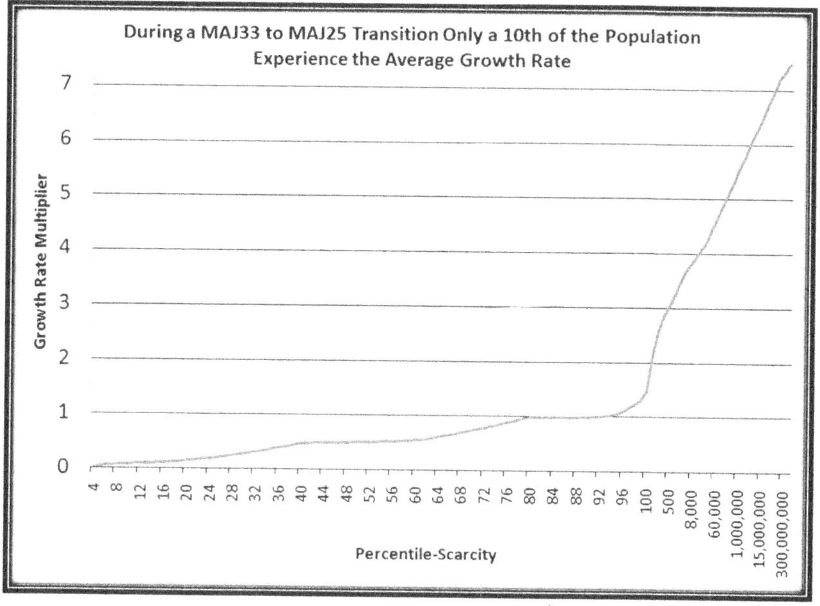

People at the one-in-125-scarcity level more than double their real income growth during the MAJ33 to MAJ25 transition. By the time you get to the one-in-a-million level, your growth rate is 5.5 times faster than the average. All key leaders in the economy above this point gain more (and in some cases much more) by promoting decisions and policies that accelerate maldistribution than they do by employing honorable means to increase their income. *Maldistribution is oligarchy capitalism. It is vastly different from equitable free market capitalism.*

The principle of equal opportunity for all is obviously sacrificed in a 30-year maldistribution transition. Those at the top advance spectacularly. Those in the bottom 75% majority are crucified. Adam Smith's free market relies on motivated self-interest to produce a desirable outcome. His guiding principle is turned on its head by ever-increasing maldistribution. A person at the high strata can achieve far more by increasing maldistribution than by pursuing customary honorable income growth.

Disruption of status among highest earners.

The fracturing of relationships between low and high earners as maldistribution progresses is well known. To the extent that social relations are enhanced when people are of roughly the same economic class and that they are reduced when people are of vastly different economic strata, maldistribution disrupts the relationship among people of certifiably high levels of scarcity and ability.

#26

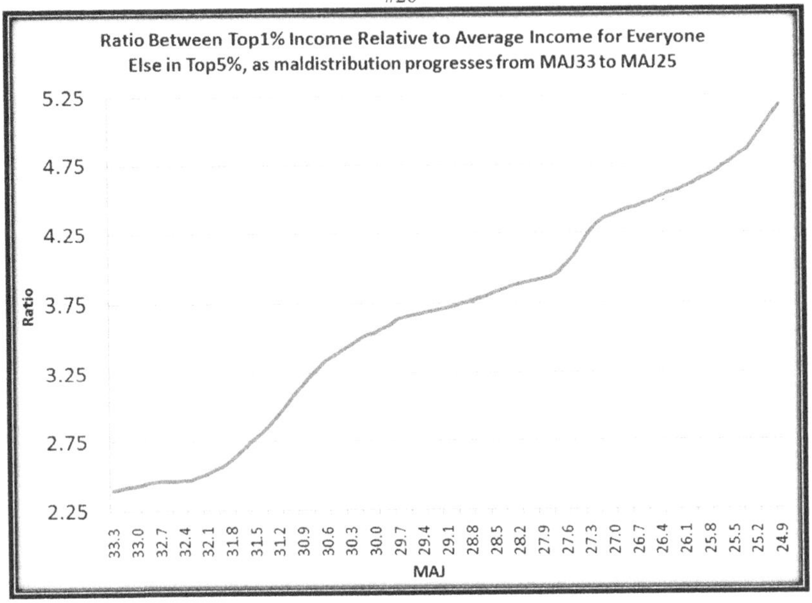

A fracturing of great importance also occurs within the Top5%. Prior to maldistribution, the ratio between the income of the Top1% and rest of those in the Top5% was about 2.5 to 1. By the time one reaches MAJ25, this ratio is almost 5 to 1. The status of everyone else relative to the Top1% plummets as illustrated in the above graph-26.

It is a common misconception that maldistribution results only because there is a great divide between people of low or intermediate status (say a person at the median) and those of elevated status and ability. True enough, there are usually vast differences in ability and justifiable differences in remuneration between these two groups which can be accentuated by lack of education and lack of abilities at the low end. However, it is wrong to think maldistribution is exclusively caused by the difference in true abilities or education, or that maldistribution can reliably be corrected by educating those of lower rank or by increasing their productivity. History teaches us that maldistribution marches to its own drummer.

A distinction should be drawn between a component like education that is needed for economic growth and the influence that education may separately have on maldistribution. Education and productivity are, of course, necessary for economies to advance, but recent U.S. history has shown increasing productivity and rising educational levels have taken place at the same time that maldistribution worsens. Maldistribution is defined by shifting incentives along the curve to disproportionately benefit the upper strata rather than any lower strata.

Ruling the roost.

Maldistribution increases the spread between those of high rank and anyone of lower rank. The increasing spread is evident within the upper reaches of the Top1% earners. This spread is especially clear when you examine the 400-case lookup table in the files accompanying this book.

#27

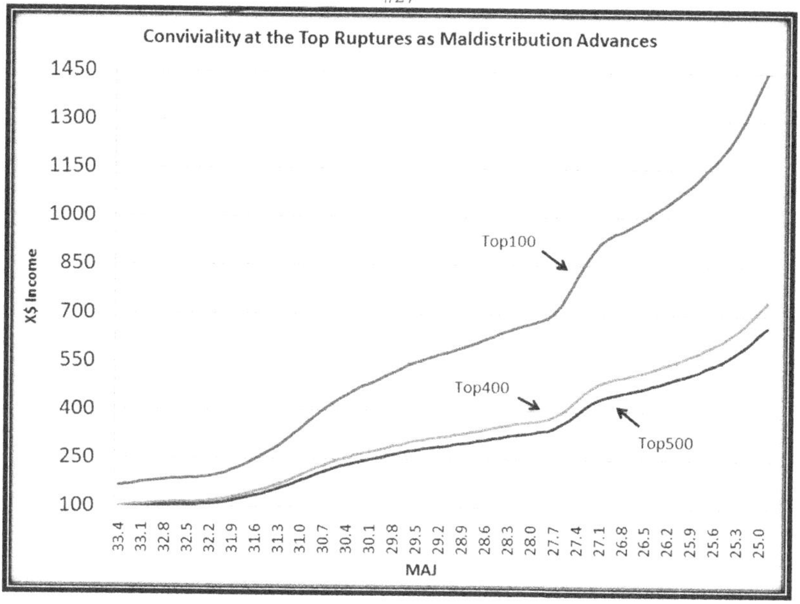

As can be seen in graph-27, at MAJ33 and thereabouts, the Top100 earners are close to others within the Top500 subgroup; but by a MAJ25 distribution, the spread increases substantially.

Similarly, the following graph-28 compares the income of a person at a one-in-500-scarcity level with a person at a one-in-240,000 level. We see that at MAJ33, the higher-income person's income is 8.3 times more than his lower-earning colleague; but at MAJ25, it is a whopping 20x greater.

#28

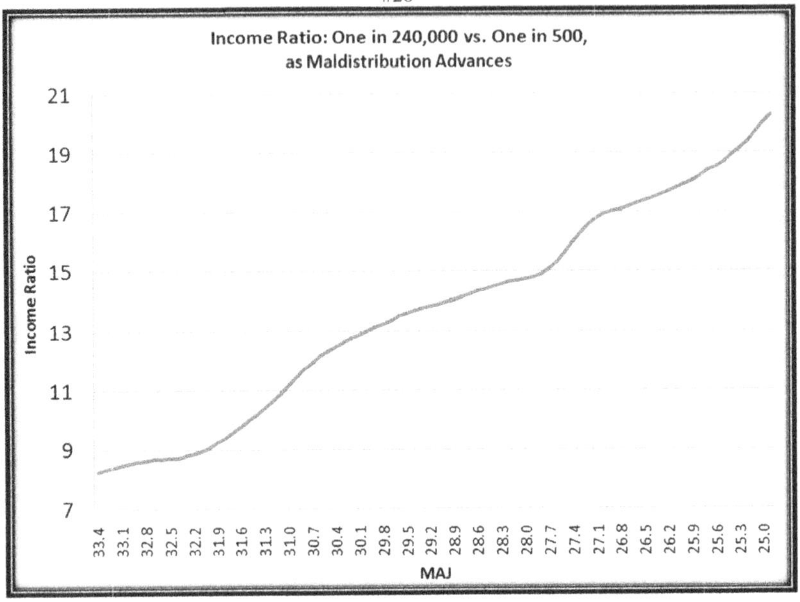

The spread between these two was always large. But ask yourself: At MAJ25 did the lower income person at the one-in-500 rank suddenly become less intelligent, less able, less productive, or less educated? Hardly.

No economic necessity or proper working of the market economy compels the increasing spread. When it occurs, it is a cultural decision – the maldistribution ethic. With maldistribution, these spreads enlarge between any higher and lower income person, independent of any change in the scarcity of abilities that are brought to the marketplace. If you want to get a visceral feeling of how great the spread between the super-rich and common folk can be in some instances, take a look at Jamie Johnson's DVD "Born Rich."

It is a dangerous spread because it increases the domination of the few (whether within the executive suites or elsewhere), and because it increases dominance of a few lucrative sectors over other sectors that may be of greater true value to the economy.

It makes it easy for a high-income bond trader to look contemptuously at a manufacturer who struggles to keep an organization together that does not bring in the big bucks, but that does employ workers and does produce a product. In view of many such businesses being abandoned, the arguments favoring maldistribution hardly benefit nations or their people. Consider career choices. A future physician may become a bond trader.

Maldistribution distorts proper relationships. Irrationality, already abundantly available, tends to become increasingly concentrated at the top. In a "wiki" thinking world where the contributions of widely diverse people, the wisdom of crowds, emergence, and complexity drive societies, a reduced incentive for the majority is antithetical.

Taking a peak at the Top1%.

We know more about the Top1% than ever before, thanks to Emmanuel Saez, Thomas Piketty, and others who have thoroughly studied top income earners.[11] They have provided a huge service to everyone by doing so. Their work has made it possible to estimate the all-important ratio between the income of the Upper½% and the Lower½% in the Top1% – a ratio which is central to the computer programs I write.

#29

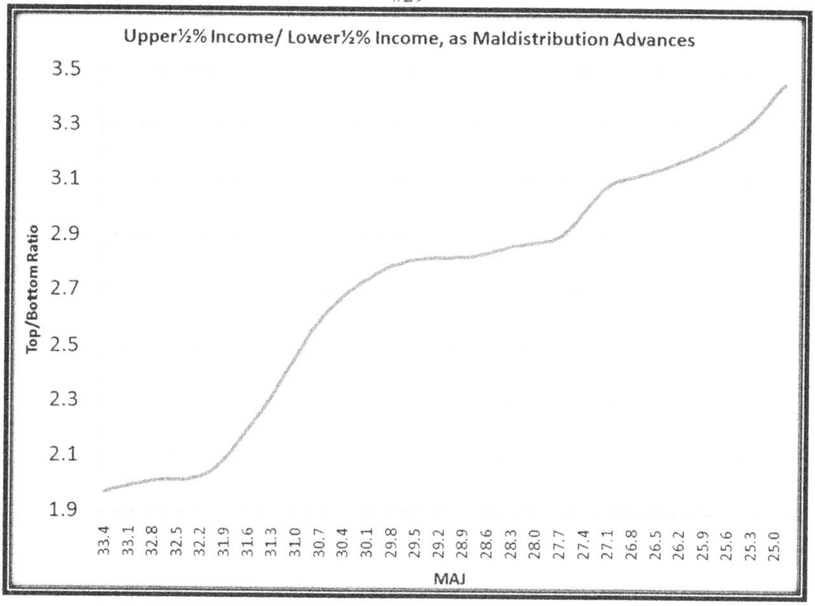

This ratio in many nations is entirely unreported and unstudied. The job of illustrating central tendencies in the Top1% will never be completely known until all governments are forthcoming. Governmental income-distribution reports need to be adequately audited and contain Top1% income data of the kind you have seen in the spreadsheets.

The above graph-29 shows an estimated smoothed trend line for the Top/Bottom Ratio. You will see those at the Upper½% not only distance themselves from mere mortals at lower percentiles, they also increasingly distance themselves from the Lower½%. The ratio becomes ever-greater as maldistribution advances.

At the distribution ranges that we have been primarily considering – MAJ33 and MAJ25 – the ratios between the Upper½% and Lower½% are approximately 1.98 and 3.40, respectively.

The ratio has a practical back-of-the-napkin importance because, without difficult computations, it can be used to quickly determine the average X$ income for the Lower½% and Upper½% sections of the Top1% [Lower½% X$= 2*(Top1%/(1+ratio)); Upper½% X$= Lower½% X$*ratio].

#30

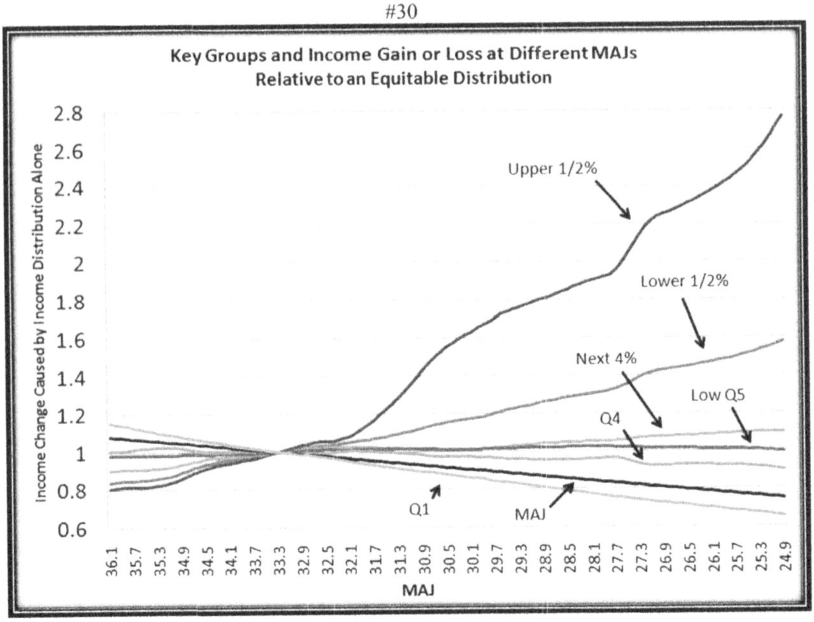

From the highest to lowest segments, all major segments of income earners are shown in the above graph-30. On the right side of the graph, they are represented in descending order from those who benefit the most to those who are hurt the most. On the left side of the graph, the graph lines are mirrored and inverted. Points in close proximity to MAJ33, whether to the right or left, are reasonably equitable.

We see at MAJ25 that the obvious maldistribution gainers, the Upper½% and Lower½% incomes, are in each year respectively 1.6 and 2.8 times higher than they would have been under MAJ33. At one step down in the hierarchy, the average income increase for the Next4% (the four percentage points beneath the Top1%) does not tend to exceed 10%. The incomes for the Low Q5 (everyone in the top 1/5 less the above top5% already graphed) are in a more ambiguous state, sometimes increasing 2% and at other times losing a half percent. All other groups are solid losers. Q4 (the next lower 1/5th of the population) loses of its 10% income. The MAJ income falls 25%. Income for Q1, the lowest 1/5th, drops 35%.

The group averages shown in the chart identify the influence on different segments; but as you have already seen, it is necessary to drill down to the X$ for each individual to comprehend the full range of incomes within any segment.

Who smiles? Happiness.

Kahneman and Deaton have done valuable work on economically induced happiness.[12] They indicate that a logarithmic principle applies to how we emotionally respond to income. This principle, Weber's Law, also applies elsewhere. For example, the relationship between stimulus and perception such as vision (brightness) and sound (intensity) is logarithmic. Kahneman and Deaton make the important observation that a person's sense of emotional well-being (happiness) in the U.S. *does not* continue to increase beyond a $75k income. But on the other hand, they observe that one's evaluation of life (sense of satisfaction) *does* continue to advance without stopping as income increases. These general tendencies have been noted to apply worldwide.

I do not pretend to be a deep thinker in the happiness field, but it struck me that the analysis here of income distribution serves nicely as a means to explore – let's call it – economically induced overall happiness. In a nub, this is the measure of happiness, shown in the upcoming graphs. It is simply the average of the "emotional well-being" and "sense of satisfaction", each being logarithmically determined [log(income)], but the former not advancing further once it reaches the designated stop point ($75k in the U.S.).

In poor, maldistributed nations, unhappiness can accrue both from a low average income for the nation and from the influence of maldistribution. In the spreadsheets, happiness is shown to reflect these influences. But in the following graphs, average income is held constant so that we can see the influence that maldistribution *alone* would be expected to have on happiness.

In the following graph-32A, 1.00 is the average national happiness at MAJ33. Even in nations with the most even of distributions, average happiness can advance no more than 2.2% above the national MAJ33 happiness. However, beneath MAJ33 maldistribution can reduce happiness in a nation by 9% in the most unequal nations.

#32A

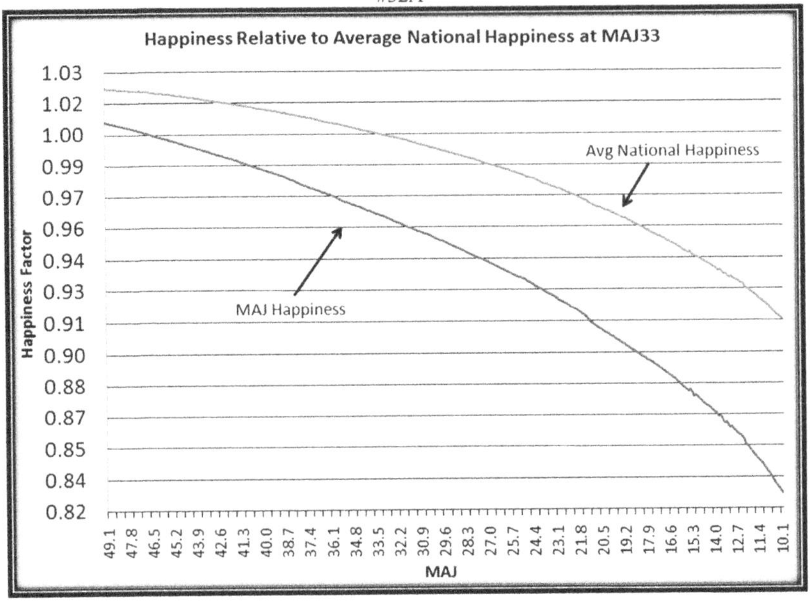

Happiness for the majority is always less than average national happiness because income at the MAJ is always less than the nation's average income. We see this principle in all lookup-table X$ curves.

In the following graph-33B, when we focus on the MAJ36 to MAJ21 range (instead of the full range shown previously) and look at the relationship in a slightly different manner, we see that national happiness falls 1.98% and MAJ happiness falls 3.18% once MAJ25 is reached. At MAJ10 (beyond the range of graph-33B), MAJ happiness drops 14% beneath the MAJ33 level.

As shown in the graph-32A and 33B, the opportunities for increasing happiness via more equal distributions exist primarily when nations are gripped by maldistribution. Once MAJ33 is reached, national happiness can only be increased slightly via changes in income distribution.

#33B

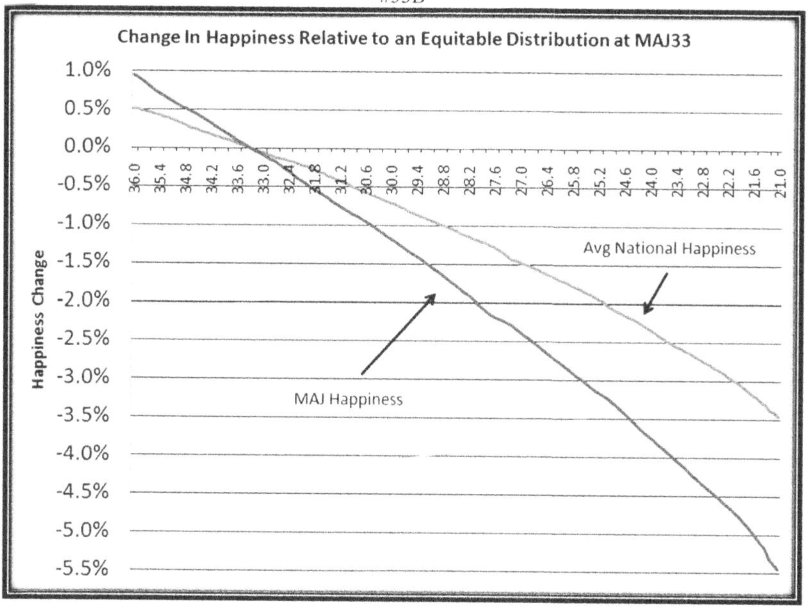

#33C

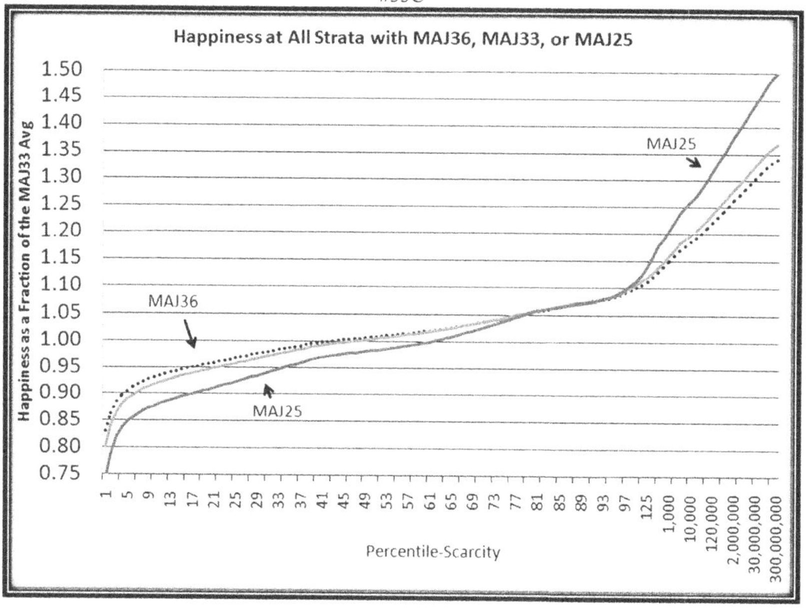

Taking a look at three curves – MAJ36 (maximum prudent equality), MAJ33 (the proposed fair case), and MAJ25 (frank maldistribution) – we see in the above graph-33C that happiness remains close throughout much of the range for MAJ36 and MAJ33.

#34D

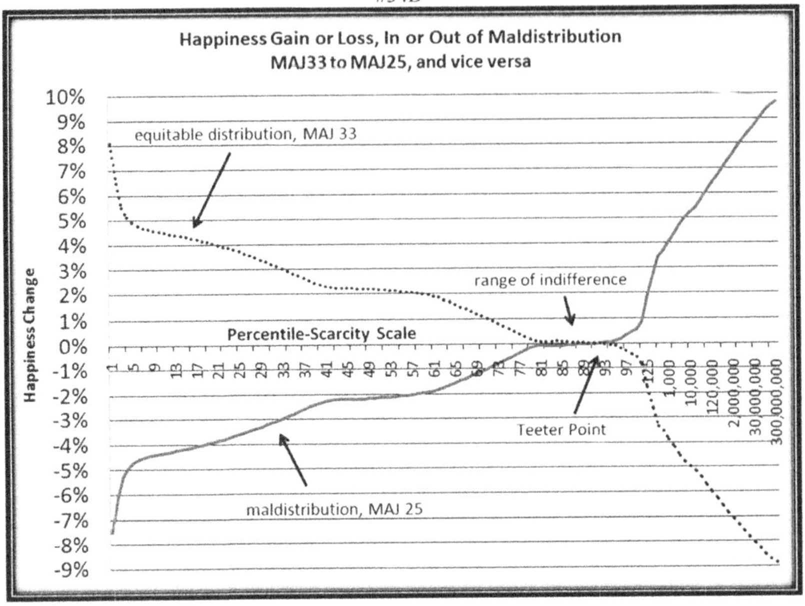

The above graph-34D shows that the happiness of all people beneath the teeter point fell, and the happiness of those above the teeter point rose with the change from a MAJ33 to MAJ25. And we can see how a change from the maldistributed MAJ25 back to MAJ33 inverts those changes to the benefit of the majority. A few unhappy pirates is the price always paid when going from maldistribution to an equitable distribution.

If maldistribution is reversed to a fair MAJ33, one can expect vigorous opposition from the Upper½% because they will be reluctant to forfeit the happiness gains that they derived from maldistribution.

The stick, stick, and the carrot.

Our instincts seldom allow us to see a full range of income distributions, such as previously illustrated in graph-14. For most of us, our reference point is apt to be more natural and closer to the income midpoint. Graph-35 attempts to duplicate this view.

For us working men and women, we principally experience the region shown here using the median as the reference point (1.0). Beneath the 50th percentile, incomes relative to the median are close; but from the midpoint upwards, they diverge appreciably.

#35

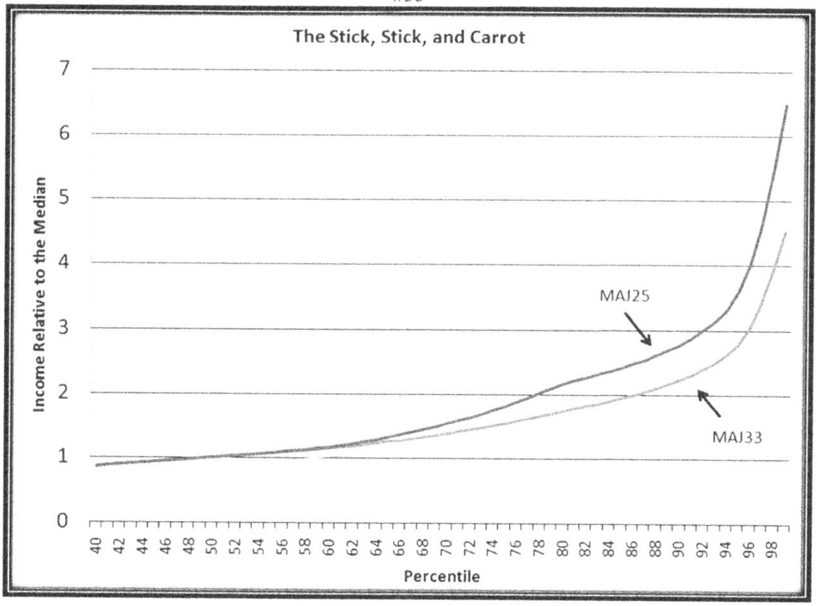

The MAJ25 and MAJ33 distributions represent two distinct compensation philosophies. Each involve the carrot and the stick: better pay for doing better, lower pay for doing worse or making a less valuable contribution. This principle conforms to the theory that high inequality is necessary to give people incentives and tends to be attractive for economists who like to see large increments associated with a particular outcome. For example, a sharply rising pay scale as scarcity increases.

In MAJ25, we see such a rise. The MAJ25 philosophy is also attractive for personalities who derive joy from dominating, and the minor potentates they collect along the way. The pirate-in-chief makes a great to-do about the rewards (carrots) and shows how far you will fall (stick) if you do not perform. The MAJ25 curve bears it out. By the 78th percentile, you make twice as much as the guy at the midpoint; and by the 92nd percentile, three times as much. It looks like MAJ25 is leaving MAJ33 in the dust.

Think again. If you believe the pirate flimflam, you have been snookered. Before anyone came into the MAJ25 game, a bigger stick had already been applied. In addition to the customary stick and carrot, the maldistributed economy adds the additional stick: a sharply rising pay scale.

As you may recall from the previous graph-14, everyone at a MAJ25 distribution beneath the teeter point (the 92nd percentile) already got a smaller income than MAJ33. The MAJ25 crowd had been fooled. They were donkeys with blinders. They were not worthy of those mentioned incomes two and three times larger than those at the median. Throughout the scale, they were actually getting a smaller income than those who elected the MAJ33 route (graph-14). Those who chose MAJ25 participated in an illusion – a more brutal one than necessary. If you have any doubt about this, turn back to graph-14 and look again at the standing of those on the MAJ25 curve beneath the teeter point

Beneath the teeter point, those on the MAJ33 curve had higher incomes. They came into the workplace ready to do a decent day's work without illusions of grandeur relative to their cohorts. They came into a workplace where everyone from top to bottom got a fair shake. Their smoothly increasing compensation scale shown in graph-35 did not contain the drama of MAJ25. It did, however, contain a sensibility and higher income completely lacking at MAJ25.

Maldistribution – paying more for people of lower ability.

#36

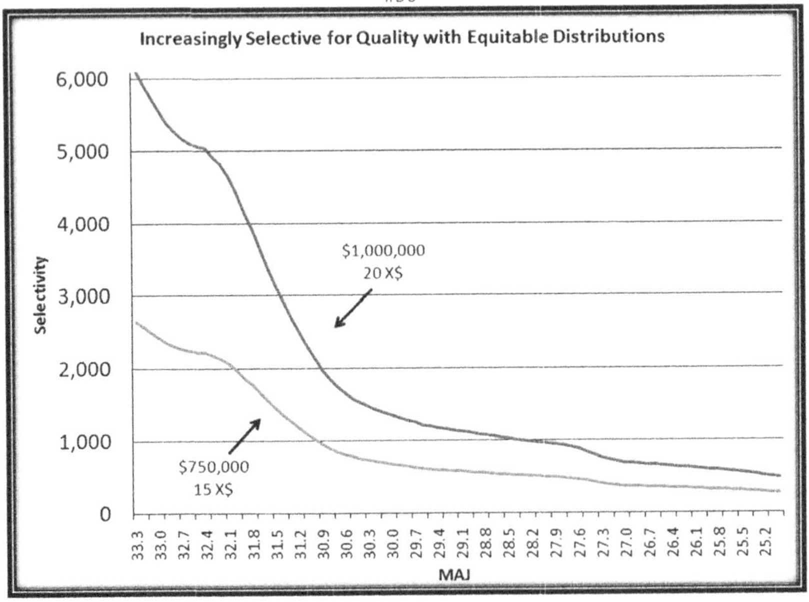

To anyone visiting or living in a country where a tinhorn potentate rules and preserves his position and those of his cronies by enforcing acute maldistribution via the power of office, it is blindingly clear that the majority of those at the top have stunningly low ability in terms of economic usefulness. Think deeply.* Throughout the scale, there is a continuum of reduced ability as maldistribution becomes ever more intense. This continuum is the feature illustrated in the above graph-36. The concept is simple. It took the computer program less than a second to deliver all the data on this topic.

Graph-36 shows constant earning rates of 15X$ and 20X$ (corresponding to incomes of $750,000 and $1,000,000).

People earning high amounts such as 20X$ ($1,000,000) are obviously scarce, but the standards drop to low levels as an economy moves to a MAJ25. Explicitly, take the 20X$ selectivity curve. At a MAJ33, the system is highly selective allowing only one in 6,150 to attain the million dollar rank. But the profligate MAJ25 it is far less selective, paying that same relative income to a mere one-in-480. And at the 15X$ income, the selection criteria similarly drops from one-in-2,650 to one-in-265.[13]

Looking through the news, I see the Bloomberg Billionaire Index and various remarks of braggadocio. Whenever a nation proudly boasts that it has increased the number of millionaires or billionaires, the cautionary flag should wave fiercely because the mechanism for doing so is usually the drive to maldistribution. The nation typically becomes less selective for those who rise to high levels. This is especially dangerous in a free market and democracy because less able people proliferate in high decision-making positions. Those of true merit can be muscled out. High quality decision-making is one of the casualties of maldistribution.

In contrast to pure selectivity, the *selectivity ratio* illustrates selection relative to an equitable distribution base. The selectivity ratio in graph-38 indicates the degree to which high earners at the 15X$ and 20X$ income levels ($750,000 and $1,000,000) are scrutinized in the face of maldistribution.

At the fair MAJ33 distribution, only one-in-13.2 at 20X$ and one-in-10.3 at 15X$ of those who achieved their incomes in the MAJ25 case would have made the cut. As shown in graph-38, at MAJ33 the selectivity ratio is 1.0, indicating that no greater selectivity was necessary. But as

---

* Please do not interpret the expression "Think deeply" as a command. Many of you are, have been, and always will be in a deep thinking mode. The expression is used as punctuation for those of us who scoot along on a level of thinking just sufficient to get through the day. The "thinking deeply" is a reminder that we are approaching a curve in the road and may want to shift into another thought zone, slightly different (but no harder) than our customary cruising along.

maldistribution increases, selectivity was insufficient, corresponding to the ratios shown in graph-38.

#38

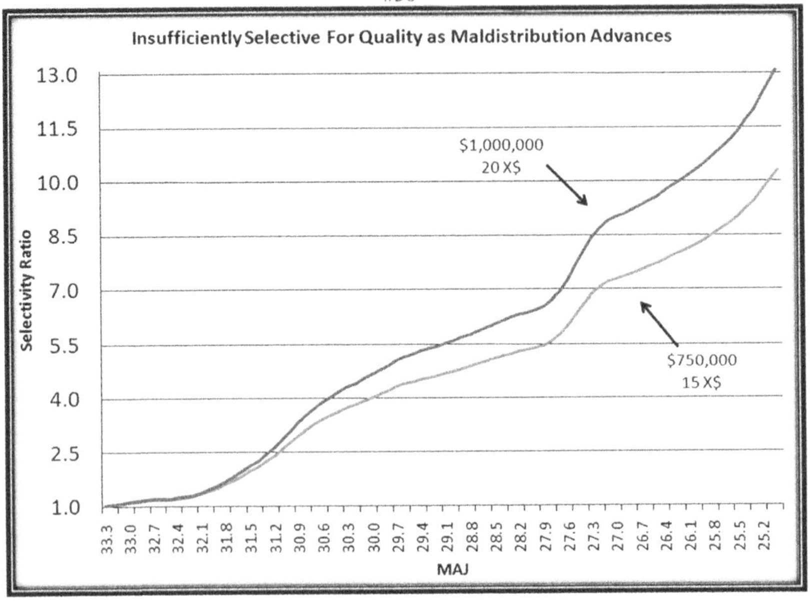

In the lookup table we see that at the one-in-a-million-scarcity level at MAJ33, the earnings are 115.1X$ ($5,755,000 in this case). Yet at MAJ25, one out of 17,627 are earning this same amount. At this point, the selectivity ratio is 56.7 – profligacy reigns. A proliferation of people of low ability in high places reduces quality of decision-making at precisely the point that a market economy requires superior decisions.

Correction without recrimination.

Revolutionaries, often through violence accompanied by a vision of an improved world, have slaughtered or removed a ruling class in a broad stroke. I believe this is wrong and counterproductive.

To look at class conditions and attempt to rectify them at the barrel of a gun is ill advised. Those who use violence seldom have the capacity to significantly advance economies. Nations in greatest distress too frequently have been driven into ever-greater misery by war. Although force and honeyed promises to a desperate people can inspire great foolishness, look at the spreadsheets. There is a trove of data that shows the impact of income and wealth at any period in history. Once the blasting and words have been given a few years to clear, the populace frequently ends up in a puddle more disagreeable than the one it left.

I do not come to this world with lily clean hands. I was raised in the segregated South in the U.S. under privileged conditions. As I saw it, the segregation we lived under was not virulently mean, as it was elsewhere. But it was unremittingly debilitating and wrong. So I know a bit about starting off with daft notions. This gives me a perspective on the capacity for change. Some will be unreservedly recalcitrant; but more often than one may be prepared to believe, opposing positions can change when reasons are compelling and persistent.

Quiet heroism is capable of rising unexpectedly. This was recently brought to my attention in the Scottsboro Boys Case. Nine rough, black, teenage hobos were wrongly accused of gang raping two white women in Alabama in 1931 during the Great Depression.[14] In that era, lynchings were frequent. The story begins at a scene where a lynching appeared to approach certainty. However, even in the intensely racist South, the Sheriff and law enforcement stood strong to prevent it – an act of courage under unfavorable odds. Then came trials that proclaimed guilt at numerous junctures but which were successfully appealed.

The point of heroism and rectitude for me came when the judge, of pure Southern tradition, set aside the jury verdict of guilty because the evidence did not support it. His decision cost him his job. Judge Horton was never elected to the bench again. He was widely opposed. Another judge handed down guilty verdicts, some of which were mitigated by parole or pardon. The larger story is that even in an imperfect world, we can move forward as long as motivations are proper. Allies like Judge Horton can be found in unlikely places. They, others, and our inner voice have the power to inspire and move us.

So be accurate. Be persistent. Be tough and strong if necessary. Be wise. It is just as impossible to reverse evolution in economics as it is in nature. Even when beneficial changes are made, you will return to a state differing from the original conditions.[15] Goals will seldom match outcomes.

Do not be violent. Too frequently the vitality of nations is laid low by the disproportionate force of a few. This wrong can be substituted for one just as great if the majority ill-advisedly resorts to violence. The majority can always triumph when guided by reason, accuracy, and fairness. I say this because I do not want the sometimes forceful words and plain picture painted here to cause evil.

In the selectivity ratio graph-38, we saw that somewhere in the neighborhood of one out of ten people at high rank possesses sufficiently great ability to justify his or her present high income. If they are removed, not only from this level of remuneration but from the decision-making process, the nation loses a valuable component required in a successful economy – broad-spread high quality decision-making. It may take more than a generation to replace it, in which case the entire society can falter, or worse.

Once an economy reaches a MAJ25, the normal selection process that would have occurred in a MAJ33 market economy has already been breached. There are no rules or easy ways to filter out or demote those who have been wrongly promoted to high income. The least worthy are apt to have the biggest mouths, have the ability to hire agents, and have sufficient contacts and power to employ governments to perpetuate their windfall.

About nine out of ten of those at the top have achieved their high income by virtue of maldistribution. As you read these pages, you may want to retain these few paragraphs in the back of your mind because if a nation is ever to get to a MAJ33 again, it needs to be done by correct and persistent means. The opposition from the unworthy will be loud, intense, ruthless, and rich.

The great danger of excessive income equality.

#40

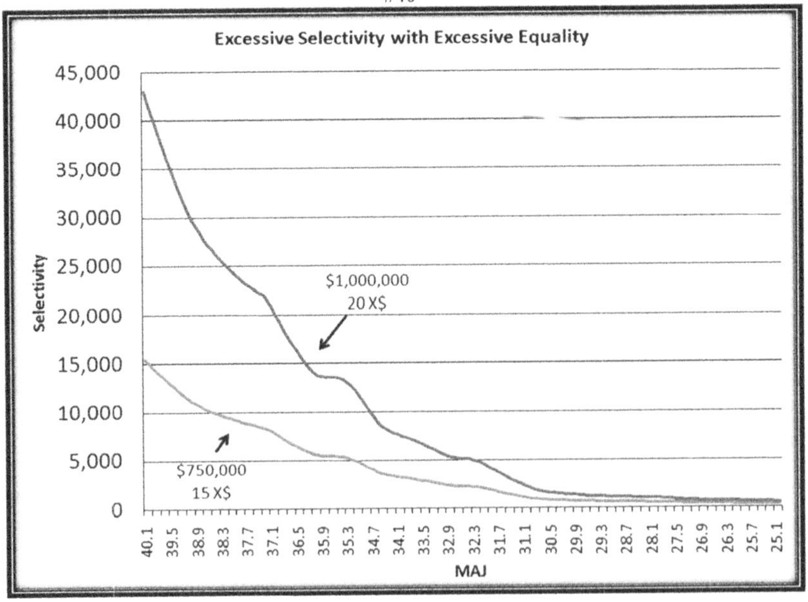

To this point, the data has decried maldistribution. Here, it will illustrate the great danger of excessive equality. Graph-40 opens the window to a *wider range* (MAJ40 to MAJ25) to show how selectivity comes into play, particularly in highly equal distributions.

In graph-40, we see that from MAJ36 through MAJ40, there is a sharp increase in selectivity at 15X$ and 20X$. this sharp rise in selectivity, especially at 15X$ ($750,000), is dangerous. If selectivity is excessively stringent, you remove precisely the kind of people necessary for quality decision-making and quality action. The economy and society suffer greatly.

I want people to be in positions of high authority who have more ability than I do. I benefit from it. I do not want to lose them. There may be fair and legitimate debate about what degree of selectivity is appropriate, but distributions significantly more equal than MAJ36 throw up a wall of dramatically increasing selectivity. It seems to me that to cross into this territory would provide little advantage to the 60% majority by way of improved income or happiness and it would create a likely prospect of reduced desirable economic activity and, perhaps, worse. The data tells us that MAJ36 is the stopping point. History tells us that MAJ33 widely works well. I like proven things that work well.

With particular reference to the above case, one of the practical advantages of defining distribution curves using MAJ numbers is that it makes it trivially easy to instantaneously determine how much better (or worse) off the 60% majority would be by a move in income distribution. It is a ready measure of how a democracy treats its people.

For example, when we consider the option between a MAJ36 (which I hold to be the maximum equality that most nations should seek) and MAJ33 (the reliable workhorse), we can easily calculate the maximum advantage the 60% majority would derive from a change in income distribution alone, before other factors are considered. The answer: 9% [9%= 36/33-1, and simple calculations of this kind can be used for any of the distributions]. However, in my mind, the 9% gained by a change of income distribution above MAJ33 would often be lost in spades by reduced economic and social vitality.

Hidden behind the Gini.

Look again at the simple calculation in the previous paragraph using MAJ numbers. You cannot perform such calculations with Ginis. [16] Most people have never heard of a Gini – with good reason. Although it is the most common measurement of income distribution, it is very cumbersome to use. We (as normal people walking down the street, in cafes, or on the job) can neither discuss it comfortably nor the income distribution to which it pertains. Even academically, it hobbles the process of modeling and understanding how economies work.

Income-distribution language has been so imprecise that the topic is practically unmanageable. By not being able to discuss income distribution or easily model it, we have been rendered powerless to understand or correct the vast adverse effects of income distribution gone awry. I disparage the Gini because I feel it has stymied valuable public and academic thinking.

Throughout the foregoing we have seen how easy it is to make calculations using MAJ numbers. We have also seen how easy it is to see how everyone from top to bottom is doing in any distribution using X$ graphs. These methods differ substantially from methods you will find elsewhere. For me, however, customary income-distribution discussions using the Gini are utterly bewildering.

Ginis are especially useless on the crucial topic of democracy. A democracy must serve and protect the majority, and it must provide a standard of fairness for all. To the extent that it does not do so, it is no democracy at all. The MAJ speaks directly to the wellbeing and status of the 60% majority, and by extension, to how fairly the remaining 40% are treated. The Gini does not.

To hide and obfuscate on a topic so vital is pedantic, perverse, and dangerous Try telling anyone what Ginis such as 34.0, 37.8, and 50.2 convey. Try telling them that the 60% majority of citizens are getting 36%, 33%, or 25% of the income earned in their nation. *Which numbers speak to you with greater clarity?*

If the majority of citizens in any nation were given complete and accurate income-distribution reporting, *would they not* be able to elect more appropriate officials? *Would they not* choose more beneficial policies? And *would not* their leaders inside and outside government be able to make better decisions ____? (Again, please fill in the blank yourself)

The Gini is no mystery. You can see its approximate relationship to the MAJ in the following graph-43. Coincidentally at 35, both are approximately equal.

#43

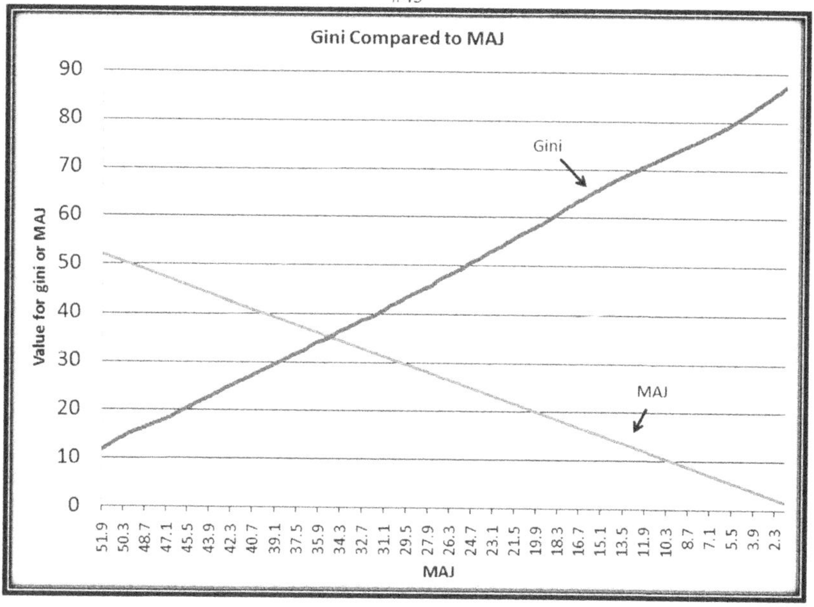

Gini numbers – such as 34.0, 37.8, and 50.2 – are dull as mud and carry little or no meaning for me, no matter how many times I see them. Granted, the Gini provides a valuable, uniform technical standard for measuring income distributions. I use it daily for technical purposes, but for conversations between normal folk – why would anyone choose to use them? [17] If you want a reliable audience for discussing Ginis, I suggest goldfish. They seem receptive.

To Gini aficionados, I might also mention that as Ginis increase linearly, people of identical ability at the high end of the scale receive incomes that expand approximately exponentially. And since people do not receive incomes in Ginis, but in real currency, it might be wiser to stay closer to the topic at hand. A small move in a Gini can spell a large change in income at the top. Focusing on Ginis is a superb way to obfuscate vast changes in top incomes and to provide little information about how the majority is doing.

The complete initial 2,500 worldwide nation-years of data available for this study is shown in the following graph-44.[18] It illustrates the real world relationship between reported MAJs and Ginis. Since it contains all the available real world quintile data, you see Ginis and MAJs at the approximate frequencies at which they occurred, with the percentage rate of occurrence also shown in the graph-44. Real world MAJ variations from the MAJ trend line tend to be small.

#44

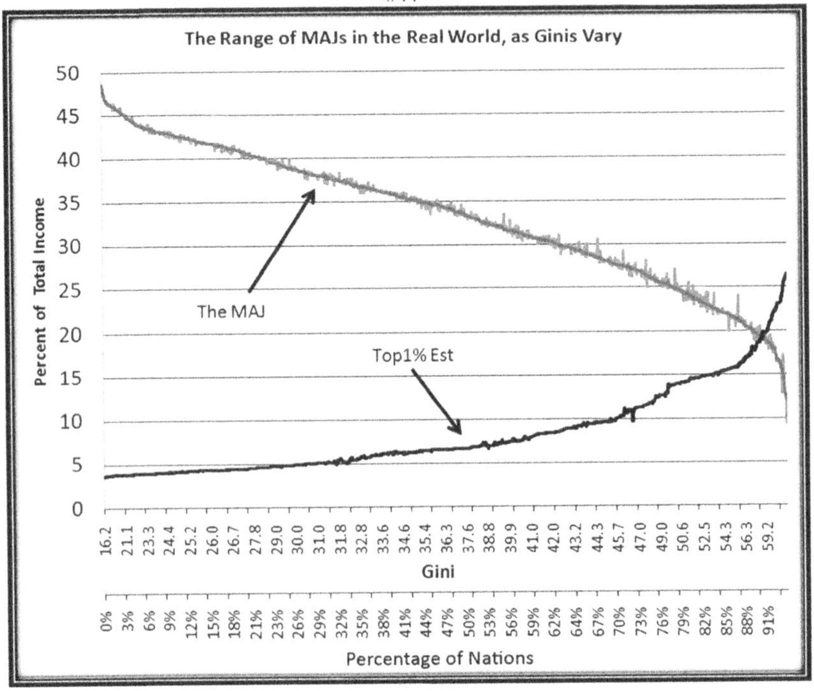

Nations that dip below a MAJ25 are outside the norm, as evidenced by the percentage designation in the graph. As can be seen at the intersection of the two curves, from a MAJ19 downward, distributions are so outlandishly inappropriate that the Top1% receives more of the total income than does the 60% majority. To have the Top1% receive a greater share of the income than the bottom 60% is an irrationality of the most grievous sort.

Frequently Gini users are remarkably inept at their craft. Ginis are so often wrongly calculated that the literature abounds with "corrected" Ginis. By contrast, income distributions are widely published in 20% increments. Given that the MAJ is the sum of the first three of them (quintiles), the MAJ gives greater assurance that the calculations are at least mathematically correct.

The fondness for imprecise income-distribution reporting is spectacular and unnecessary. If Ginis were not bad enough, try quintiles (1/5ths). That is the standard many nations use to report income distribution. Sometimes they *do* report the Top 10% or the Top5%. But reporting the Top1% ... well, for the most part, that only happens in your dreams. The U.S. Census doesn't even do that.[19]

Quintiles.

The reporting you would typically find would be the percentage income shares for each quintile. In following Table-45, the data would look like this for a MAJ33 and MAJ25 respectively:

#45

	gini	Q1	Q2	Q3	Q4	Q5
MAJ33	37.8	6.2	11.2	16.0	22.4	44.3
MAJ25	50.2	4.1	8.2	12.8	20.3	54.7
Maldistribution Influence		-34.24%	-26.82%	-19.98%	-9.67%	23.67%
Equitability Influence		52.08%	36.66%	24.97%	10.70%	-19.14%

A listing of quintiles (Q1, ... Q5) such as in Table-45 and the Gini would be as much as many governments would reveal. And the data in many instances can be decades old. Reporting percentage share is ripe for misconstrual. Governmental data certainly would not report the "maldistribution influences" and "equitability influence" shown in the table.

Take the change at the lowest quintile (Q1). The move from 6.2% to 4.1% is apt to be interpreted as a 2.1% drop in income, say over a 30-year period – hardly something to raise one's heart rate. But within the low quintile, these folk had so little income to begin with that their drop in income share would have been devastating: a full 34.2% drop in the income that they would have received if maldistribution had not occurred [34.24= 4.07 /6.19 -1]. Every year into the indefinite future while the MAJ25 prevails, the average person in this quintile gets an income 34.2% lower than it would have otherwise had at MAJ33. The real drop in status for this class was 34.2% – not the 2.1% inferred by the customary quintile reporting.

From Table-45, it is plainly apparent that with maldistribution, all quintiles were losers except Q5. But from the table, one might have inferred that the 20% of the population in Q5, principally the college educated, benefited. Wrong. You must struggle to find individuals who reap great rewards from maldistribution. They do not appear in abundance, even in Q5.

As shown in the following graph-46, no group beneath the Top1% benefited by more than 15%. All those beneath the 92nd percentile were losers. None beneath the 97th percentile benefited by more than 4.5%. How then can Q5 show a 23.7% beneficial maldistribution influence? No problem: The Lower½% got an average 56.78% benefit and the Top½% received an average 172.12% benefit. Their increases are so great that they cannot be reasonably shown in graph-46. All of this can easily be seen by dividing the MAJ25 case by the MAJ33 case in the lookup-table spreadsheet. Though the precise numbers may vary in particular cases, the maldistribution thrust remains in the same general direction.

#46

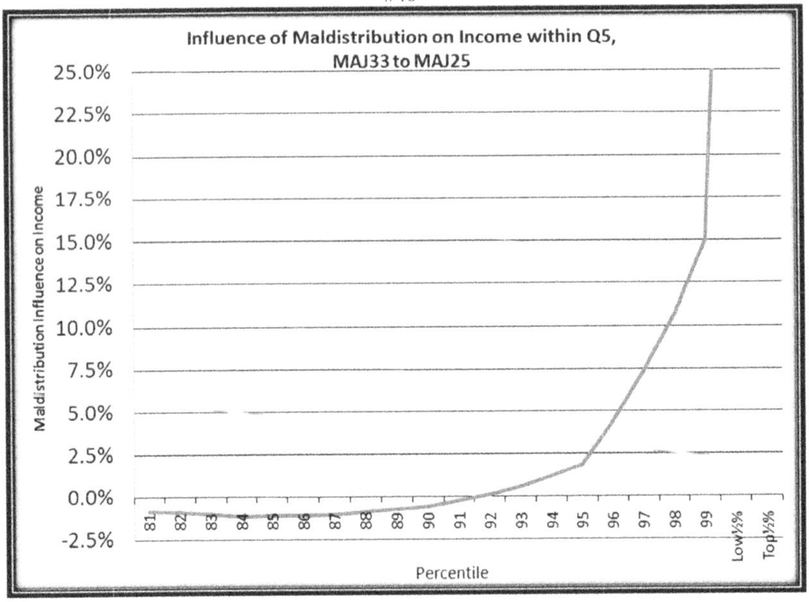

We can quickly see the consequences of falling from a MAJ33 to a MAJ25 and then returning to an equitable position at the original MAJ33 (the "maldistribution influence"). The fall results in an average 25% drop in income for the majority [25%= 25/33.333-1]. The return to an equitable distribution results in a 33% increase in income for the majority [33.3%= 33.333/25-1].

The "equitability influence" row in the previous Table-45 shows the vast benefits of returning to an equitable distribution. As previously mentioned, the reason that the return from maldistribution is more potent than the initial fall is that the base income for the majority had been reduced so greatly by maldistribution that returning to the original 33 level produces a sea change. This is one reason why the move from maldistribution is massively beneficial. It was the crucial component that pulled the USA out of the Great Depression and kept the economy vibrant. By 1939, the nation had gone from a MAJ24.6 in 1929 to a MAJ28 and real GDP was higher than pre-crash levels. The cure was well in progress, with the MAJs going ever-higher. The world of macroeconomics is now in love with interest rates, stimulus, tax policy, and financial manipulations of various kinds. The majority of these, even when appropriate and beneficial, carry a less potent influence than a break from maldistribution.

Let me show in graph-47 what quintile reporting looks like in a typical MAJ25 distribution compared to individual reporting.

#47

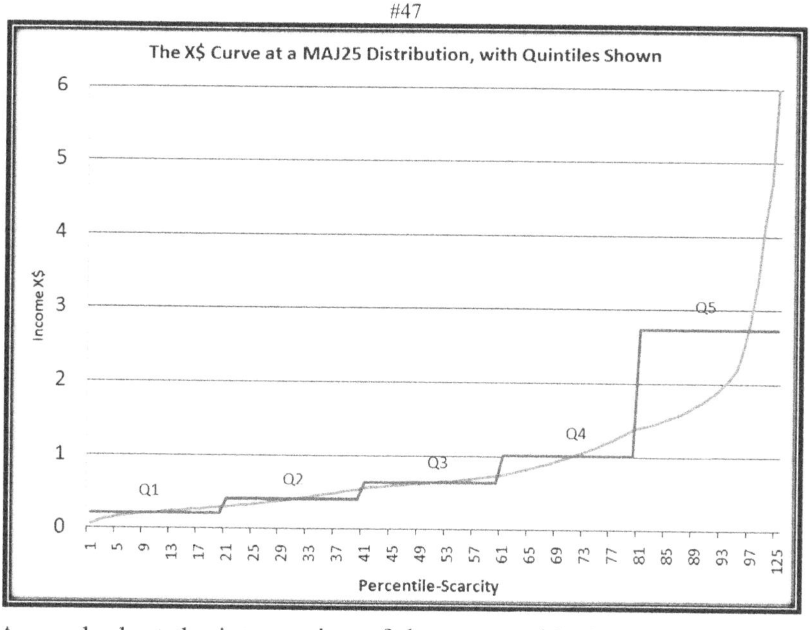

As we look at the intersection of the curve with the quintile horizontal lines, we can see that at approximately a single point, each quintile intersects with the income-distribution curve. At all other points, quintile data is erroneous. With quintile reporting alone, the spread becomes so enormous within the fifth quintile (Q5) that one cannot tell what is happening. Q5 would report a single 2.7 multiple for the entire group. A person at the low end of Q5 would be earning 1.4X$. A person at the one-in-a-hundred rank would be earning 4.7X$. By the time one reaches one-in-a-thousand, it is 28.6X$. Of course, it sharply escalates from there. All these people are within Q5. It is not the guy at the low end of Q5 that is bending the curve, but the folks at the top.

To speak of Q5 as an income-distribution group is especially useless. By not reporting the changes within the key portions of Q5, the main effects of maldistribution are almost completely disguised.

To show the data in graph-47 required an analysis that is accurate but seldom used. When you divide each of the quintile values by 20 (the number of positions in a quintile), then you get the average X$ for each quintile level shown in horizontal quintile lines in the graph.

All of this begs the obvious: Why is data reported in quintile form at all? With modern computing and file storage, the difference between 5 data points and 130 data points is trivial. Should you doubt the value of more precise reporting, take a look at the spreadsheets that my programs have created from U.S. governmental data.

It is sad that we miss many of the great stories of income distribution because income distribution is reported so convolutedly. Studies indicate that income Q3+Q4 for New England colonies in 1774 was 52.8%.[20] Such a high degree of equality at this point on the curve is unprecedented. You would know this instantly from looking either at the 400-case lookup table or histories of the 100-point distributions in particular nations.

If this figure is indeed true, we would be missing one of the great stories at the cradle of democracy – modern democracy was born under an extraordinary equitable income distribution. We would have missed the story because convoluted methods for reporting income distribution ensured our ignorance.

Gini and quintiles have a central defect. Intuitively our first instinct, and rightfully so, is to look out for "number one" – the "me." Gini and quintiles are counterintuitive because they force us to look at the general condition first and then leave us hanging without ever letting us know how the "me" is doing. The X$ curve starts with the "me" and then provides sufficient information so that you can determine how any larger group or any person elsewhere on the scale is faring.

Anyone who delves into the data will see that there is a range of highly inequitable distributions where any single description of the curve (whether it be Quintile, Top1%, Gini, or MAJ) breaks down and can no longer adequately describe the distribution. Any one of these values could stay the same or vary slightly when some other condition changes significantly. This is more than a passing theoretical point. Wealth distribution, for example, is so much more inequitable than income distribution that many of these terms often lose any significant meaning. Short of an X$ curve, you have insufficient information to understand what is going on.

#49

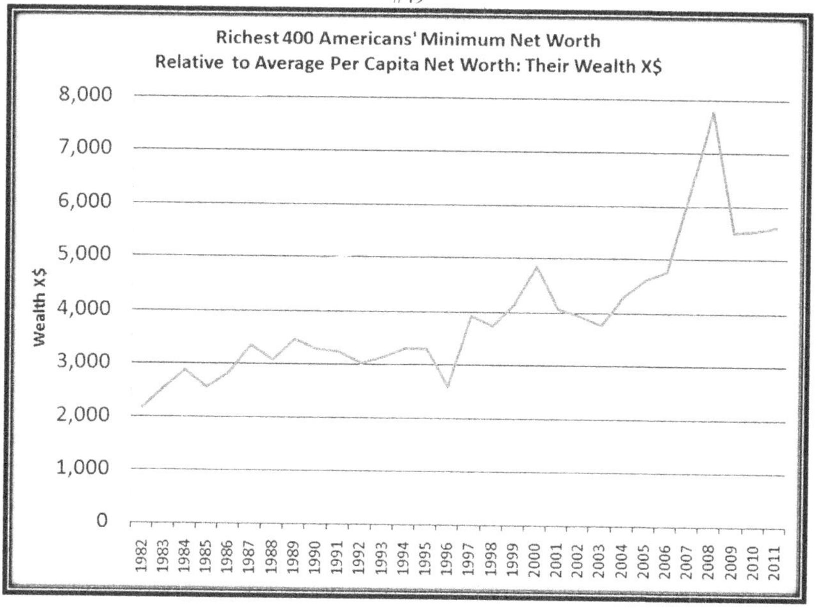

By way of example, at current population levels, only one in approximately 767,500 people are included in the Top400 wealth holders in graph-49. This is now the scarcity level for this group. In the graph, we see the ratio between the average net worth for everyone in the U.S., and the minimum net worth required to be included in the Top400. During the past decade, the U.S. MAJ has owned only about 4% to 5% of total net worth.

Without data at this level of precision, you would know very little about distribution at the extreme top, especially if you were given only the Gini. When the Forbes 400 was first reported in 1982, the minimum required net worth for the Top400 was about 2,200 times average U.S. net worth. At its peak in 2008, it was approximately 7,800. In the same period, the Gini for these distributions ranged from 71 to 84.4 – numbers which don't tell the story.

With 130 points you have sufficient detail to get a good working knowledge of the incomes and wealth of everyone from the very lowest to the very highest. Many people are doing studies of unimaginable variety and importance. They need to know the precise standing of individuals worldwide, from the lowest to the highest. Even a novelist is entitled to better information than is currently available. Quintile reporting benefits no one. It is not science. It is not reason. It certainly is not serious economics. It is hide and seek. Anyone who hides the data is not a steward, but a scoundrel.

Percentage	Scarcity
50%	**2**
75%	**4**
87.5%	**8**
90%	10
91%	11
92%	**12.5**
93%	14
94%	17
95%	20
96%	**25**
97%	33
98%	**50**
99%	**100**
99.5%	**200**
99.75%	**400**
99.88%	**800**
99.94%	**1,600**
99.97%	**3,200**
99.98%	**6,400**

Scarcity.

Though scarcity has been mentioned many times within these pages, we have not looked closely enough at it. Let's turn to it now. Income distribution is usually discussed in terms of percentages. Inadvertently, this can be seriously misleading because compensation, if fair, must be related to the scarcity and utility of the performance delivered.

Let's start with the percentage and scarcity Table-50. The points in a light-type font illustrate conventional percentiles alone. At 50%, to 75%, to 87.5%, the bold font indicates a doubling of scarcity, which is intended to show that the performance brought to the marketplace is twice as rare at each step, and compensation should reward those doublings. Similarly, doublings shown in bold occur at 92%, 96%, 98%, 99%, 99.5%, et cetera.

By way of example, looking at percentages alone in the table might suggest to you that since the percentages 99% and 99.5% are close, people at those levels should be compensated at approximately the same level. That would be wrong. The person at the one-in-200 level (99.5%) is, or at least should be, bringing a performance to market that is twice as rare as a person at the one-in-100 level (99%) [2= 200/100]. Always keep your eye on scarcity, not percentile.

Scarcity is the reason that income-distribution curves sharply rise once you get to high percentiles on the curves. A sharp rise is natural and does not imply a problem. The problem is the more delicate one that this book focuses on. When the rise is excessively sharp, the result is maldistribution. So we need also to have a fine-tuned understanding that can distinguish between an appropriately rising compensation at the high end and one that is excessive.

It is so hopelessly impractical to speak in terms of percentages within the Top1% that the only workable method for evaluating high remuneration is scarcity. When we speak in percentages at the lower end of the scale, we need to be aware that scarcity is the motor behind compensation.

The explicit purpose of the following graph-51 is to show *pure scarcity.* Previously, you have seen comparisons between MAJ33 and MAJ25, and the percentiles shown in a separate row at the bottom. But you have not seen pure scarcity. We benefit from looking at it now.

#51

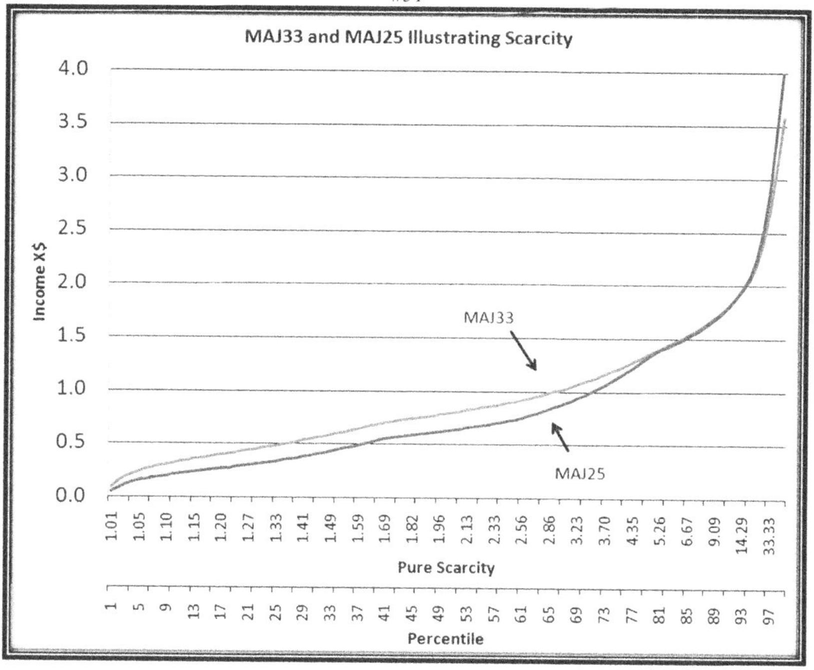

In graph-51 you see income rising slowly at the start. You also see that the pure scarcity numbers in the first row increase slowly in tandem. More to the right you see income sharply increasing as do the scarcity numbers. With graph-51 and the prior page 50 table, we get an idea of the general link between income and scarcity. And as we see in the various distribution curves, this relationship varies in form depending on which distribution prevails. By contrast, the percentile row at the bottom marches to a different drummer. It increases linearly.

For this reason, logic using percentages to describe distributions, as one might use in customary conversation to estimate appropriate norms, often tends to be wildly misleading. Although we often must talk in percentages, we need to know that at the core, scarcity directly moves distributions, not percentage. At best, percentages do so in an indirect manner [scarcity= 1/(1-percent probability)].

The dictator game.

Economist Joseph Stiglitz in his book, *The Price of Inequality*, summarizes a field of economic inquiry sometimes referred to as the dictator game.[21] At risk of further summary, here goes: There are two players. Player #1, the dictator, is given $100 and instructed to divide it between himself and player #2. The dictator usually takes the greater share and gives player #2 about $30 to $40.

The purpose of the game is to measure fairness and to see how player #2 responds. There is a limit to how much inequality player #2 will endure. When offered less than about 20% of the total ($20), player #2 revolts and refuses to accept any payment whatsoever. He would rather receive nothing than be treated unfairly. Now let's consider this in light of this chapter's heading "... one third or one fourth." The one fourth is 25% – the MAJ25 income share. If we are to assess the degree to which the 60% majority would be disgruntled, it seems they may well be nearing an arguable 20% threshold for revolt. That threshold is close to a 21.3% to which we will soon enough turn.

Oh, by the way, in the dictator game, when player #2 got about one third plus, there was no revolt. It is possible to placate the MAJ by being passably fair with us.

The time machine, now in reverse only.

Studies by King, and revised by Lindert, provide sufficient data on the 1688 income distribution in England and Wales[22] that my programs could roughly reconstruct a full range of the 300-year old distribution (with the same Gini, Q5, and Top5% as originally supplied). The program produces a MAJ21.3 distribution for 1688. Other analyses of data of the same approximate era yield similar results.

This makes it easy for us to look at and get a better understanding of income distributions of the kind that existed a century before the U.S. Declaration of Independence was written, and similarly more than a century before Adam Smith published *The Wealth of Nations* – the book which so nicely details the essence of a market economy.

The following graph-53 compares modern income distributions in a democracy and market economy at MAJ25 and MAJ33 with those of antiquity when King James II was on the throne in England, and neither modern democracy nor market economy were words on the tip of one's tongue.

#53

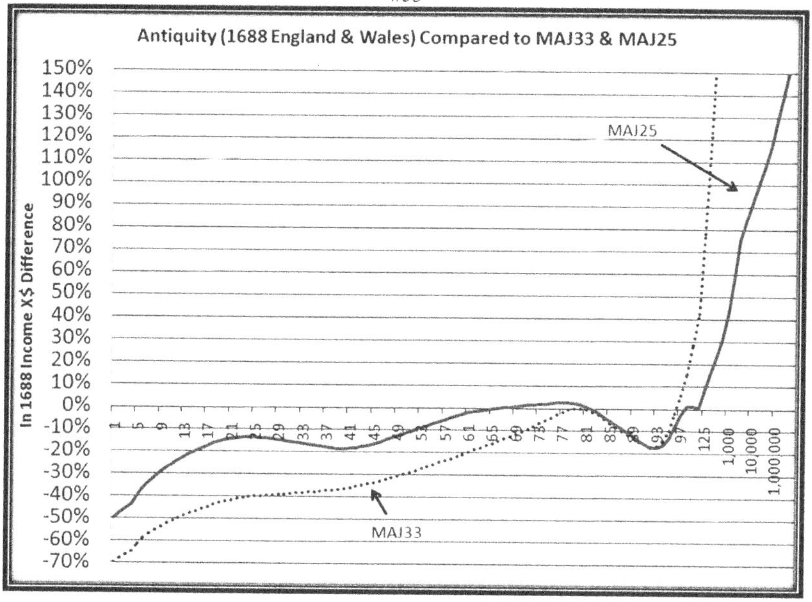

The zero line in graph-53 corresponds to conditions roughly as they existed in 1688. The graph shows that in 1688 people beneath the 80th percentile obviously faired much worse than their counterparts at MAJ33. Maldistribution proponents may argue that the recent dive into a MAJ25 maldistribution is fairer than income distribution 300+ years ago (the year 1688). Yet even there, the argument is not entirely accurate.

The recent maldistribution move to MAJ25 has put about 1/5th of the population at roughly the same relative X$ position that they would have experienced in antiquity, as evidenced by the points where the MAJ25 curve hovers near the zero point. It will take only a continuation along the current maldistribution path to bring the complete population beneath the 80th percentile to the approximate status experienced in antiquity.

Maldistribution enthusiasts are undoubtedly troubled by the observation that at the high end of the income scale, the relative status of the nobility, kings, and the like remains considerably higher than their modern counterparts under a MAJ25 regime. They need not despair. Remedy is in sight. It is still possible to move back those 300 years. The move from 33% to 25% MAJ was accomplished in 30 years. At this pace, the move from MAJ25 to MAJ21.3 can be performed within 17 years; the year 2029 or thereabouts might well be the date of interest. [16.7= ln(25/21.3) / ln((33.333/25)^(1/30)); 2029= 2012+ 16.7]. The rate at which equitable income distribution has collapsed gives hope of a quick return to the King James II era. Only 7% of nations in the recent historical record have reached MAJ21.3. Their illustrious example can inspire all King James II aficionados.

Maldistribution proponents may now proudly march with confidence under the banner "King James II in 2029 or bust." The "or bust" adds a fine folksy (if not literal) American touch to the ancient concept – don't you think? That nicely wraps up the science of going back more than 300 years in about half a century without troubling yourself with science fiction.

CH. 3

WEALTH

Wealth for the majority.

To draw attention to what Wealth is: As in a business or nation, it is net worth – the value of all your assets, less all your debt. So even though you may regard your car, house, and valuables as an indication of wealth, for true wealth, you need to subtract your debts. Net worth is an important component of economic wellbeing. Do not let income dominate your worldview to such an extent that net worth is forgotten.

As with income, wealth[23] can be estimated by using MAJ techniques. We just use the WealthMAJ rather than the IncomeMAJ (previously and customarily referred to as MAJ alone) to indicate the percentage of total wealth held by the 60% majority.

By way of introduction, the WealthMAJ is universally much lower than the IncomeMAJ. A wide difference between the two is common worldwide. In a sample of worldwide data that I had, the WealthMAJ was about 39% of the IncomeMAJ at the median (range 14% to 77%). In U.S. history, it seems to follow a path similar to the one shown in the following graph-56.[24]

As maldistribution advances, the MAJ increasingly does not have ownership. Ownership is net worth. That ownership shifts to the already wealthy. A monstrous dislocation and wrong is that *magnified reductions in net worth at the low end of the scale result from income maldistribution.* It is inevitable. And it is precisely the matter that distribution concerns itself with.

The relationships between components are not difficult to picture in your mind. If you have wealth, you are in a position to lend money and to control assets. If you do not have wealth, you are certainly in no position to lend money. Instead you are apt to become a borrower.

#56

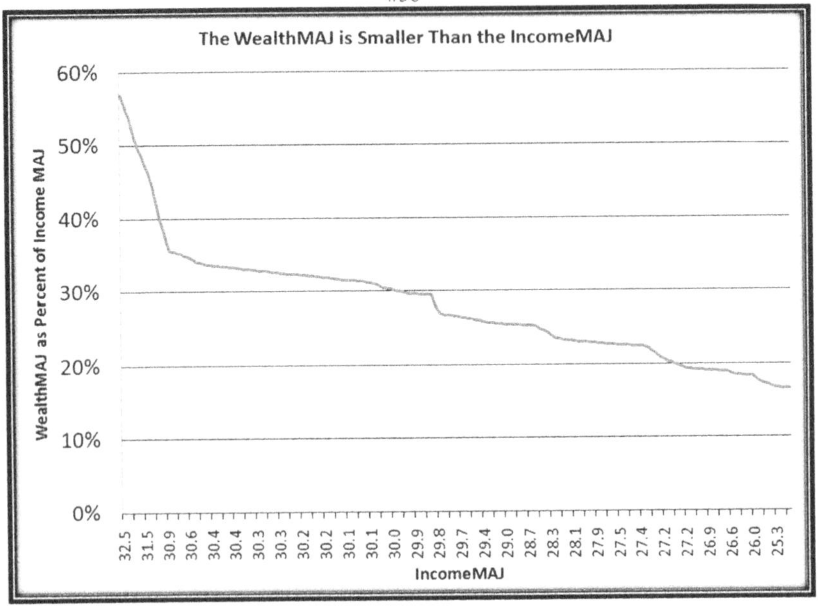

As the wealth at the low end of the scale is progressively reduced by maldistribution, those at the top are forced into unnatural machinations to lend money to people who neither have the assets nor income to support their borrowing. Their incomes can stagnate or be reduced by way of maldistribution. The MAJ's capacity to purchase may also be slight, causing them to purchase less from businesses that the wealthy own. Unholy distortions of wealth and income distribution played dominant roles in the Great Depression and the 2008 Calamity.[25]

In acute cases, the wealthy, too, are damaged by maldistribution because they no longer have means for effectively employing their assets through investments or for deriving good interest rates through sound loans. From the various combinations of these components, opportunities for crises and sharp business cycles thrive.

Guided by traditional economic thinking, I can remember many years ago being impressed by the commendable economic calming in the post WWII era through the 1970s in stark contrast to the wild swings of standard deviations in prior eras of booms, panics, and busts in U.S. economic history. I attributed this beneficial outcome largely to prudent monetary and fiscal policy. Now I tend to think another great hand was also at play: the removal of prior maldistribution.

#57

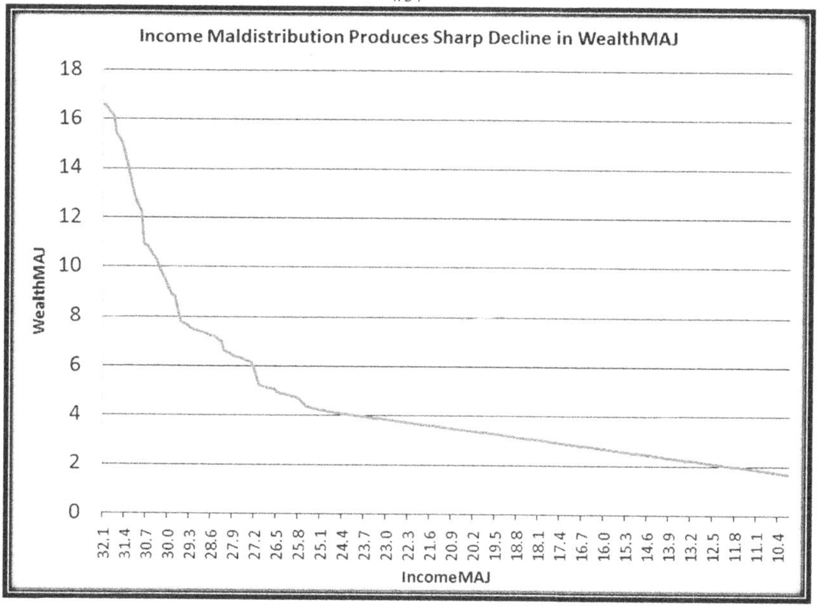

We see in the above graph-57 that wealth distribution is highly sensitive to income distribution. A small change in the IncomeMAJ is often matched by a large change in WealthMAJ. A pathetic picture appears to the right in graph-57. In the real world, the relationship is highly variable and not as ironclad as it may appear in the graph, notwithstanding that the tendencies are in the same direction. It may interest you to know that graph-57 was created by multiplying the percentages in graph-56 by the series of IncomeMAJs shown on the horizontal axis.

Lest you think that the 60% majority having a mere 4% or so of the total net worth of a nation would occur only in extraordinarily barbaric nations, you may want to observe that since 1997 the WealthMAJ has usually been less than 5% in the United States.

For half of all U.S. history, the IncomeMAJ has exceeded 29.7 and WealthMAJ has exceeded 7.8. The recent vigorous and concerted efforts of many people over many years have now moved the U.S. into rare territory. *By both distribution measures, U.S. conditions are more adverse in 2007 than in 97% of the nation's history as shown in graph-58.* And other recent years during the past decade are close to these values. In 2003, WealthMAJ was reported to be at 4%.[26]

#58

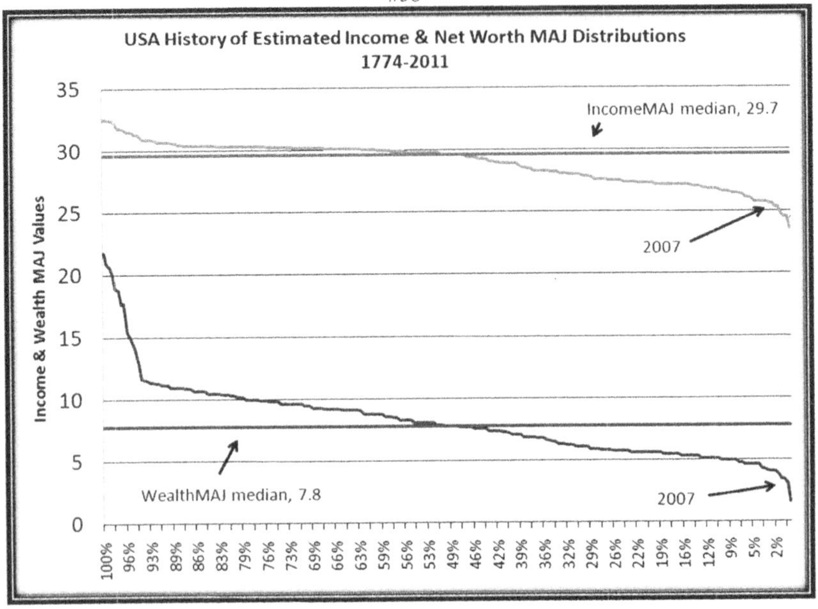

You may not be accustomed to WealthMAJs and feel that their values are so miniscule that there could be no possible remedy. Please take heart. A short mental exercise may help you to see that a solution is possible for the MAJ.

As in the methods used with IncomeMAJ, you can do quick calculations with the WealthMAJ to determine how the wealth of the 60% majority changes when the WealthMAJ changes. In the 2009-2011 period, the WealthMAJ was approximately 4. A move to the customary U.S. median WealthMAJ7.8, when other conditions remain the same, would mean that within the MAJ, wealth would be 95% larger on average [95%= 7.79/4-1].

The following graph-59 shows similar changes at other points in real world estimates for those in the 60% majority [1.948= 7.79/4]. A huge increase in wealth resulting from such changes can be looked at from the inverse perspective, too. A wealth that normally would have been available for the MAJ has been removed. The return is not so much an augmentation of the MAJ's wealth as it is a return to the approximate standard that made common economic activity possible in the past.

#59

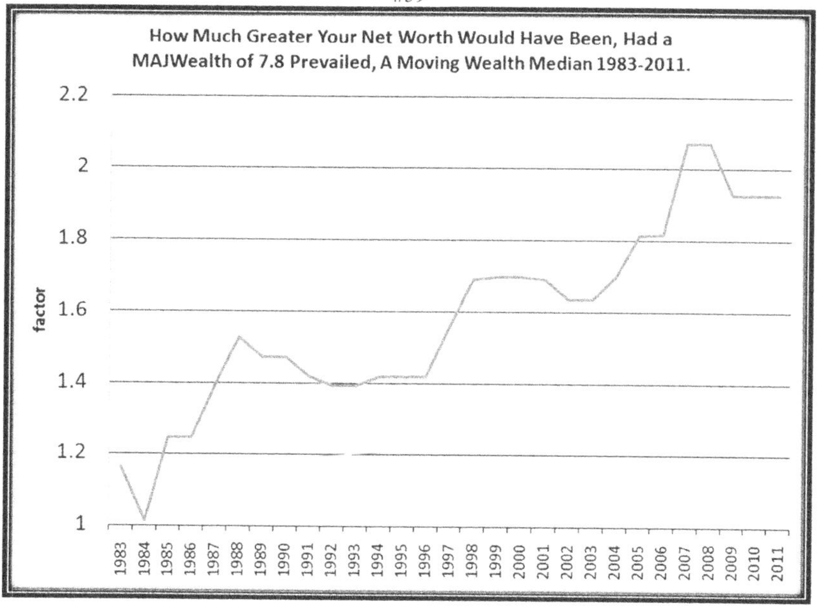

#59B

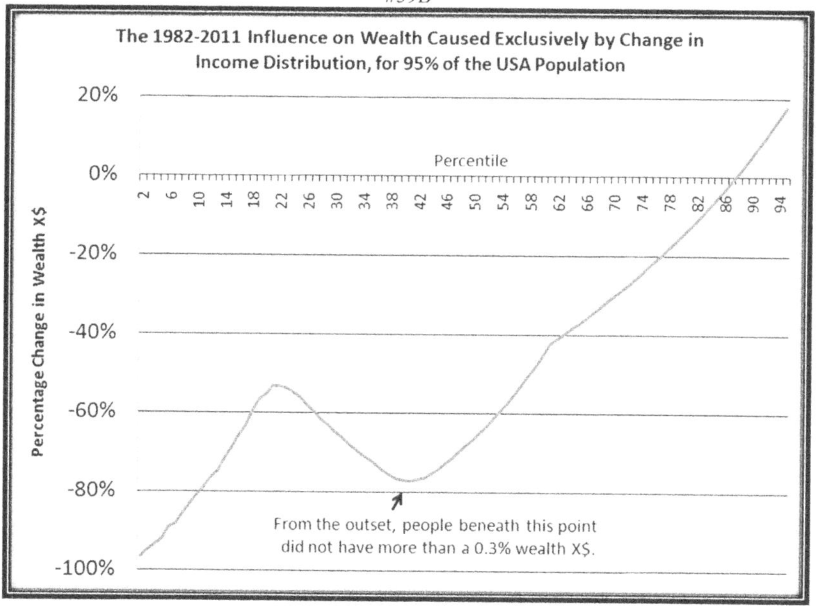

When circumstances conspire to provide the extremely wealthy with a significantly greater share of wealth than exists under median conditions, remedy is required. The MAJ needs to be provided with conditions that make it possible to accrue at least 7.8% of a nation's wealth. Otherwise, how can citizens consider their nation to be a beacon of economic fair play? The foregoing is an exceptionally modest goal.

These concepts apply to the real world in graph-59B. From 1982 to 2011, wealth distribution changed so significantly in the U.S. that there was a 65.7% reduction in the WealthMAJ during the period. The onset of this reduction of wealth for the MAJ began long ago. By 1990, the WealthMAJ had dropped 54.9%, and by 1999 the downward move had gone further south to a -61.7%. These great drops in wealth for the majority are ingredients sufficient to feed numerous future difficulties.[27]

#60

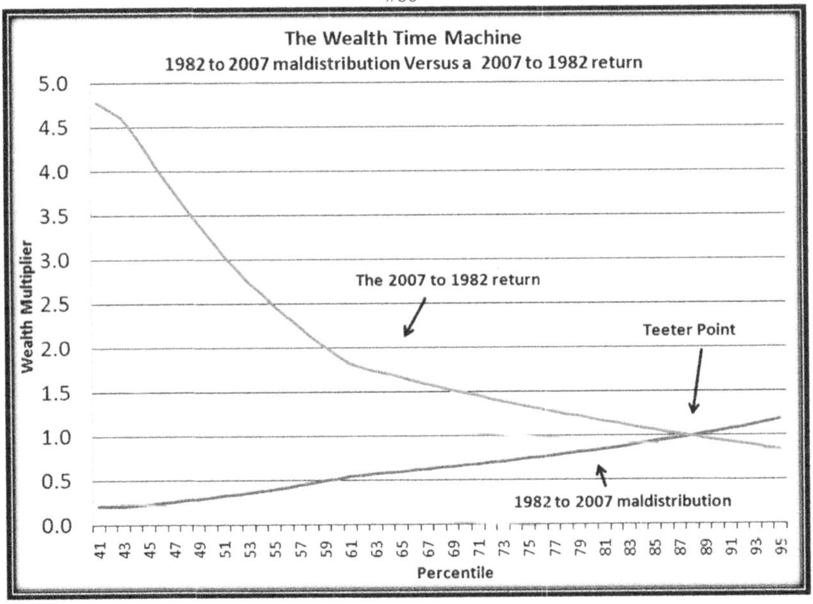

The period of most extreme difference in recent wealth distributions for which I have a consistent data series are the years 1982 to 2007 in the United States. Focusing on the 41st to 95th percentile in graph-60, we have a picture of wealth distribution changes that significantly differs from income distribution.

Beneath the *income* teeter point, there was a broad zone of indifference from the 76th to 92nd percentile, where changes in income distribution had slight influence (graph-14). With *wealth*, the picture is different.

In the graph, net worth sharply diverges at points beneath the wealth teeter point – the 88th percentile. In the income-distribution indifference range, wealth by contrast was significantly reduced by maldistribution, dropping, on average, to 84% of its former X$ level and presenting an average 1.19 wealth multiplier upon returning to the more equitable 1982 wealth distribution.

From this we see that the broad group close to the income teeter point, who initially appeared within a zone of indifference, now is significantly hit by the change in wealth distribution. The clear maldistribution losers expand to about 76% to 88% of the population, depending upon whether you take an income or wealth view.

The wealth converter.

The Wealth Converter is the ratio between wealth and GDP. It is a fundamental number for analysis, and it has practical implications in your life. Its effect can be seen in the private and public sphere.

In the late 1960s, I worked in Manhattan and lived in Brooklyn. The impact of converting money into wealth (items of long-term value) is profound. The wonderful old public library only two blocks away was a treasure, as were Prospect Park, Central Park, the museums, the art galleries, and the universities. All of these forms of wealth significantly contribute to the value of life, with unexpected results in my case.

My night courses at NYU serendipitously resulted in my becoming a director, editor, and cameraman, and later, starting a small business that manufactured motion picture editing equipment. The business, for many years, was the source of my livelihood and satisfaction. When you think back on your life, aren't there instances where wealth significantly benefited you? The prudent application of wealth touches us all.

For the past 40 years, I have lived in a section of Appalachia where most folk have, to state it politely, modest income and wealth. To state it sharply, too many of us are dirt poor. Notwithstanding poverty, one house in a nearby mountain neighborhood always stood out. The lady there had a beautifully maintained vegetable garden and flowers everywhere – a very nice place. Often even in resource-poor times, individuals and business can make extraordinary advances because they take the little bit they have and employ it to great advantage. Sweat equity becomes equity (Wealth).

And there are fluctuations in circumstances. I recall a West Virginia back road that I regularly traveled many years ago. The times were always tough there, but one year in the 1970s, folks seemed to have a little more money. That year, a striking number of homes were suddenly painted and put into reasonably decent shape.

On an international scale, you can see the capacity of some nations to more effectively convert income into wealth. A few years ago, I felt the need to quit relying on secondhand reports and made a trip around the world to see it for myself, traveling and living, much as locals do.

I recall crossing the border from Kyrgyzstan into Uzbekistan. I was struck by the number of roses, well maintained vines and homes, recently manufactured small cars and trucks, and the activity of the people in Uzbekistan. Yet upon returning and looking at statistics, both nations were shown with the same per capita income. Unless the region that I saw was doing disproportionately well, I was certain that the figures were incorrect.

A few years later the data changed to reflect the higher per capita income for Uzbekistan. Never underestimate "walk down the street" economics: people growing more roses and having the capacity to be proud of their homes and lives. That justifiable pride and order is so difficult to achieve. And once it is achieved, it is wonderful when it can be perpetuated. Such events etch on my thinking the importance of being there on site and relying on your own eyes and ears.

To make another comment on "walk down the street" economics: To significantly draw down net worth unnecessarily and often is a reliable impediment to wealth. We had a landlord in town who universally rented to the most disreputable folk. Whenever a family moved out, the yard was littered with discarded mattresses, furniture, appliances, and the like. Poverty is exacerbated by imprudent management of assets. Reducing your net worth by unnecessarily buying and replacing mattress, appliances, or covering costs of other imprudent decisions keeps the ratio between net worth and income low – in many instances a low wealth converter existing for the rest of your life.

To exclusively employ income to cover expenses of titillation and short-lived consumables can also ensure that you never have significant wealth or a nickel in the bank. Wealth requires discipline, not necessarily obsession.

So, there it goes. Just as in your own life, some people are more adept at converting income into wealth. This relationship between income and wealth as we see it in economies has powerful mathematical implications.

The U.S. Wealth Converter is equal to the ratio of net worth of households to GDP.[28] Knowing this value is fundamental to estimating wealth. Since the process is straight forward, it may interest you to know the three steps used to get both wealth and income estimates for all income strata from the lowest to the highest. The method follows:

> First, the appropriate IncomeX$ curve (shown in the foregoing curves) is multiplied by the average GDP per capita to get income estimates in dollars and cents, or whatever other currency you desire. This gives the income for each person on the curve. Second, the average GDP per capita is multiplied by the Wealth Converter (which is also GDP based), to get the average wealth per capita. Third, using the same principle as the first step with income, the above average wealth per capita is multiplied by the appropriate WealthX$ curve. And presto! The job is complete. From the lowest to the highest, you have estimates of wealth and income for everyone.

Regardless of what mechanisms are the motors behind the workings of an economy, four components ultimately determine our income and wealth: GDP per capita, the Wealth Converter, the IncomeX$ curve, and the WealthX$ curve.

From this summary, I trust you can appreciate how crucial wealth and income distribution is to our economic lives. You depend on these components. They constitute the highway to your pocketbook.

Pause. Think. When we talk of income or GDP, we think of money coming into our hands. This emotion dominates – be it personal or national.

Financial health is the consequence of income (GDP) and net worth (wealth) together. These two peas need to be in the same pod. But net worth is such an odd item. Valuations of assets may be wrong. And net worth involves an inconvenient calculation: Assets less debts equal net worth. We are so fond of forgetting that last item that we wrongly relegate it to a separate discussion, as if debt were separate from wealth. Wrong. Wealth is always another word for net worth. As inconvenient as it may be, wealth will always be assets less debts.

Wealth distribution (WealthMAJ) drives home the point: Who will be the debtors? Who will be the lenders? As long as net worth is maldistributed, lower classes will be excessively indebted to upper classes or foreign sources of funds. When a nation talks of excessive debt, it talks about a sick net worth.

And Income distribution (IncomeMAJ) tells how we value people: Which classes we elect to treat with dignity. Which classes we treat with disdain. Who we give opportunities to. Who we do not. From this we see how central both IncomeMAJ and WealthMAJ are to the financial health of people and nations.

The canary: the wealth converter.

So far we have discussed the salubrious side of the wealth converter. It also contains an unhealthy component. We see that up until about 1995, the Wealth Converter stayed within a customary range, moving about a median of 3.5. For the U.S. at the time, that was the range of wisdom. Then it exploded. Twice.

#64

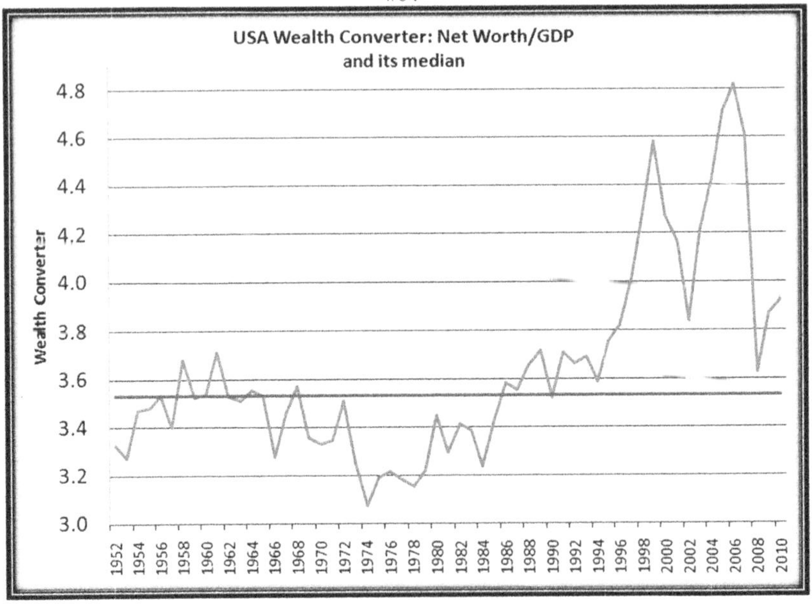

The Converter in graph-64 was trying to tell a story. Hardly anyone was listening. However, in this drama, Robert Shiller of Yale picked up on the rumbles in both instances prior to calamities. He attempted to alert the nation. In the first version (year 2000) of his book, *Irrational Exuberance*, he correctly identified (using PE ratios) a key dragon: overvaluations of stocks. In the second version (2005), his Chapter 2 spotted the second dragon, housing. In clear language, we were told why stock market and housing prices were irrationally high and doomed to fall. The books were met with widespread discussion, excitement, respect, and inaction.

In two of the most worthwhile downloadable databases on the web, Shiller provides sufficient stock market and housing data that anyone can go from the present into data that reaches as far back as the late 1800s.[29] With these databases in hand, you can see how the two bursts in the Wealth Converter occurred.

#65

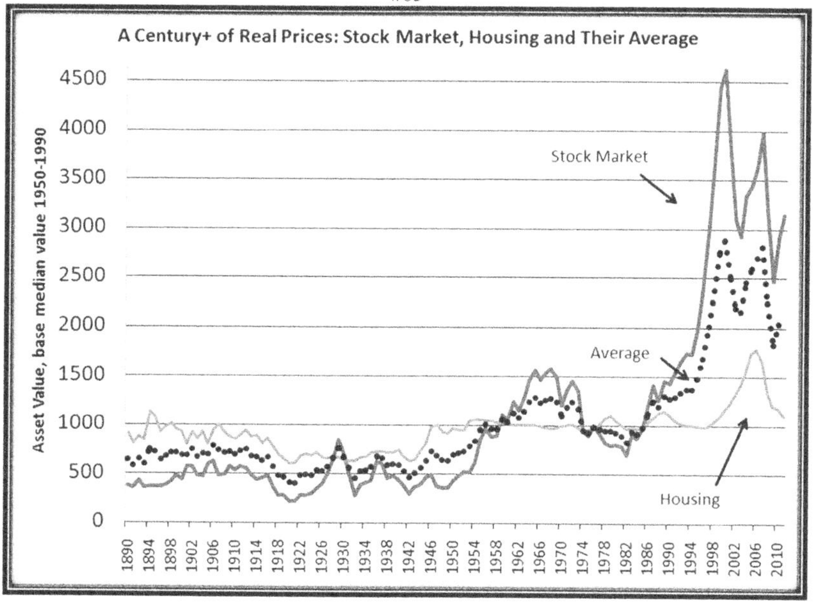

An instance in everyday life where we see the relationship between income and assets is the Home Price-to-Income Ratio. The common understanding is that to be able to afford mortgage payments, a base income sufficient to make mortgage payments is necessary. For bankers to go beyond sensible ratios and the common practice of verifying income would induce mortgage failures. In the United States, from the mid-1970s through the late 1990s, the ratio for new homes was usually between 3 and 3.5.[30] Starting in about the year 2000, the ratio rapidly rose to exceed 4.5 by the middle of the decade, systematically placing homes in the hands of owners who could not afford them. Further, a new and unconscionable form of mortgages appeared, formally called "stated income loans" (informally "liars' loans"), in which bankers systematically did not verify the mortgage applicant's stated income.[31] A PBS online video is persuasive, showing 2004 FBI warnings and more being ignored.[32] Mortgage failures followed.

In wealth converter history, most seriously distorted relationships between income and wealth compel correction.

The previous graph-65 is derived from the Shiller datasets. It was modified so that 1,000 would represent the median income-adjusted value in the U.S. during the 1950-1990 period. With this scaling, the graph represents the differences in prices of assets as if you started out at a median point somewhere between 1950 and 1990 with $1,000 invested.

Look at housing. The graph shows more than a century of housing price data. Never had there been such a huge burst in real (inflation-adjusted) housing values as the one that began in 1997. Suddenly it shoots up (as does the Home Price-to-Income Ratio). Not hard for competent management to spot a problem long before a crisis. Plenty of time to take corrective action by quelling the fervor.

Take a nap. Let it crash.

Now glance at the stock market (real S&P500,* scaled). I reserve comment. Being sardonic twice a day is excessively stressful. Let's touch on that later.

More relaxing and to the point, recall the twin humps that you saw in the Wealth Converter. They are similar to the average of the stock market and housing values shown by the dotted line in the graph. It is possible, but usually unnecessary, to go deeper. An analysis of key asset classes and debts, and the proportions in which they are held substantially does the same thing that the Wealth Converter does.

The Converter measures the relationship between income and wealth. When wealth unnaturally and wrongly expands, the impact is evident. The Converter is the proverbial canary in the coal mine.

The great advantage of the Converter is that, even without lengthy analysis, it is possible for management to spot trouble brewing well in advance and to take corrective action. With it, you can easily perform DIY economics and keep management on its toes.

The Wealth Converter moving standard deviation is one of the most reliable ways to spot ensuing trouble. The following graph-67 shows it.

---

* The S&P500 stands for Standard & Poor's index of 500 large companies traded in the U.S. stock market. It generally represents performance of industries in the U.S. economy.

#67

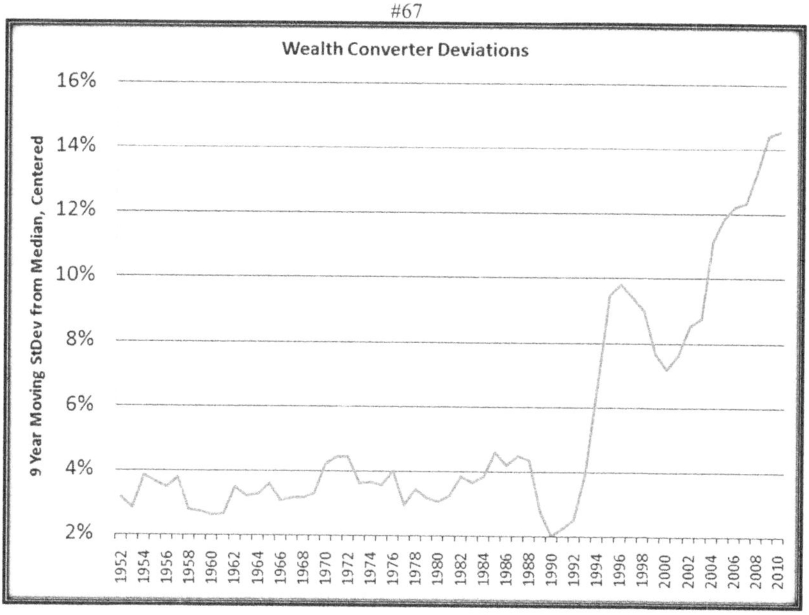

Looking at deviations is preferable to looking at absolute values because nations have vastly different Converter levels. Graph-67 focuses on unnatural deviations from the median. If the deviations cannot be explained by healthy moves in the economy, even a casual observer is forewarned. You don't need to be an expert. Keep an eye on the upswing. We will return to it much later.

Wealth worldwide.

Estimating wealth for individuals worldwide is fraught with difficulties. Net worth (wealth) data is nonexistent for many nations. About 30 of 150 nations provide some wealth distribution data, often decades old. This is in sharp contrast to the 2,500+ income-distribution cases used to develop the income-distribution curves in the lookup-table spreadsheet.

The lack of wealth reporting makes it difficult to calculate reliable Wealth Converter values. The following graph-68 shows Converters for 161 nations in the year 2000.[33] The median on the horizontal line is 3.71.

The Wealth Converters used in graph-68 cover most nations and are the only data I have access to. I use these Converters in the spreadsheets knowing that true Converter values vary from year to year. When annual Converters are not available, wealth estimates in the spreadsheets are susceptible to error. With such little reliable wealth data, I have restricted most of the wealth calculations to the spreadsheet, where perhaps you can improve on them

#68

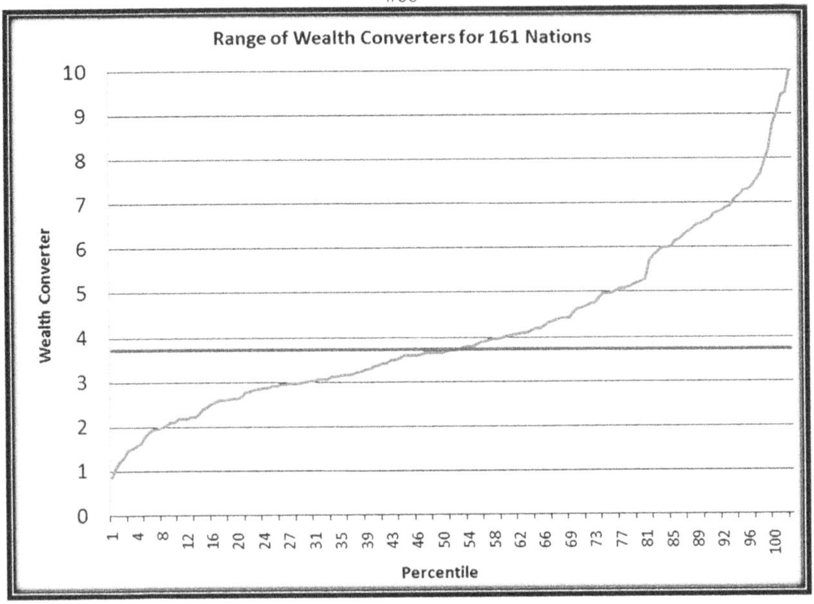

The Wealth Converter tells us how efficiently a nation converts income into wealth. This capacity varies between nations for numerous reasons. One of the less happy reasons is that in some poor nations, wealth holders invest much of their wealth outside the country where it is created.

Ancient Bolivia gives an example of conquistador wealth machinations and plunder of a kind that still continue in some regions. The *Insight Guides, South America* observed: "The amount of silver that was taken from Potosí [Bolivia] is staggering: 16 million Kg (16,000 tons) arrived in Seville between 1545 and 1660, three and a half times the entire European reserves of the day. The wealth was squandered on Spain's futile religious wars, or wasted by the extravagance of its nobles and clergymen, almost all of it ending up in the coffers of Flemish, German, or English bankers."[34] The expression "Rich as Potosí" became a synonym for wealth and opulence. The wealth came principally from a single mountain in Bolivia. Its extraction resulted in the death of thousands of indigenous Bolivians by brutal means. Effectively, none of the wealth remained in Bolivia. Exploitations of this kind do occur. The wealth converter can help ferret them out.

The wealth curve.

The Wealth Converter has a cousin. Indeed, a family of 100+ points: the Personal Wealth Converters on the Wealth Curve, as we see in the following graph-69 [achieved by dividing wealth by income at each data point].

#69

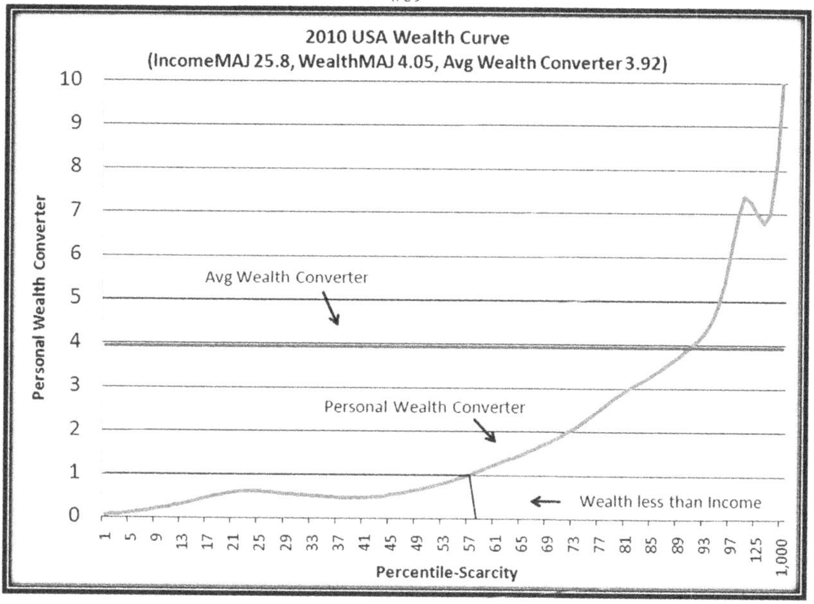

The average Wealth Converter at 3.92 is on the horizontal line. As you see, the average Converter (and by extension average wealth) tells us little about how individual people fare. The average intersects the curve at a single 92nd percentile point. For this reason, news reports of wealth approach complete uselessness. The range of wealth values are so vast that you must drill down to each point on the curve to get the drift of what is happening.

The Personal Wealth Converter curve is produced by dividing the U.S. net worth curve in 2010 by the income curve. By doing this, we can see how much wealth a person tends to have for each unit of income. The curve tells the approximate wealth relative to income for people at all points on the percentile-scarcity scale. For example, if your Personal Wealth Converter is 2, this means that your net worth is twice your income.

The wealth curve tells two stories. First, if catastrophe struck, you had no income, and you were compelled to sell all of your net worth for purposes of having enough money to live, the values on the curve indicate how many years you would be able to sustain yourself on your own resources at a level of expenditure equal to your current income. Under this scenario, 57 percent of the population has less wealth than income, as pointed out in graph-69. They would tend to exhaust their wealth within a year. Zero wealth is reached within 2 years for all beneath the 73rd percentile; within 3 years beneath the 82nd percentile; and for the person at the one-in-2,000 level (not shown on the graph-69), it would be 12.7 years. Of course, selling net worth makes one increasingly vulnerable to the point of desperation in extreme cases.

These conditions can be ameliorated by more equitable income and wealth distributions, but the magic of distribution in this area is modest. Instead of the dire scenario, people usually must adapt by having some source of income and reducing expenses. The lucky and sometimes wise few at all strata can build a more secure financial condition by having a good income, being attentive to keeping debt low, investing, and saving a sensible fraction of their income. Good luck, as well as fortunate starting circumstances, are sweet beyond a recitation of the didactically obvious.[35]

Another story told by the curve is that accumulating wealth takes time, even when one saves. The wealth curve multiples seem to be related to the average years to accumulation. It is not inconceivable that many of the very wealthy accumulated their fortunes within relatively short periods, say in about 40 years or so, given that this was the Wealth Curve value at one-in-a-million point in 2010.

A handy feature of the wealth curve is that it makes it possible to make a crude first approximation of income when net worth is known, but when income is unknown. Dividing net worth (wealth) by the corresponding point on the wealth curve gives an estimated income.

Are you better off now than you were 38 years ago?

Ah ... Dear reader ... Perhaps you had not hatched at such a distant date. But I trust you grasp the drift. Long, long ago in a world with many bright and blissful days, equitable wealth and income distributions were so plentifully common that we thought they came with the rising and setting of the sun. Never in a dream did we think otherwise. They were bright but ignorant times.

For practically all people, wealth comes at uncertain times and in uncertain ways, but it bears one consistent, unwavering property. To sustain wealth requires the capacity to conserve it. In an instant, wealth (large or small) can be lost through imprudence or by a turn in the wind of fortune.

Wealth can seldom withstand the constant pressure of irresponsibility. Building and sustaining wealth usually connotes responsibility and discipline.

In the USA, the necessity for a level of responsibility to have and sustain property was not lost on the Founders. They required holding property to be a precondition for voting rights. They did not want mob rule. They wanted enlightened rule. For good reasons, we no longer require the holding of property to be a precondition for the right to vote. But, correctly so – a link between wealth and responsibility will continue to exist. Longstanding wealth fosters the responsibility necessary to maintain it.

#71

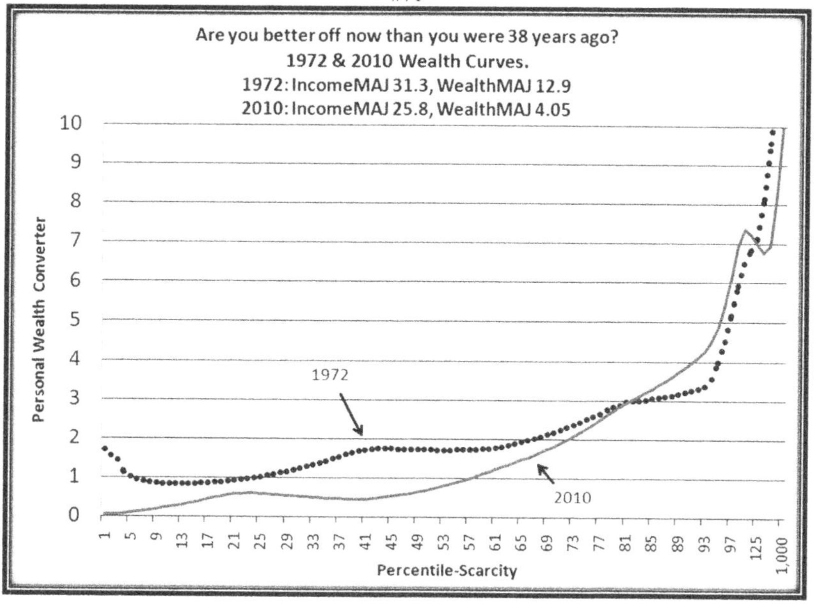

In the above graph-71, you see that beneath the 80th percentile, people had very little wealth, often not even enough to sustain themselves for one year in the event of catastrophe. By contrast, in the 1972 curve, many would have had enough wealth to sustain themselves for about two years.

The transformative impact of the 2010 curve by comparison to the 1972 curve is that modern maldistribution removes a desirable wealth-income relationship from a huge proportion of the population. The essential grounding of responsibility in wealth (even when it is a small amount of wealth) has been systematically removed by the income and wealth distribution curves.

For those not at the high strata, it was beyond the power of the individual to correct. It left a large portion of society no longer grounded by the responsibility and discipline inherent in prudently sustaining wealth. Now, the wealth for much of the nation relative to income is so slight that the ethics that were once a part of the normal social fabric necessarily change. A change I do not welcome.

Fish in the tummy. Nets.

In high school, I had the rare opportunity to have an economics teacher (Yale graduate) who was rumored to be worth in the neighborhood of thirty million (oil) – at the time, a lot of money, as it still is. He did a good job. I still recall a few of articles we studied. No customary text books. Myron Joseph's *Economic Analysis and Policy* (1963) is where we started. It was stiff reading in parts – difficult for a young high school student. The phrase I took away from the class was: "Capital is foregone consumption."

Capital can be property or invested money. Or it can be more abstract – say a Robinson Crusoe, on an island spending several days making nets instead of eating fish which he might snag by hand in tidal pools. By foregoing the immediate consumption of tidal pool fish – to take the time to build nets for catching future fish – Crusoe builds for himself capital (nets) which (until the nets need to be replaced) will make the rest of his life easier and food more readily available. By contrast, if Crusoe had continually focused on immediate consumption (snagging and eating fish), instead of expending his time building nets which became capital, his life would have been more primitive and poor.

The wealth curves provide a handy means for approximating how much people on the percentile-scarcity continuum save (invest) and consume. By these methods, we can examine the workings of the economy and see approximately how much goes to immediate consumption (fish in the tummy) and how much goes into capital (nets). Capital in the modern economy comes from savings (foregone consumption which works its way through the system to become capital). By using the wealth curve, I will show how income maldistribution has a perverse influence on a market economy.

Regardless of one's income level, a chief advantage of a certain amount of savings (and thus wealth) in your life is that it has the potential to bring tranquility. It is akin to the psychological concept of delayed gratification, which is also a measure of maturity.

But there are no easy answers. An economy requires consumption for businesses and employees to prosper. If there were a wild run to excessive savings, it would reduce necessary consumption.

USA history – the 50-year advance, the 30-year collapse.

Never had the working man gained so much as he did from 1929 until about 1977 – the timeframe subsequent to World War II that became the Golden Age of Capitalism. The chief feature of income-distribution history in the U.S. is the unprecedented fifty-year increase in the MAJ and its subsequent thirty-year collapse.

#73

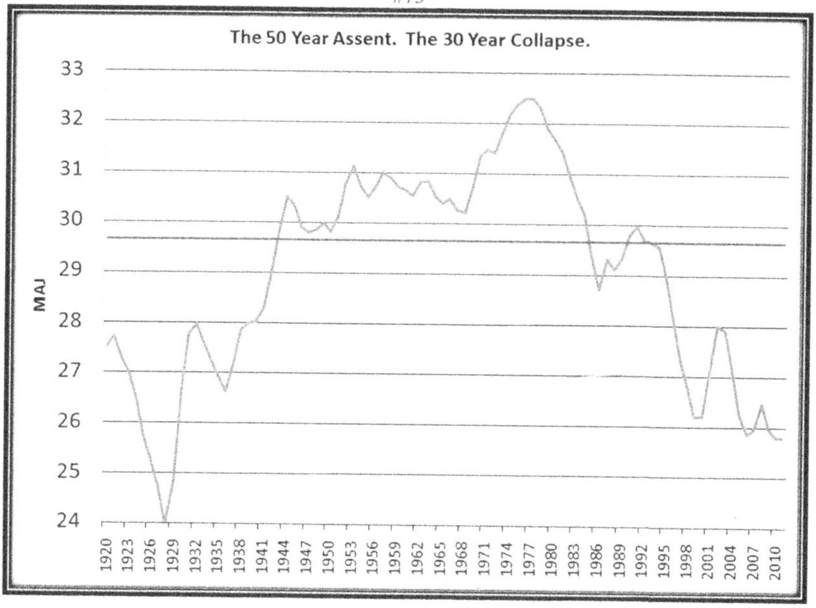

From 1921-1928, the MAJ sharply declined from 27.9 to 23.6 to welcome in the Great Depression. In the decade from 1936-1944, the MAJ increased from 26.4 to 30.6, reaching the most favorable levels of the century, as of that date.

For the forty-year period from 1943-1983, the MAJ remained above the 29.7 median, shown by the horizontal line in graph-73. From its peak of 32.5 in 1976-7, the MAJ sharply declined to 25.8 in 2007, in the range it was prior to the Great Depression.

In 1938, the MAJ was 28. Throughout the Great Depression it was lower. Historically, both in the amount and in the direction, the adverse effects of maldistribution are consistent with the earlier analysis that states: The efficient market system functions at its best when income distributions are equitable.

During the Golden Age of Capitalism, the MAJ was well above the median. At the MAJ pit, we had the Great Depression. It is counterintuitive and wrong to expect that removing income from 80% of the population will foster a healthy economy.

By the hand of maldistribution, at least 80% of U.S. citizens have been removed from the honor of fully contributing. They no longer can feel to the fiber of their being: This is the nation I helped build. I am proud of it. I am a player. If income growth reflects contribution, those words can now only be voiced with authority by the few at the top. Why did they care so little about the rest of us? Aren't they doing the math? Don't they see the numbers? Don't they know what they are doing? It is our economy. It is their economy. We all must make it work and live in it.

I make no apology for emotion. The subject is serious enough to require reason and emotion. There are occasions when individuals and groups do dastardly things. Maldistribution is one of the most monstrous of those cruelties.

If any of what is contained within these pages should strike you as passably logical, please do not expect that it might have penetrated macroeconomic thinking. As Nobel Prize winning economist Joseph Stiglitz writes, "standard macroeconomic models don't even recognize that the distribution of income matters."[36]

It may amuse you to compare your income and its advances with some of the recent bright lights. For its first two centuries, the U.S. never saw incomes at the top of the kind that are now the norm. The following graph-75 shows the inflation-adjusted annual income for those at the one-in-a-million level of income ability throughout all of U.S. history. The recent increase has put legs to the word: maldistribution. There are roughly 300 people at this general level of income in the U.S., many of whom presumably can be found among the now 400+ U.S. billionaires.

We have seen the consequences of the MAJ going from one third to one fourth of the income. In raw dollars, you can plainly spot it in the upward inflation-adjusted spike subsequent to 1980 in graph-75.

#75

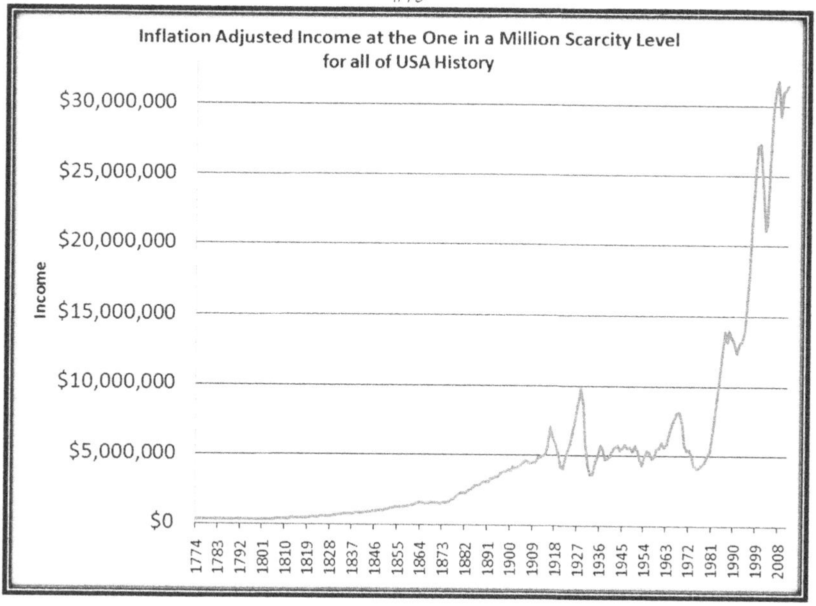

To consider the issue of economic reward, let your eyes rest on the upcoming pages.

CH. 4

THE ART OF COMPENSATION

Here we show:
CEO compensation at various income distributions.
Wealth income relative to customary income.
The roles of the KeyRatio, Productivity, and Scarcity.
The role of "Not-IQ" and its opposite.
The low and underclass & influence of income in those quarters.
The capacity of the market to limit high-income psychopaths.

The CEO.

Cut to the chase. Income distribution is how we value people.

Nowhere is high compensation more plainly obvious than executive compensation. The heads of corporations lead not only their own business, they lead the income scale culture. The standard they set moves through their business, society and the wider economy. It is wrong to think that executive compensation decisions can be made in isolation without broader influence.

The MAJ designations at the head of the columns in following Table-78 and 79 show CEO compensation at the indicated dollar amounts. As seen by moving to columns to the right, the amounts that CEOs receive ultimately define the income shares at the MAJ.

The corporate names in the tables are used as placeholders for corporations having the designated number of employees. *Do **not** attach significance to any corporate name at any particular point.* The corporation moves up or down in the table depending upon its current number of employees.

#78

	Employees	MAJ36	MAJ33	MAJ29	MAJ25	MAJ21	MAJ17
Wal-MartStores	2,055,000	$4,663,911	$7,074,322	$23,800,925	$55,649,074	$113,474,297	$175,580,965
StateGridChinaNational	1,486,000	$4,211,369	$6,328,818	$20,724,309	$47,546,388	$95,423,578	$146,220,234
ChinaNationalPetroleum	1,117,345	$3,849,786	$5,738,345	$18,348,826	$41,400,935	$81,936,686	$124,483,383
UnitedStatesPostalService	826,955	$3,501,754	$5,174,751	$16,136,212	$35,773,893	$69,763,389	$105,035,309
Sinopec	634,011	$3,220,758	$4,723,401	$14,405,758	$31,445,511	$60,529,090	$90,407,982
HonHaiPrecisionIndustry	550,000	$3,079,796	$4,498,308	$13,557,444	$29,348,988	$56,101,254	$83,437,494
Carrefour	490,042	$2,969,882	$4,323,444	$12,905,484	$27,749,842	$52,745,168	$78,174,656
SiemensAG	480,000	$2,950,586	$4,292,804	$12,791,899	$27,472,351	$52,164,762	$77,266,359
DeutschePost	475,100	$2,941,069	$4,277,700	$12,735,980	$27,335,862	$51,879,498	$76,820,150
McDonald's	465,000	$2,921,239	$4,246,243	$12,619,667	$27,052,228	$51,287,150	$75,894,047
PetroChina	464,000	$2,919,260	$4,243,104	$12,608,071	$27,023,974	$51,228,176	$75,801,879
AgriculturalBankofChina	447,519	$2,886,209	$4,190,719	$12,414,880	$26,553,715	$50,247,574	$74,270,186
Gazprom	436,096	$2,862,809	$4,153,663	$12,278,575	$26,222,531	$49,558,025	$73,194,111
UnitedParcelService	428,000	$2,845,969	$4,127,012	$12,180,727	$25,985,095	$49,064,200	$72,424,002
ChinaTelecommunications	391,864	$2,768,020	$4,003,841	$11,730,508	$24,895,998	$46,804,992	$68,906,391
Hitachi	389,752	$2,763,314	$3,996,415	$11,703,472	$24,830,777	$46,670,010	$68,696,525
InternationalBusinessMachin	386,558	$2,756,164	$3,985,135	$11,662,426	$24,731,795	$46,465,228	$68,378,191
Industrial&CommercialBanko	381,713	$2,745,242	$3,967,907	$11,599,789	$24,580,843	$46,153,081	$67,893,117
Citigroup	380,500	$2,742,492	$3,963,571	$11,584,036	$24,542,896	$46,074,645	$67,771,254
Target	366,000	$2,709,149	$3,911,025	$11,393,456	$24,084,378	$45,127,837	$66,301,184
CompassGroup	365,630	$2,708,287	$3,909,667	$11,388,537	$24,072,557	$45,103,450	$66,263,344
DaimlerAG	362,063	$2,699,940	$3,896,523	$11,340,966	$23,958,277	$44,867,760	$65,897,684
HomeDepotInc	355,000	$2,683,246	$3,870,244	$11,245,972	$23,730,267	$44,397,861	$65,168,971
SearsHoldingsCorporation	355,000	$2,683,246	$3,870,244	$11,245,972	$23,730,267	$44,397,861	$65,168,971
TATAGroup	350,000	$2,671,290	$3,851,432	$11,178,069	$23,567,440	$44,062,579	$64,649,279
VeoliaEnvironnementSA	349,000	$2,668,884	$3,847,649	$11,164,422	$23,534,732	$43,995,255	$64,544,959
Tesco	345,754	$2,661,044	$3,835,318	$11,119,967	$23,428,226	$43,776,100	$64,205,420
Sodexo	342,380	$2,652,841	$3,822,421	$11,073,506	$23,316,974	$43,547,285	$63,851,016
Volkswagen	329,305	$2,620,519	$3,771,637	$10,890,934	$22,880,426	$42,650,499	$62,463,023
FordMotorCo	327,531	$2,616,066	$3,764,646	$10,865,845	$22,820,514	$42,527,555	$62,272,869
GeneralElectric	327,000	$2,614,730	$3,762,548	$10,858,320	$22,802,547	$42,490,696	$62,215,863
Kroger	323,000	$2,604,618	$3,746,675	$10,801,409	$22,666,727	$42,212,130	$61,785,141
HSBCHoldings	322,282	$2,602,794	$3,743,812	$10,791,151	$22,642,255	$42,161,959	$61,707,580
HewlettPackardCo	321,000	$2,599,529	$3,738,690	$10,772,802	$22,598,492	$42,072,246	$61,568,906
ArcelorMittal	319,578	$2,595,898	$3,732,992	$10,752,400	$22,549,844	$41,972,540	$61,414,811
ToyotaMotor	316,121	$2,587,024	$3,719,072	$10,702,583	$22,431,110	$41,729,285	$61,038,932
AT&T	309,050	$2,568,664	$3,690,284	$10,599,708	$22,186,150	$41,227,837	$60,264,492
MatsushitaElectricIndustrial	305,828	$2,560,203	$3,677,023	$10,552,383	$22,073,574	$40,997,572	$59,909,045
LaPoste	299,010	$2,542,094	$3,648,657	$10,451,290	$21,833,325	$40,506,565	$59,151,480
ChinaConstructionBank	298,868	$2,541,714	$3,648,062	$10,449,170	$21,828,292	$40,496,282	$59,135,625
GeneralMotorsCorp	284,000	$2,501,207	$3,584,676	$10,223,975	$21,294,274	$39,406,872	$57,456,674
SamsungGroup	277,000	$2,481,631	$3,554,077	$10,115,610	$21,037,874	$38,884,784	$56,652,973
Nestlé	276,000	$2,478,807	$3,549,664	$10,100,002	$21,000,973	$38,809,699	$56,537,438
RobertBosch	271,265	$2,465,339	$3,528,627	$10,025,654	$20,825,312	$38,452,447	$55,987,893
ChinaRailwayGroup	266,474	$2,451,546	$3,507,094	$9,949,664	$20,645,959	$38,088,003	$55,427,584
MetroAG	263,794	$2,443,757	$3,494,938	$9,906,816	$20,544,908	$37,882,808	$55,112,238
EdekaZentrale	253,531	$2,413,416	$3,447,623	$9,740,378	$20,152,966	$37,087,893	$53,891,531
Sberbank	251,208	$2,406,432	$3,436,739	$9,702,172	$20,063,124	$36,905,897	$53,612,256
DeutscheTelekomAG	248,519	$2,398,292	$3,424,058	$9,657,694	$19,958,590	$36,694,248	$53,287,570
Telefónica	248,487	$2,398,194	$3,423,906	$9,657,163	$19,957,343	$36,691,723	$53,283,697
VerizonCommunications	242,000	$2,378,304	$3,392,936	$9,548,704	$19,702,727	$36,176,672	$52,494,023
FedEx	238,935	$2,368,779	$3,378,113	$9,496,879	$19,581,204	$35,931,082	$52,117,711
BankofChina	237,379	$2,363,912	$3,370,540	$9,470,424	$19,519,203	$35,805,844	$51,925,863
DeutscheBahn	237,078	$2,362,968	$3,369,071	$9,465,294	$19,507,185	$35,781,574	$51,888,686
Onex	237,000	$2,362,723	$3,368,691	$9,463,965	$19,504,069	$35,775,281	$51,879,053
BerkshireHathaway	217,550	$2,299,875	$3,271,046	$9,124,195	$18,709,997	$34,175,004	$49,431,152
UnitedTechnologiesCorp	215,000	$2,291,353	$3,257,825	$9,078,378	$18,603,221	$33,960,343	$49,103,268
CasinoGuichardPerrachon	213,000	$2,284,621	$3,247,383	$9,042,224	$18,519,021	$33,791,147	$48,844,919
LowesHomeImprovementWa	210,000	$2,274,441	$3,231,599	$8,987,626	$18,391,951	$33,535,963	$48,455,408
SaintGobainSA	208,000	$2,267,599	$3,220,994	$8,950,980	$18,306,719	$33,364,896	$48,194,385
PSAPeugeotCitroenSA	207,200	$2,264,849	$3,216,733	$8,936,265	$18,272,509	$33,296,256	$48,089,669
Safeway	207,000	$2,264,161	$3,215,666	$8,932,581	$18,263,946	$33,279,076	$48,063,463
NipponTelegraphandTelepho	205,288	$2,258,249	$3,206,506	$8,900,963	$18,190,468	$33,131,701	$47,838,686
BankofAmericaCorp.	203,425	$2,251,776	$3,196,480	$8,866,384	$18,110,152	$32,970,677	$47,593,151

#79

	Employees	MAJ36	MAJ33	MAJ29	MAJ25	MAJ21	MAJ17
Aramark	200,000	$2,239,770	$3,177,891	$8,802,335	$17,961,500	$32,672,842	$47,139,182
Oracle	200,000	$2,239,770	$3,177,891	$8,802,335	$17,961,500	$32,672,842	$47,139,182
SuperValuInc	200,000	$2,239,770	$3,177,891	$8,802,335	$17,961,500	$32,672,842	$47,139,182
AltriaGroupInc	199,000	$2,236,239	$3,172,424	$8,783,517	$17,917,852	$32,585,438	$47,006,001
FranceTélécom	191,000	$2,207,536	$3,128,024	$8,630,979	$17,564,521	$31,878,688	$45,929,854
AXAGroup	189,927	$2,203,624	$3,121,977	$8,610,243	$17,516,556	$31,782,855	$45,784,031
FederatedDept.Stores	188,000	$2,196,560	$3,111,060	$8,572,835	$17,430,063	$31,610,115	$45,521,253
ThyssenKruppAG	188,000	$2,196,560	$3,111,060	$8,572,835	$17,430,063	$31,610,115	$45,521,253
Unilever	179,000	$2,162,896	$3,059,076	$8,395,142	$17,019,926	$30,792,182	$44,278,081
LGGroup	177,000	$2,155,258	$3,047,292	$8,354,963	$16,927,354	$30,607,837	$43,998,152
JPMorganChase	176,000	$2,151,417	$3,041,367	$8,334,776	$16,880,865	$30,515,303	$43,857,671
Delphi	171,400	$2,133,553	$3,013,824	$8,241,059	$16,665,246	$30,086,449	$43,206,929
UniCreditSpA	170,000	$2,128,051	$3,005,346	$8,212,252	$16,599,034	$29,954,868	$43,007,370
Walgreen	168,600	$2,122,517	$2,996,821	$8,183,307	$16,532,540	$29,822,780	$42,807,097
PepsiCo	168,000	$2,120,136	$2,993,154	$8,170,860	$16,503,955	$29,766,015	$42,721,043
AllianzAG	167,193	$2,116,925	$2,988,207	$8,154,079	$16,465,427	$29,689,518	$42,605,092
ToshibaCorp	166,651	$2,114,762	$2,984,876	$8,142,783	$16,439,496	$29,638,043	$42,527,077
YumBrands	166,600	$2,114,558	$2,984,562	$8,141,719	$16,437,053	$29,633,194	$42,519,729
KoninklijkeAholdNV	163,866	$2,103,571	$2,967,647	$8,084,401	$16,305,564	$29,372,312	$42,124,456
FiatSpA	162,237	$2,096,964	$2,957,480	$8,049,989	$16,226,682	$29,215,901	$41,887,576
SonyCorp	162,000	$2,096,000	$2,955,995	$8,044,966	$16,215,171	$29,193,088	$41,853,026
HCA	161,500	$2,093,961	$2,952,858	$8,034,354	$16,190,859	$29,144,900	$41,780,062
SuezPublic	160,700	$2,090,689	$2,947,825	$8,017,338	$16,151,880	$29,067,656	$41,663,121
CVSCaremarkCorporation	160,000	$2,087,818	$2,943,408	$8,002,408	$16,117,690	$28,999,922	$41,560,585
WellsFargo&Co	160,000	$2,087,818	$2,943,408	$8,002,408	$16,117,690	$28,999,922	$41,560,585
CargillInc	158,000	$2,079,566	$2,930,718	$7,959,545	$16,019,581	$28,805,631	$41,266,550
DardenRestaurants	157,300	$2,076,661	$2,926,251	$7,944,469	$15,985,091	$28,737,357	$41,163,255
FujitsuLtd	157,044	$2,075,596	$2,924,614	$7,938,946	$15,972,458	$28,712,355	$41,125,427
TheBoeingCompany	157,000	$2,075,413	$2,924,333	$7,937,996	$15,970,286	$28,708,055	$41,118,923
ElectricitédeFranceSA	156,152	$2,071,877	$2,918,898	$7,919,662	$15,928,358	$28,625,083	$40,993,415
J.C.Penney	155,000	$2,067,053	$2,911,483	$7,894,663	$15,871,210	$28,512,032	$40,822,436
Gap	154,000	$2,062,845	$2,905,017	$7,872,875	$15,821,426	$28,413,580	$40,673,569
MarriottInternational	150,600	$2,048,396	$2,882,824	$7,798,187	$15,650,900	$28,076,593	$40,164,240
OAOLUKOIL	150,000	$2,045,823	$2,878,874	$7,784,906	$15,620,603	$28,016,760	$40,073,842
Starbucks	145,800	$2,027,613	$2,850,927	$7,691,080	$15,406,750	$27,594,756	$39,436,582
StarwoodHotels&Rsrts.	145,000	$2,024,104	$2,845,543	$7,673,033	$15,365,659	$27,513,735	$39,314,297
VINCI	142,000	$2,010,824	$2,825,182	$7,604,845	$15,210,516	$27,208,040	$38,853,088
LockheedMartin	140,000	$2,001,864	$2,811,450	$7,558,927	$15,106,148	$27,002,572	$38,543,256
Pemex	138,215	$1,993,793	$2,799,085	$7,517,626	$15,012,350	$26,818,031	$38,265,097
BNPParibas	138,000	$1,992,816	$2,797,588	$7,512,631	$15,001,011	$26,795,730	$38,231,487
Procter&Gamble	138,000	$1,992,816	$2,797,588	$7,512,631	$15,001,011	$26,795,730	$38,231,487
JohnsonControls	136,000	$1,983,677	$2,783,594	$7,465,949	$14,895,086	$26,587,488	$37,917,747
CréditAgricoleSA	134,000	$1,974,446	$2,769,465	$7,418,872	$14,788,356	$26,377,816	$37,601,988
WaltDisney	133,000	$1,969,796	$2,762,348	$7,395,182	$14,734,685	$26,272,433	$37,443,340
CostcoWholesaleCorporation	132,000	$1,965,121	$2,755,196	$7,371,390	$14,680,805	$26,166,680	$37,284,170
HondaMotorCoLtd	131,600	$1,963,244	$2,752,325	$7,361,845	$14,659,194	$26,124,275	$37,220,355
ElectronicDataSystems	131,000	$1,960,421	$2,748,008	$7,347,495	$14,626,714	$26,060,555	$37,124,476
RenaultSA	130,573	$1,958,407	$2,744,928	$7,337,260	$14,603,553	$26,015,124	$37,056,126
GrupoSantander	129,749	$1,954,508	$2,738,966	$7,317,454	$14,558,747	$25,927,260	$36,923,947
BestBuy	128,000	$1,946,174	$2,726,227	$7,275,176	$14,463,155	$25,739,895	$36,642,176
EmersonElectric	127,800	$1,945,216	$2,724,763	$7,270,320	$14,452,182	$25,718,394	$36,609,850
NissanMotorCoLtd	127,625	$1,944,377	$2,723,481	$7,266,067	$14,442,573	$25,699,567	$36,581,546
CanonInc	127,338	$1,943,000	$2,721,375	$7,259,087	$14,426,798	$25,668,665	$36,535,090
RWEAGPublic	127,028	$1,941,509	$2,719,098	$7,251,536	$14,409,740	$25,635,249	$36,484,857
Alcoa	123,000	$1,921,912	$2,689,167	$7,152,451	$14,186,111	$25,197,577	$35,827,263
Johnson&Johnson	122,200	$1,917,968	$2,683,146	$7,132,551	$14,141,249	$25,109,862	$35,695,547
NorthropGrumman	122,200	$1,917,968	$2,683,146	$7,132,551	$14,141,249	$25,109,862	$35,695,547
WachoviaCorporation	122,000	$1,916,979	$2,681,637	$7,127,565	$14,130,010	$25,087,890	$35,662,559
SociétéGénérale	120,000	$1,907,029	$2,666,455	$7,077,439	$14,017,094	$25,087,890	$35,662,559
TheRoyalBankofScotlandGrou	120,000	$1,907,029	$2,666,455	$7,077,439	$14,017,094	$24,867,252	$35,331,378
ChinaMobileCommunications	119,000	$1,902,011	$2,658,801	$7,052,197	$13,960,273	$24,867,252	$35,331,378
INGGroupNV	115,000	$1,881,646	$2,627,757	$6,949,994	$13,730,496	$24,756,290	$35,164,887
Bouygues	113,300	$1,872,844	$2,614,348	$6,905,940	$13,631,596	$24,308,043	$34,492,743
sum (thousands)	34,545	$300,503	$429,196	$1,213,984	$2,517,723	$4,647,506	$6,769,050
MAJ33 Multiple		**0.70**	**1.00**	**2.83**	**5.87**	**10.83**	**15.77**

The number of employees is the key component.[37] It gives us a starting estimate of scarcity, given the presumption, for example, that if a person is head of a corporation with 1,117,000 employees, then he or she is at the one-in-1,117,000-scarcity level. On this assumption, as the number of employees change, so does demonstrated scarcity. In lockstep, CEO compensation changes. Within the broad scope of a functioning economy, the fewer the number of employees, the less the CEO should be paid.

No current CEO compensation for any particular company is shown. The estimated pay scales in the columns are based on the assumption that the average compensation for all of the employees, including all levels of management, is $48,000 – approximately the same as U.S. per capita GDP. Clearly this does not apply for each individual case, but there is a remedy. Use the correction factor.*

When CEO total compensation exceeds an amount shown in a column, CEO pay drives the MAJ distribution downward (as suggested by the progressive increase in pay as your eye moves towards MAJ columns at the right-hand side of the table). Over a long period of time, many companies paying salaries higher than the MAJ schedule are the motor that creates nation-wide maldistribution. The CEO pay scales here are consistent with the MAJ distributions in the lookup-table spreadsheet.

You may be tempted to say, "I do not begrudge the CEO a high salary. Look at the job that is being done. It is fantastic. It is central to the wellbeing of the company." But this well-meaning logic cannot translate all the way down the system. People at all levels do a fantastic job in a well-run company. That is why they are on the job in the first place.

If the leader takes a disproportionate amount, then people under him/her are under-compensated for the great work that they do. Those at the top are in a delicate position, since their compensation translates all the way down the scale. If their share is disproportionately large, then someone else's share is disproportionately small (whether they be in labor or management). The math is inevitable. The circumstances are far more delicate than commonly appreciated.

---

* Correction factor = "Average CompanyX Compensation" /48,000. Just multiply this number by the indicated compensations in the columns MAJ36 through MAJ17, and you will have the proposed compensations for the CEO, at the scarcity level conforming to the indicated number of employees and your chosen average compensation.

If the CEO is compensated at an amount equal to the grossly inequitable MAJ17, go study the spreadsheet lookup table at MAJ17. Look at how such compensation works its way down to the MAJ. It becomes brutally ugly once you enter the MAJ.

A business can readily select to compensate its employees according to any distribution curve in the lookup table. To do so within equitable ranges presumably promotes fair pay for all, without a necessity for labor-management bickering about the form of the curve. You can look through the curves to find the fairest ones for your business. Labor and management can have a shared destiny linked to equitable compensation curve, top to bottom. Customers can know it. Employees can know it. Stockholders can know it. The nation can know it.

Just as there are upper rational limits for CEO compensation, there are floors beneath which it should not fall. The MAJ33 is such a floor. And MAJ36 provides entirely insufficient compensation given the responsibility and difficulty of the CEO job.

The last line of Table-79 shows the position of other distributions relative to MAJ33. For example, a MAJ29 compensation is 2.83 times greater than the MAJ33 case. The next to the last line shows the sums for the previous columns. One hundred twenty-nine companies of the sizes indicated would employ more than 34 million people. At MAJ33, total CEO compensation would have been about $429 million ($1.2 billion at MAJ29), assuming a $48,000 per capita average.

There will be the few who contribute so extraordinarily that they deserve commensurately high compensation. That is the rub. The Top1% is a treasure when properly compensated; a malignancy when it is not.

Extending back as far as recent memory reaches for most people, we, in the USA, are now anchored at disproportionately high top-end incomes. But if we look in the spreadsheets at a variety of scarcity levels during the post WWII era, we get a better picture of our nation and condition that caused it to thrive.

A CEO compensation consistent with MAJ33, or thereabouts, is apt to change compensation and allocation of responsibilities throughout executive suites. Equitable distributions and a greater leveling at the higher reaches (the reduced spread between people at the top seen in earlier graphs #26 through #29 and the upcoming IQ analysis cause me to speculate that equitable distributions are conducive to improved decision-making at the top.

Income distribution does not decrease or increase the total payroll of a business. Products can sell at the same price. Competitive strength is not reduced by equitable distribution. Any constant total amount for combined labor and management, reallocated along a different curve, leaves cost of production unchanged within a business. As far as accounting is concerned, the same amount is going to company employees, just in different proportions.

If excessive compensation goes to the Top1%, beyond their true value, someone else pays for it: the customer by a higher price, the lowly worker by reduced income, the stockholder by reduced value retained in the firm and by reduced dividends, and everybody by a less vibrant business.

We have previously seen that a MAJ36 provides little likelihood of significant increases in wellbeing and happiness for the majority: It does so by insufficiently compensating the most able people at the top. To do so is wrong. The MAJ36 column in Table-78 and 79 provides the evidence that supports the argument. MAJ36 compensations are insufficient to get high quality and interesting leadership.

The MAJ29 in the tables is the midpoint between MAJ33 and MAJ25 (in the event that you are not inclined to cast your lot with either of them). The rest of the argument is that a MAJ25 maldistribution is destructive, and distributions south of it are extremely dangerous.

In a high earner's life, compensation is not made in isolation. It eventually comes back to influence the high earner's extended family. For parents in the upper 10% of income earners with three children, there is roughly a one in three chance for each of their children to end up as an adult in one of the following income groups: 1) the Top 10%, 2) the MAJ, or 3) the group in between (the respective probabilities more precisely being 29.6%, 31%, and 39.4%).[38]

You can anticipate that a maldistribution culture will ultimately disadvantage the clear majority of a high earner's descendents and extended family who in adulthood will find themselves in the MAJ or near to it. To impoverish the MAJ is to impoverish a portion of the high earner's family and its offspring in the future.

There also is roughly a one in three chance that those who come into the top 10% will come from parents from the following income groups: the Top 10%, the MAJ, or the group in between (the respective probabilities being 29.6%, 28.2%, and 42.4%).[39] The MAJ needs to be appropriately compensated in the present generation for future generations to prosper.

The ongoing health of corporations and businesses requires that leadership provide sufficient economic advantages to classes other than the top 10% because, as shown, about 70% of those in high position normally come from lower classes. The people who spend their youth in the MAJ, or nearby, need conditions where they can flourish [70.4= 100-29.6]. Explicitly, this 70% resides beneath the teeter point. They are the group damaged by maldistribution.

It is myopic and selfish in the extreme for a high earner to assert that disproportionately high compensation is his exclusive right. To whom much is given, much is expected. The maldistribution culture damages his family, his company, the economy, and the nation.

Table-78 and 79 have covered enough ground already, but it is well to keep in mind the distinction between CEO pay and CEO income. The CEO also benefits from wealth income that will result from investing his high income. What starts as narrowly considered compensation is, in practice, an entry into an income stream with a large flow coming from wealth, as well as customary compensation. Any compensation schedule carries with it the added wealth income bonus. To have money is to make money.

Wealth income.

Whenever a person earns a salary or gets income by other means, job status carries with it the income stream derived from wealth. For those of us at the low end, this wealth bonus is usually so small that we neglect to consider it. At the upper strata, the wealth bonus is often grand. In the statistics, this bonus is mixed in with the income shown in the income distribution curves. Let's try to carve it out from the whole and take a look at it.

The carving is not completely accurate, as we will soon see, but it does serve to estimate a floor for the income that would normally be generated by wealth. We multiply the ten-year bond rate in the Shiller database (listed back to 1871)[40] by the wealth indicated in the spreadsheets for all scarcity levels. This gives an estimate of the average lower limit wealth income for everybody. Wealth income, as shown here, is not necessarily received in cash each year, and may take the form of asset appreciation or indirect advantages derived from the wealth.

The following graph-84 shows a smoothed version of wealth income at scarcity levels of one-in-240,000 and one-in-a-million. An artifact of the smoothing is that the steep increase wrongly looks like it occurred about four years earlier than it actually did. The late 1970s and early 1980s experienced high interest rates that also increased wealth income. That period was followed by increased wealth inequality that kept wealth income high.

#84

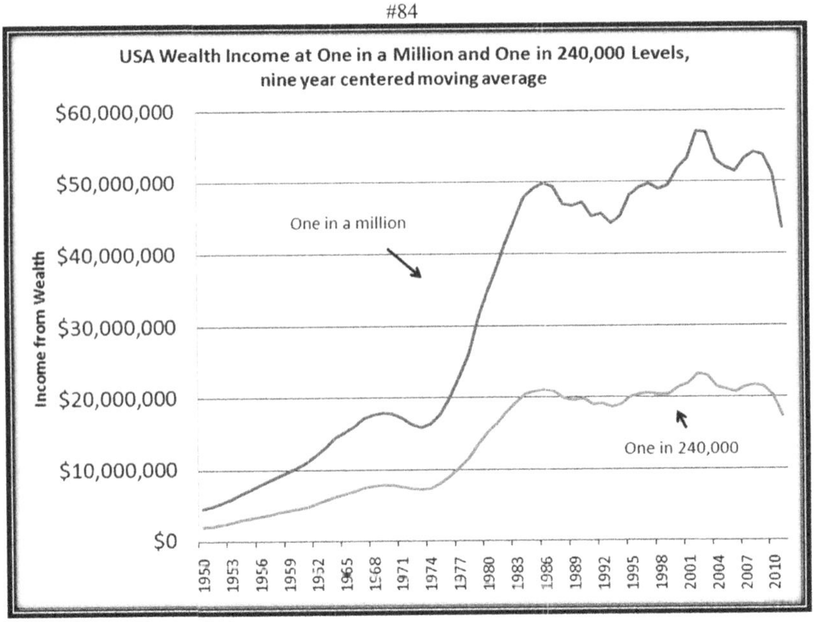

The common target for excessive compensation is the CEO. As you can begin to appreciate, the full blame should not fall on the CEO alone. As much as we may feel CEO compensation is excessive, we need to acknowledge that in most instances, the CEO has great responsibility and often great ability. The CEO presumably will seek a compensation that is keyed to those who automatically receive a high wealth income flow from their accumulated riches, which can exist irrespective of the wealth holder's ability.

In the following graph-85 for the U.S. from 1950-2011, we consider what the stream of income coming from wealth looked like compared to the customary incomes shown in the spreadsheets. As shown by the wide spread between Max and Min values in graph-85, there is great variability in the relationship between wealth income and customary income (assuming that the scarcity levels for income and wealth are identical).

#85

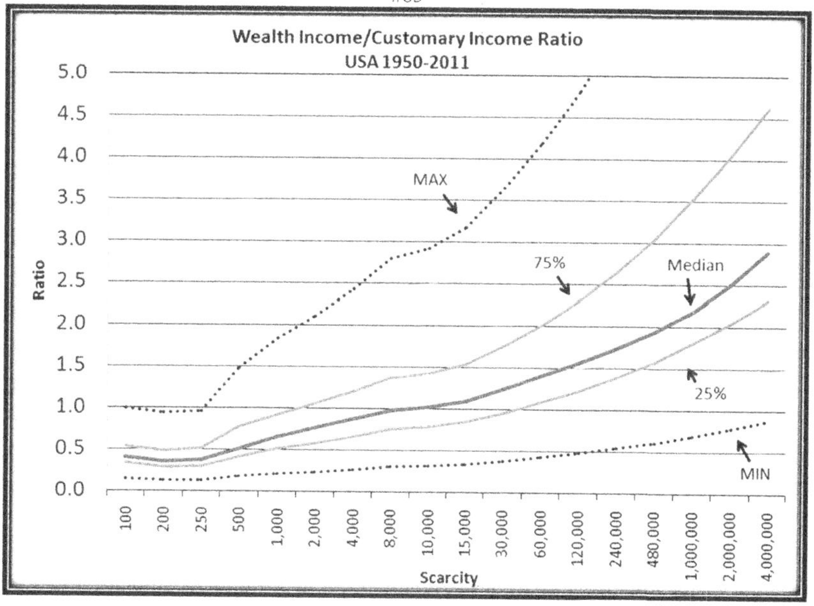

#85B

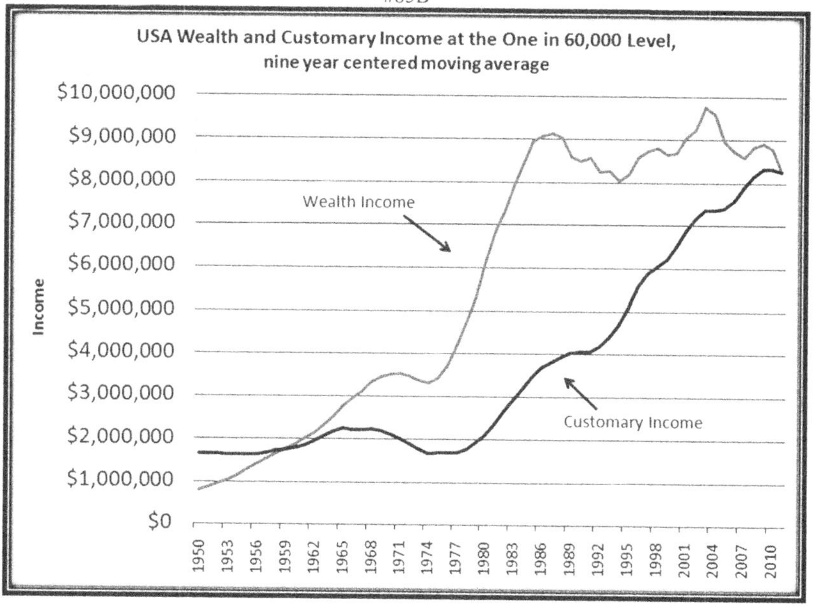

Notwithstanding, patterns emerge. At low scarcity levels, wealth income seldom approaches customary income. By the time we reach the one-in-8,000 point, the median is customarily above 1.0, indicating that from this point upwards the tendency is for wealth income alone to exceed customary income at identical scarcity levels.

By the time we reach the one-in-60,000 point, wealth income exceeds customary income in 75% of cases. We can see this particular relationship over time in graph-85B.

People with vast fortunes and exceptionally high incomes are not apt to be providing access to their private financial affairs, making mathematical probing of this kind all the more useful. The people in the above graph-85B are vastly rich. Until the mid-1960s, they often hovered in the neighborhood of $2 million annual income, coming either from wealth or conventional income. By the mid-1980s, high wealth holders had achieved most of their advantage. The high customary income earners achieved their advantage through maldistribution at a more consistent, but slower pace.

We now make a necessary distinction that we have not previously discussed. In the above graph, we are looking at two groups, separately, at the one-in-60,000 level: 1) those with vast fortunes (high wealth income), and 2) those with exceptionally high income. At times, the people in these groups overlapped, but in the main they did not.

Within the range of income and wealth with which most of us are familiar, there is a closer correspondence: Those of us with high income have high wealth; those of us with little income have little wealth – as previously implied in the wealth curves. But at the very high end, the relationship is more problematic. Sometimes those at identical scarcity levels, with very high customary incomes, make far less than those with vast fortunes that produce an enormous wealth income stream.

For example, in Table-87 let's take 1986 and 2007 USA as examples. In 1986, the interest rate was high at 7.68% producing a very high wealth income stream. And the MAJ also still had a substantial share of the wealth at WealthMAJ6.29, which provided a wealth share 1.68 times greater than its 2007 condition [1.677= 6.29/3.75]. In 1986, the wealthy were still making most of their wealth income from high interest rates rather than the acute wealth maldistribution that followed. On the income side, the MAJ in 1986 had about a 10% greater income share than in 2007 [9.69= 28.3/25.8-1]. These items draw attention to the real world where numerous relationships act in different directions to produce the ultimate outcome.

The table shows that up until about the one-in-4,000 wealth holder scarcity, customary income scarcity in 1986 and 2007 was usually less than wealth holder income scarcity. This means that up until about this level of scarcity, it was more likely that it would be easier to earn customary income rather than exclusively earning wealth income.

When we look at the very high end of the table, we see that customary income scarcities in 1986 and 2007 ballooned once wealth scarcity reached high levels. For example, at 480,000 and above, it would be nearly impossible to earn as much by conventional income as was earned by wealth income alone.

IncomeMAJ:	25.8	28.3
WealthMAJ:	3.75	6.29
Interest Rate:	4.63%	7.68%

Scarcity Level Matching Points, Where Income From Wealth Equals Conventional Income Earned

Wealth Holder Scarcity	2007 Income Earner Scarcity	1986 Income Earner Scarcity
500	136	264
1,000	203	686
2,000	975	1,780
4,000	3,424	4,620
8,000	8,891	11,988
10,000	12,095	16,300
15,000	21,141	28,492
30,000	54,918	73,952
60,000	142,697	192,007
120,000	370,779	498,386
240,000	963,376	1,293,667
480,000	2,502,569	3,359,098
1,000,000	6,878,782	9,222,942

At the one-in-8,000 wealth holder scarcity level and above, it is easier to make money by wealth income rather than by customary income. It is easy to spot this effect in the earlier graph-85 of the "Wealth Income/Customary Income Ratio." Whenever the ratio in the graph exceeded 1.0, it became more likely that it would be easier to earn income by wealth income alone than to earn it by customary income. At 1.0 and above, wealth income can no longer be carved out of conventional income by these methods as initially proposed because it exceeds it. Above 1.0, the table scarcities tell the story.

Here we see the important interplay between wealth distributions and income distributions. The high-income CEO, of great ability, is apt to be guided in his compensation demands, at least in part, by the large income-earning advantage that high wealth holders (often of lower ability) have. When wealth becomes seriously maldistributed, it holds out a tantalizing carrot-like incentive to push CEO pay higher. Income distribution, too, then edges toward being increasingly maldistributed. Where would the stopping point be? What will produce the stopping? Mull it over. Time to move on.

KeyRatio.

The lion's share of important work done by a nation is done by those between the 50th percentile level and the one-in-200 level of scarcity. This group is a bedrock of society. Many of those at the 200 level of scarcity are often capable of scoring about 670 on either the math or verbal SAT and may well have an IQ of about 140. They frequently are professional people: medical doctors, engineers, or similarly skilled professionals. Those at the 50th percentile have already made the cut to the upper half of society by being the higher one out of two.

The KeyRatio is the ratio between the incomes of these two groups: those at the one-in-200 level divided by the income of those at the 50th percentile. In order for the market economy to function, all people within this range need to be compensated at a high rate consistent with their contribution to the economy. Otherwise, the flow of income within the economy is insufficient to support consumption and the salaries of those key people who bring the product to market.

The obvious way for those at the one-in-200 level of scarcity to advance their income is to do quality work. Less obviously, it is just as important with respect to the total economy that the level of abilities of those at the 50th percentile are fully developed and appropriately remunerated, because they are the base from which the KeyRatio determines the income of those at the one-in-200 level.

The honorable way to ensure a good income for those at the one-in-200 level is to increase the contribution, productive capacity, and income for those at the 50th percentile. (The G.I. Bill after WWII is an example of this concept in practice.) By this means, when the KeyRatio is multiplied by the income at the 50th percentile, the one-in-200 level income is also proportionally increased. The dishonorable way to increase income for those at the one-in-200 level is to increase maldistribution and thereby increase the KeyRatio.

Looking at the following graph-89, you will see that the KeyRatio at MAJ33 is 7.3. At MAJ25, it balloons to 20.7. The shortsighted temptation is to ignore the people at the 50th percentile and to settle on benefitting those who prosper because they are above the teeter point. *That would not be taking care of the tribe.* A KeyRatio in the neighborhood of 7.3 serves the tribe well.

The KeyRatio is centrally important for assessing what distribution is most appropriate for a society. Superstition, primitive thought processes, poor work habits and numerous other adverse conditions may exist in a highly uneducated nation. In such a case, an equitable MAJ33, and a 7.3 KeyRatio nationwide, may be inappropriate because of an excessively large spread between abilities and performance of the 50th percentile and the one-in-200 earner.

#89

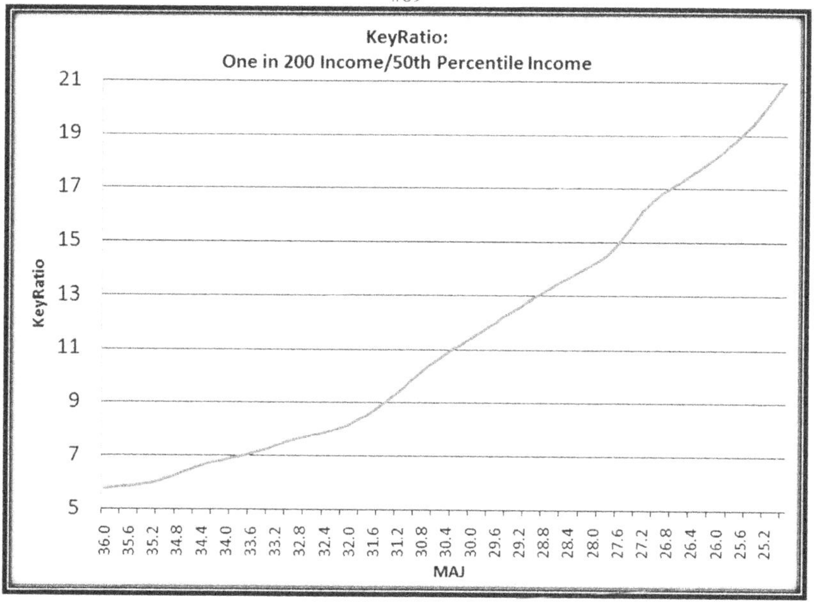

Just as there is a KeyRatio for income, corresponding KeyRatios can be constructed to measure abilities and performance brought to the marketplace. By this means, income and performance reference points together can serve to illustrate when an income KeyRatio is excessive and when it is not.

But if the starting point is a high KeyRatio, the emphasis must emphatically shift to bringing the 50th percentile up to a high standard so that the 50th percentile can receive a justifiably higher income. Lagging in this effort would suggest that the ruling class is making an insufficient effort to advance the 50th percentile, and it would suggest that the true objective is to perpetuate maldistribution and an excessively high KeyRatio, without providing any benefit to the 50th percentile.

Productivity.

In all instances, the Simon Legree School of Management holds out for "increased productivity" as a precondition for reversing maldistribution. Bunk. Productivity is important for an individual firm. I certainly kept a sensible eye on it in my business. By contrast, we can view measurements of national productivity as a means for correcting maldistribution skeptically. The dogma that if nationwide productivity in developed nations goes up, equitable income distributions will follow, is refuted by history and math. If you doubt this, look at USA MAJ history, and look at the lookup-table curves.

#90

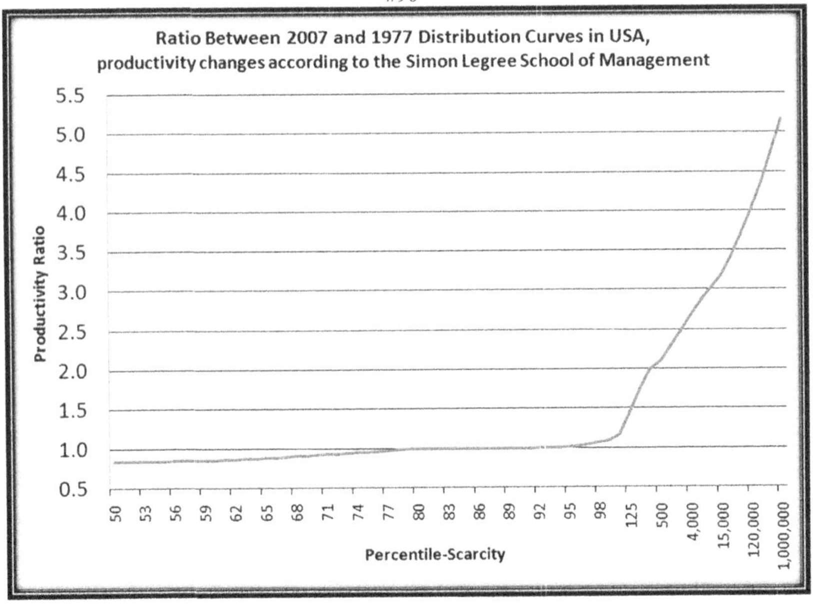

Fluidly and odoriferously, Simon Legree the fifth in his distilled, spirited manner explained the change of distribution in the U.S. during the thirty-year period from 1977 to 2007:[41]

> "Our Betterment of Legree-Like Man Society has studied the data provided in this book. We find that the above graph-90 explains the reason for the thirty-year demise of the person at the 50th percentile. That person's productivity is only 83% of what it was in 1977. The productivity of the person at the one-in-a-million increased five times during the same period. Do you expect us to pay a worm the same proportion it earned in 1977 at the very time the illustrious king of the heap has increased his productivity five-fold? I would not want the worm to touch my swizzle stick, much less give him a nickel more. I will stir my own, thank you."

The not-so-esteemed Mr. Legree *did* fish out numbers that would explain his logic. The fatal flaw is that the productivity of the average worker plainly increased since 1977, as it has done throughout U.S. economic history.[42]

#91

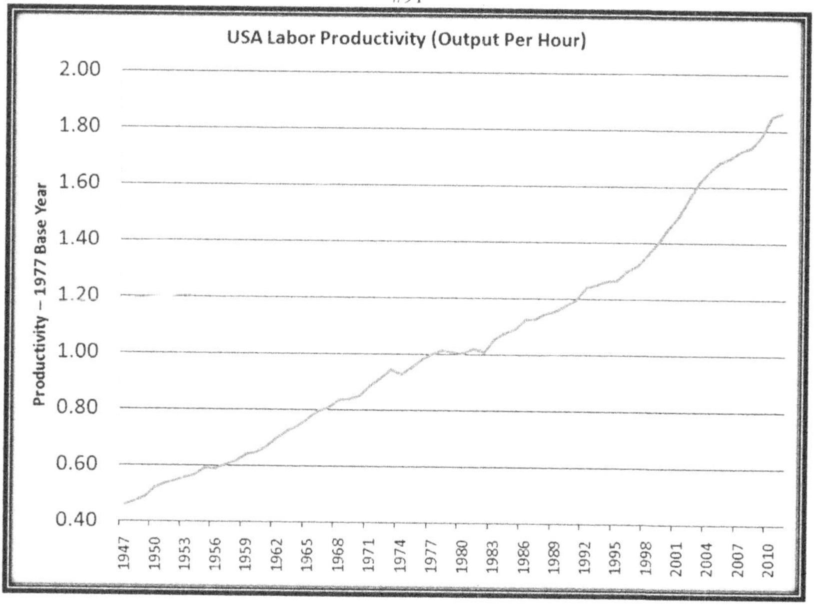

We do have firm evidence in the above graph-91 that the productivity of labor has increased about 1.86 times since 1977 – the same period in which maldistribution got legs. Productivity did not decline as Legree asserts. Productivity and maldistribution march to different drummers. In the U.S., productivity tends to consistently march upwards. Maldistribution marches to the predilections of the rich. It did so prior to the Great Depression. It is does so now.

Legree failed to show that those at the high reaches of the income ladder had increased their productivity to the extent that he asserts. This is the standard failing of those who assert that labor productivity would need to advance to quell maldistribution. The distribution curves reflect how incentives are distributed through the *complete* range – from bottom to top. Legree and his crowd ignore it.

You cannot claim that productivity on the labor portion of the curve will change the shape of the curve, without accounting for productivity at the high end of the curve. If it, too, moves in an equal upward direction, there would be no economic logic for distribution to change. The only valid economic productivity-based rationale for a more equitable distribution requires that the productivity change at the top is less than the labor productivity change.

Legree and his cohorts in all instances will always be reluctant to admit that the productivity change at the top is lower than labor's productivity change. And, *that is the precise precondition economically required to justify the productivity-cure-for-maldistribution logic.*

It is not plausible that the huge differences we have seen, say in going from a MAJ33 to a MAJ25, were caused by labor productivity deficiencies, or that labor productivity changes of a sufficient magnitude can, or will ever, reverse it. The root cause of maldistribution in the USA is culture – a Legree culture, not productivity.

Scarcity, the intuitive view.

It is often difficult to get a visceral grip on what scarcity actually means. As an aid, I developed the following informal spreadsheet Table-93. Do not take the table to be accurate. It is just a little something put together to provide a handy, albeit crude, reference while writing.

In it, the "Half SAT" college entrance exam score column is intended to indicate the highest score one receives on either the verbal or the math section.* The percentile and scarcity rankings columns refer to the total population, not just those who take the college boards or who play chess. I made estimates for chess ratings.[43] They are subject to great error. Do not take them as gospel. For percentile, SAT and IQ data, Ulf Norlinger's "Estimated IQs of some of the Greatest Geniuses" web page was used.[44]

It is ironic that economists and others employ the word meritocracy as if it conferred an advantage on a nation. Meritocracy and oligarchy have become indistinguishable.[45]

---

* A pesky point: The difference between the column, "Half SAT" rankings and conflicting SAT comments may appear confusing. The difference seems to reflect a sample size difference. The former are an expected SAT scores for a person of the indicated degree of intelligence (whether they took the test or not) and the scores in the comments indicate percentage outcomes from those who actually took the test. The differences are noticeable, most likely because many people do not take the SAT.

#93

Percent	Scarcity	IQ Stanford Binet	Half SAT	Scholastic Aptitude or Other Description
100.00%	**6,000,000,000**	201	800	Unmeasurable genius
100.00%	**240,000,000**	192	800	Highest genius
100.00%	**4,000,000**	180	800	Highest genius
100.00%	**1,000,000**	176	800	High genius; chess R. 2849. The highest ever FIDE rating was 2851, which Garry Kasparov received.
100.00%	**60,000**	166	790	High genius; chess R. 2749
100.00%	**30,000**	164	780	Genius, Nobel Prize Winners; chess R. 2649
99.99%	**15,000**	161	765	Genius, Nobel Prize Winners
99.99%	**8,000**	159	756	Genius, Nobel Prize Winners; chess R. 2549, Often having an International Grandmaster title
99.98%	**4,000**	156	741	Genius, Nobel Prize Winners; chess R. 2449, Senior Master
99.95%	**2,000**	153	727	Genius, Professors, about 99.93% (one in 1,430) of SATs lower than 800
99.9%	**1,000**	149	707	Genius, Professors , about 97% of SATs lower than 710; chess R. 2249 Life Master, National Master
99.8%	**500**	146	693	Genius, Professors, about 88% of SATs lower than 690; chess R. 2049 Expert
99.6%	**250**	142	673	Highly gifted, Intellectuals; chess R. 1949
99.5%	**200**	141	669	Highly gifted, Intellectuals; chess R. 1849 Class A
99.2%	**125**	139	659	Highly gifted, Intellectuals; chess R. 1749
99.0%	**100**	137	649	Highly gifted, Intellectuals; chess R. 1649, Class B and higher considered extremely competitive
98.7%	**75**	135	640	Gifted, University graduates, about 83% of SATs lower than 640
98.0%	**50**	133	630	Gifted, University graduates; chess R. 1449 Class C
96.7%	**31**	130	615	Chess R. 1049 Class E, bright beginner
95%	**20**	126	596	Gifted, University graduates, about 78% of SATs lower than 600; chess R. 649 Class G, slightly beneath the median chess level of 657
90%	**10**	121	572	about 72% of SATs lower than 575
72%	**3.57**	109	514	72% have not completed four years of college
60%	**2.50**	104	490	The MAJ refers to the 60% majority average income or percentage share
50%	**2.00**	100	470	about 36% of SATs lower than 475
40%	**1.67**	96	451	about 36% of SATs lower than 475
15%	**1.18**	84	393	15% have not completed High School in 2003 in USA (12 years of education); about 15% of SATs lower than 405
13%	**1.15**	82	383	Very low academic ability

In 1958, Michael Young wrote the book, *The Rise of the Meritocracy*. Young invented the word meritocracy "for purpose of damnation, not praise."[46] Indeed, in his book the protagonist is killed as a consequence of meritocracy. As the demise develops, the comment appears: "… there is nothing to be gained from social mixing, in school, in residence, or at work, because the upper class now have little or nothing to learn from the lower."[47] Young's meritocracy formula that brought about the doomed state was: Merit = Intelligence + Effort.[48]

The purpose of the prior table is not to attempt to equate income or wealth with IQ. Any attempt to find a firm, highly correlated linkage with income would be perilous from the outset.

Many years ago Judith Selvidge wrote an article that impressed me. It was about procedures for assigning probabilities to rare events. In it, she pointed out the value of "external calibration," which is to say referencing a rare event to some totally different system "whose only or main connection to the basic event is that they, too, have very small probabilities of occurrence."[49]

This is the reason for the table. Most of us know people who scored considerably better than we did on our college boards. We may also have an intuitive sense of how much smarter some people are than we are.

For example, broadly applying "external calibration," we see that a person with a one-in-four-thousand intelligence scarcity level has the mental horsepower to become a Nobel Prize winner or to make an equally outstanding contribution to society. This scarcity level implies that in many small towns (population 4,000+) and cities, there are children and adults with the mental capacity to make extraordinary contributions of Nobel Prize Winning caliber. This draws focus to the point that amazing abilities reside in unlikely places. It is a waste and a tragedy whenever maldistribution, social, or economic conditions thwart such abilities. Such people are some of our greatest resources.

The one-in-4,000-scarcity level also holds out a standard for high income earners. If you are earning an income greater than the one-in-4,000 level, you need to be making a positive contribution to society roughly proportional to a Nobel Prize winner. Otherwise you are not pulling your weight.

Table-93 is useful for viscerally "externally calibrating" what scarcity of ability means. For example, if you have a friend who scored 756 on a Half SAT, that person is rare – precisely rare at a one-in-8,000-scarcity level.

In an eminently readable fashion, Malcolm Gladwell in *Outliers: The Story of Success* points to components that delivered success to some of the greats of recent times. Ten thousand hours of hard work, deliberate practice, and effective training were a good starting point, including for John Lennon and Paul McCartney, who clearly put in their ten thousand+ hours. At 2,000 hours a year, that could occur within 5 years [365/7*40hr per week-80 hr vacation= 2005 hrs per year]. Young's meritocracy formula was: Merit = Intelligence + Effort. With a 10,000-hour threshold, it might look more like: Merit = Intelligence *multiplied times* Effort.

We see that income and intelligence are not closely aligned. Preventing maldistribution is imperative because it is impossible to know where truly great performance, talent, ability, integrity, and intelligence will arise. People at all levels must be treated fairly from birth onward because the talents we rely on as a nation will spring up in unexpected places. We never know until after the fact who will possess the vital characteristic, and who will develop it.

> "The cult of the individuals is always, in my view, unjustified. To be sure, nature distributes her gifts unevenly among her children. But there are plenty of the well-endowed, thank God, and I am firmly convinced that most of them live quiet unobtrusive lives. It strikes me as unfair, and even in bad taste, to select a few of them for boundless admiration attributing super-human powers of mind and character to them. This has been my fate, and the contrast between popular estimate of my powers and achievements and the reality is simply grotesque."
>
> – Albert Einstein[50]

With "Heritability of IQ" estimates shown in Wikipedia, we see a wide variety of possible associations, perhaps settling down to about a 0.75 heritability (where 0 indicates that none of variations in the trait is genetic in origin and 1 indicates all of the variation in the trait is genetic in origin). Although a 0.75 factor is high, it provides room for exceptions (0.25), one out of four cases. And those exceptions are often significant.

The tribe.

Pull out the napkin. Well, you may not need it. The calculations are straight forward. The reliable rule of thumb to find how much you differ from the average IQ is to divide your IQ by 100. The average IQ is 100. The peak IQ is about 200. The first percentile IQ is almost exactly half of average IQ. If you were to argue that there should be a direct proportional correspondence between IQ and income, then peak income would be twice average income and the minimum at the first percentile would be about half the average income.

In that proposed proportional IQ to income scheme, in a nation where average income was $48,000, the range of incomes would vary from $28,213 for the first percentile to $96,960 at an absolute peak IQ of 202. The Top1% would average $68,527 and a MAJ53.8 distribution would prevail. Such equality in income distribution plainly does not and never has existed in the history of nations.

Contrary to our views that have been anchored to focus on small differences at the top end, the major story is that IQ distribution within the tribe is far flatter than our emphasis on "smarts" is usually inclined to infer. And if IQ did have a direct proportional relationship with income, it would be the poor, not the rich who would primarily benefit.

#96

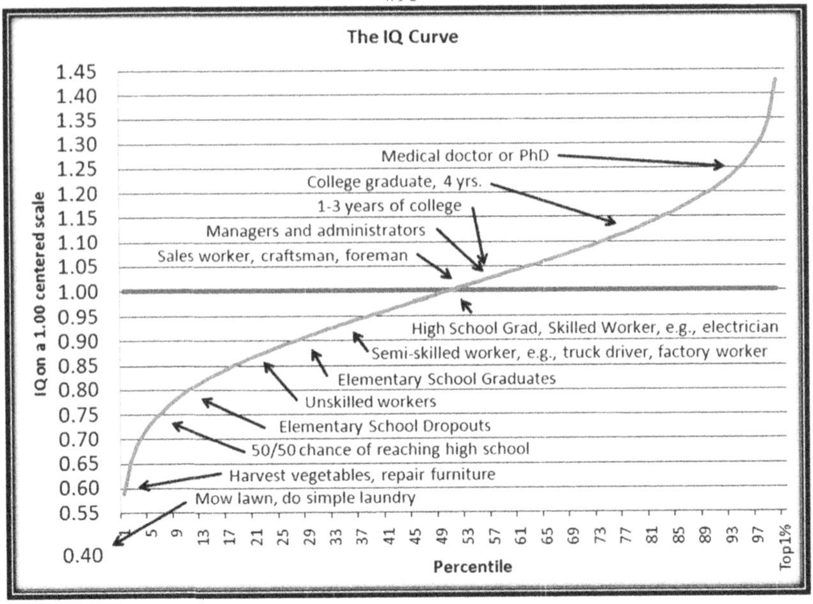

A nation, when it works well, must accommodate and provide a decent living for people of all IQ ranges, including those at the low end. To get a visual sense of IQ, some of Wikipedia's "Intelligence quotient" remarks were added to the above IQ Curve. About 4% of the population is classified as mentally retarded; 5% to 18%, as borderline intellectual functioning (below average cognitive ability).

Multiply the vertical axis in graph-96 by 100 to get IQ. Leave it as it is, to experiment with it as an X$ for determining income, as if IQ proportionately corresponds to income. However, you are apt to find such an experiment for estimating income disappointing. As shown in the following graph-97, the IQ curve is notably flat by comparison to an equitable MAJ33 income distribution.

#97

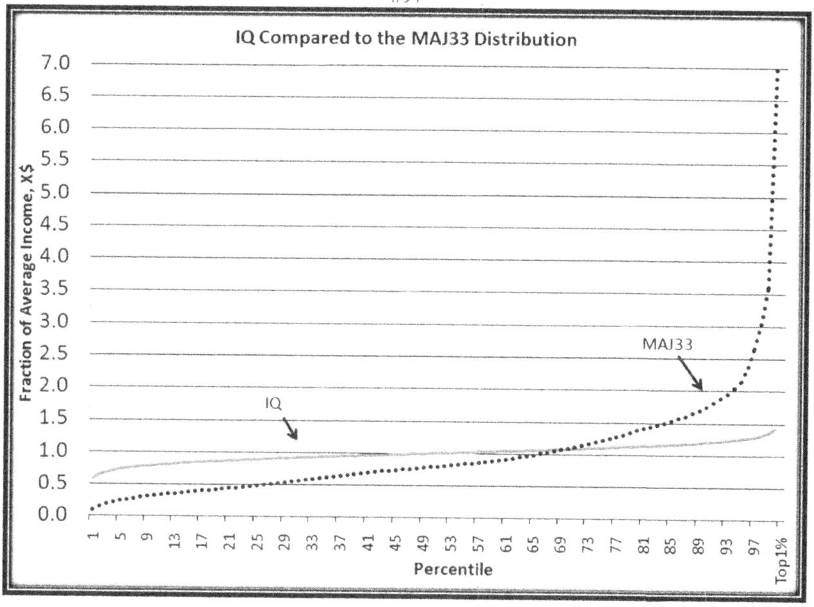

Still slugging along to find a relationship between income and IQ, the following graph-98 shows IQs that would correspond to MAJ33 and MAJ25 incomes. This graph can be made because we know the scarcity levels associated with IQ, and we know the scarcity levels associated with income. Keep in mind that Nobel Prize winners often have IQs in the neighborhood of 156+. Do you really expect the super-rich to have the extraordinarily high IQs that this graph suggests?

If you answer no, then the proposed link with income and IQ at the high end does not exist. Instead, as Gladwell has observed, once one reaches an IQ threshold of about 120, it seems that additional IQ points do not translate into an income advantages, and traits of personality and character assume increased importance.[51] About 9.1% of the population have IQs above 120.

If your answer is "yes" and you subscribe to the school of thought that the super-rich have higher IQs than Nobel Prize winners, then at MAJ33 that logic would lead to the conclusion that an approximate 156 IQ threshold for super high income would occur at an income of about one million dollars; and at MAJ25, at about three million dollars.

#98

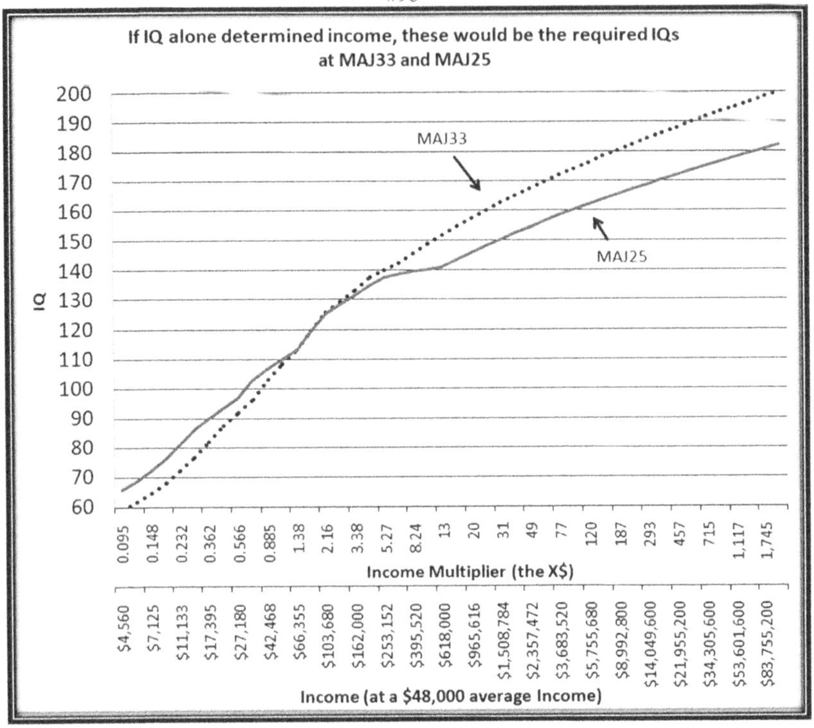

Backing away from attempting to link conventional IQ and income, perhaps there yet remains some way to hammer out a relationship. In the spirit of Selvidge's "external calibration," let's say that instead of representing conventional intelligence, IQ in the above graph-98 represents business acumen.

By this method, we see in the same graph that, at the high end of the scale, the maldistributed MAJ25 requires less ability than MAJ33, but presses for higher abilities from those at the low end – a rather twisted mentality for the MAJ25 folks.

To pay those at the top at MAJ25 more for lower business acumen – how does that strike you?

Inner Genie.

Go deep into your mind. Clear it of all heard before. Picture a world where IQ is unchanging. Picture the same world having compensations moving between MAJ33 and MAJ25. Continue thinking deeply. Ask your inner genie: "What is intelligence?" Your inner genie answers: "Intelligence, Master, is that constant quality that you have already assigned to people of the world." Ask your inner genie: "What is compensation?" Your inner genie answers: "Compensation, Master, is that changeable quality you have assigned to people of the world." As you slip out of Zen, you hear your inner genie repeating: "Constant intelligence, variable compensation. ... Constant intelligence, variable compensation. ..." As you move on, you barely hear, "Zagorsky ... Zagorsky ... Zagorsky."

Consider inner genie's brevity. A world where intelligence was largely a constant (given or developed), yet compensations went anywhere between MAJ33 to MAJ25. Clearly characteristics other than IQ are determining income variations. We do not need reams of studies to be certain of this. However, if it were possible to know baseline characteristics for compensation directly attributable to IQ, then we could estimate what fraction of income was derived from intelligence and what fraction came from characteristics other than intelligence. The inner genie's "Zagorsky" may just provide a missing link. Let's try it.

In his study, Zagorsky provides a table showing corresponding income and net worth for an IQ range of 75 to 125.[52] The computer programs I have written are able to transform Zagorsky's table into curves that explain compensation given for IQs from the 6th to 94th percentile – 89% of the population. If the data had also been available for the remaining 11%, then a full distribution curve for intelligence compensation could have been easily constructed. But the problem, as you will see, is not insurmountable. The 89% of the income curve that is available closely approximates a MAJ49 lookup-table curve. The small section of income (0.9%) beneath the 6th percentile that significantly deviates from the MAJ49 curve can be proportionally distributed to the 95th and higher percentiles without substantially changing curve shape at the backbone. By recalculating the top end with this new backbone data, the computer program gives a baseline IQ-Compensation curve (an IQ appropriate income curve) that we can compare to other distribution curves. By doing so, we can estimate how much components other than intelligence contribute to income. Don't attribute this curve to Zagorsky. Any errors are mine alone. His valuable work just made it easier for me to commit them.

To help visualize the process of creating the IQ-Comp Curve, look at the following graph-100. The data points available to me from the 6th to 94th percentile are shown in dots. The complete IQ-Comp Curve has its end points derived from the closely corresponding MAJ49 curve.[53] The final

IQ-Comp Curve was modestly less equitable than the starting MAJ49, caused partly by the difference in shape at the bottom.

#100

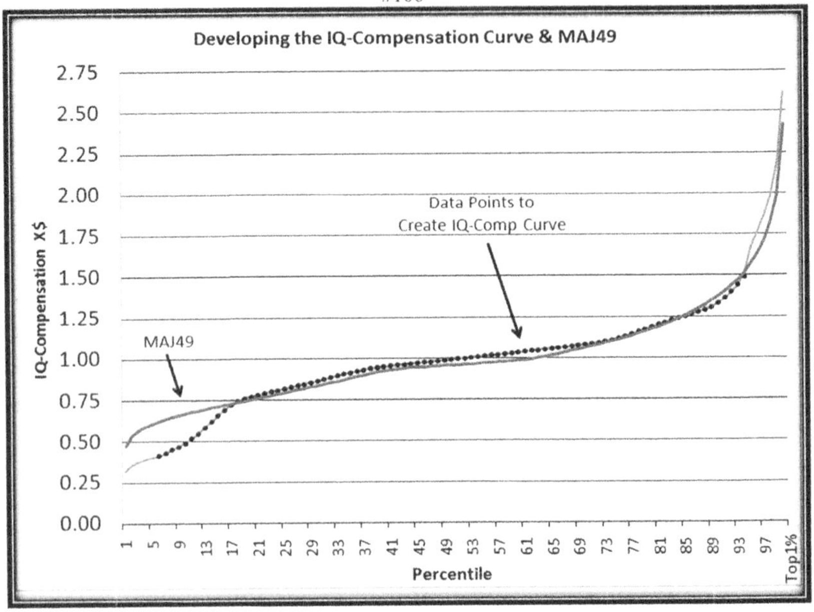

It is tempting to believe that the upper reaches of a true IQ-Comp Curve would vastly favor high IQ. I, too, would have found myself in that camp not so very long ago. But with the 6th to 94th percentile of the IQ-Comp Curve clearly defined, there is little latitude for creating other plausible shapes at the upper reaches that might greatly deviate from the shown curve. If you doubt this, try constructing a plausible curve having the same 6th to 94th percentile values, yet having other points that widely differ. Keep in mind that in the 100-point system, all points must sum to 100%. I believe you will find, as I did, that the constraints of IQ distribution and income distribution do not permit the Top1% to receive an outsized IQ advantage.

From the X$ values in the IQ-Comp Curve, we can estimate the income generated by IQ alone throughout the range. The outcome is shown in the following graph-101. This indicates about how much you would tend to be paid for IQ. The rest of your income, if higher, would come from other characteristics that the market rewards – components falling into a "not-IQ" category. *Keep the notion of "not-IQ" in mind. We can use the "not-IQ" factor to illustrate a key consequence of maldistribution.*

#101

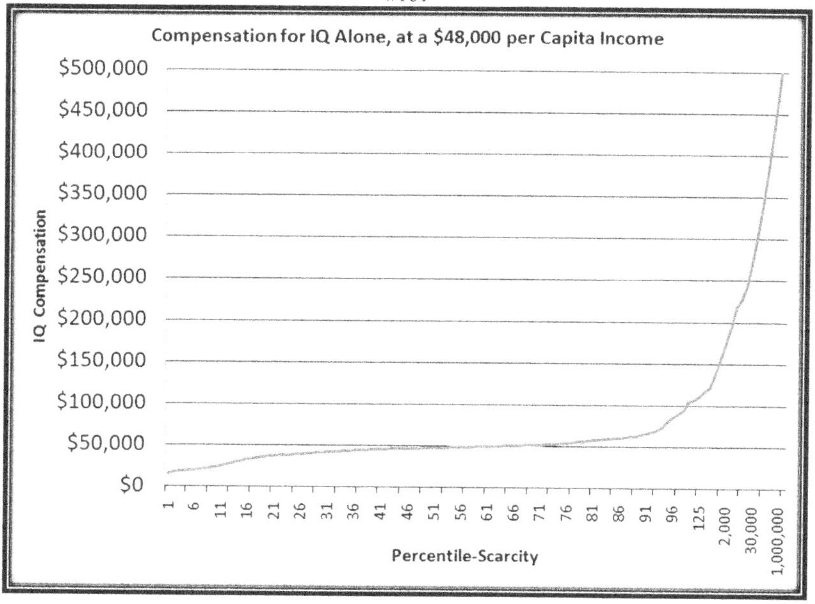

Seldom do we think it out, but IQ distribution is very flat by comparison to the huge range of incomes from top to bottom. An unavoidable consequence of the wide difference in the shape of the two curves is that people are highly compensated at the high end of the income scale for reasons that are not IQ related. They may be positive reasons, indifferent reasons, or harmful reasons – but they are not IQ. You may find the degree to which this occurs surprising

Not-IQ.

The extent to which people at the high end of the income scale are highly compensated for reasons other than IQ varies according to distribution curves. In the following graph-102, we see that the "not-IQ" component is far, far less at MAJ33 than at MAJ25. This should not be surprising. IQ Compensation distribution is relatively flat at a MAJ48 (or if you prefer a Gini of 18.9). IQ remained the same under MAJ33 and MAJ25; the component that changed was income.

The central point remains that the greater the separation between an IQ curve and an income curve, the greater will be the "not-IQ" income component.

We can divide any given curve in the lookup table by the IQ-Comp Curve to get an approximate magnitude of the "not-IQ" influences that would tend to exist throughout the curve, from bottom to top.

#102

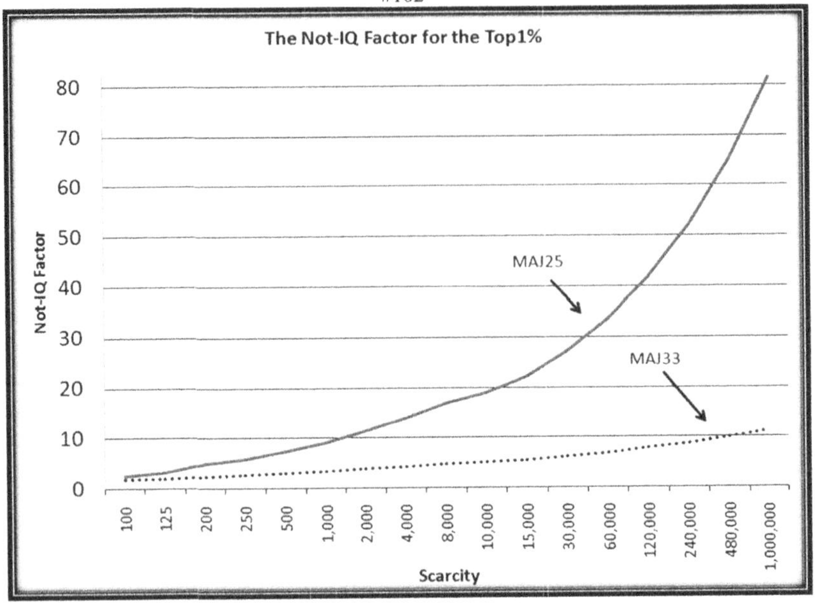

In graph-102, we see MAJ33 remains close to IQ throughout the Top1%. In sharp contrast, at MAJ25, IQ becomes a tiny portion of compensation at the high end of the curve. At the one-in-a-million-scarcity level, total compensation is more than 80 times larger than the IQ component. Obviously, this MAJ25 chasm between IQ and Income is vastly larger than the modest spread at MAJ33.

In a nation of 300 million people at MAJ33, the threshold for being in the Top500 income earners is a "not-IQ" of 10.3 – modest and sensible. At the maldistributed MAJ25 the Top500 are at a 68.3 "not-IQ." And at the highest income: a 488 "not-IQ." These guys are running on phenomenal "not-IQs."

It shows.

There is a continuum as maldistribution advances, where nations increasingly depart from intelligence-based decisions and preferences. You see this in spades when you look at a tinhorn potentate in a maldistributed economy. In such cases, in government and business, you will usually find an abundance of wing-nuts in leadership positions, and it is abundantly clear the key "not-IQ" components are coercion and a distasteful menu of items that never should have left the kitchen.

#103

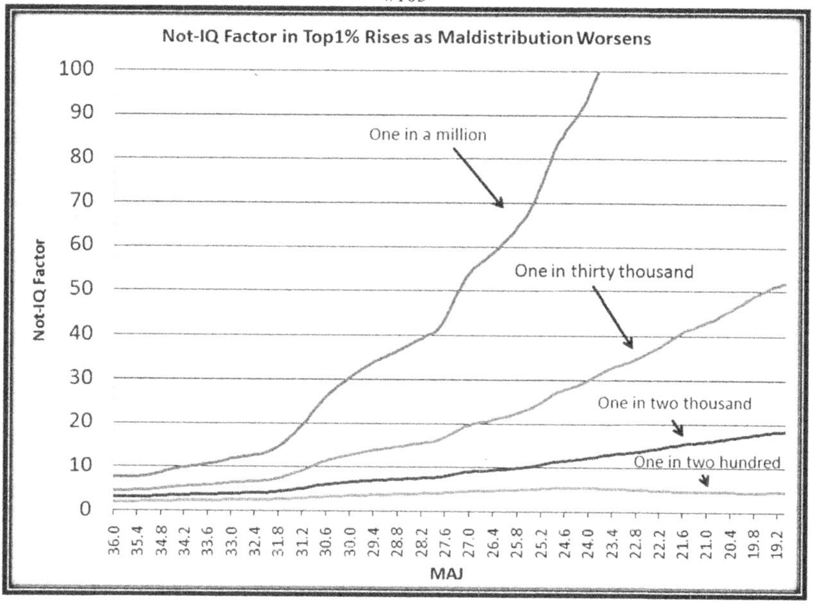

More specifically, we can see the relationship in the above graph-103. As maldistribution worsens, the high income earners at the one-in-a-million level become sharply disassociated with intelligence. The rise is quickened at MAJs beneath 31.8. It goes wildly off the scale beneath a MAJ23.7. In sharp contrast, the income earner at the one-in-200 level remains more closely grounded to intelligence with a "not-IQ" factor that ranges from about 2 to 5.5 at all points shown in the graph.

When you listen to an exceptionally wealthy person speaking in a maldistributed economy, it is well to remember that at least some of what you hear, for better or worse, is apt to be based on the "not-IQ" component. Be cautious about attributing IQ-based omnipotence to top management.

How far can economically successful nations go when enlightenment and intelligence become diminishingly small components of success? Is it not serious that as one advances to ever-higher levels of leadership, intelligence becomes an ever-decreasing component of success? Are not children the most adaptive and perceptive of us all? Will they not sense that in 73% of families, their parents are undercompensated for the intelligence they possess? Will their role models not shift increasingly away from intelligence to the more fruitful territory of "not-IQ" success? Why would a child follow the difficult route of developing education and intelligence when the plain evidence is that the greatest rewards come from the "not-IQ" (which is to say a path only slightly influenced by the classroom)? When I was in school, the window was one of the most attractive aspects of the schoolroom. But to make it the only attraction for the savvy student, would that be going too far?

As maldistribution increases, the infection of a reduced grounding in intelligence is intensely suffered almost exclusively within the Upper½%. The remaining 99½% of us are not apt to catch a debilitating case of it. It strikes with greatest force in a portion of society with whom most of us have little day-to-day social contact – the ten thousand people in the U.S. above the one-in-30,000 income level. Those at the top are the economic chiefs who indirectly determine the course of our lives. To have them making decisions without a firm and primary grounding in intelligence, would that be perilous?

#104

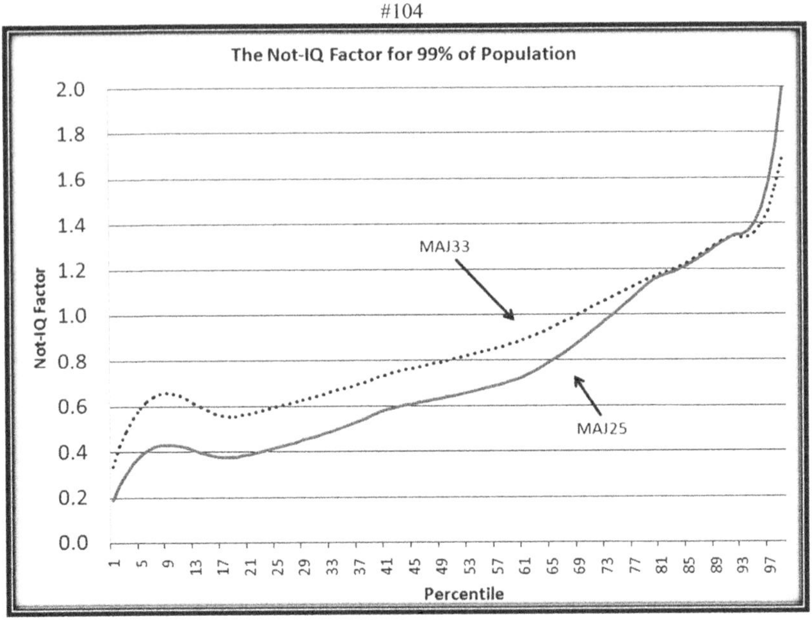

The "not-IQ" compensation that those of us in the 99% group experience does not have the drama seen in the Top1%. From about the 76th to 96th percentiles, as seen in graph-104, there is a zone of indifference between MAJ33 and MAJ25 where the differences between the two curves are about 5% or less.

When the "not-IQ" factor is equal to one, a person is compensated at an amount exactly consistent with intelligence. For MAJ33, this occurs at the 69th percentile; for MAJ25, at the 74th percentile.

When the "not-IQ" factor is less than one, a person is compensated at a rate lower than the IQ-Comp Curve. The MAJ33 keeps compensation closer to the IQ amount than does MAJ25. But no sensible distribution will keep the "not-IQ" at 1.0 throughout the range, because to do so would necessitate the nation having the same MAJ48 income distribution that intelligence does. Such a high MAJ would wrongly and dangerously under-compensate leadership, as has already been shown in another excessively equal distribution (MAJ36).

Some "not-IQ" compensation is necessary. Although a high "not-IQ" factor is deleterious, so too is an excessively low one. There are many "not-IQ" components that are valuable: integrity, hard work, discipline, desirable psychological characteristics, responsibility, conscientiousness, organizational capacity, health, creativity, experience, and the list goes on beyond the realm of didacticism to encompass numerous valuable traits, many of which we do not have the good sense to recognize.

Having said this, for a leadership to have a "not-IQ" factor of 80 (or another similarly high number) is a malady. Do you really want leadership in government and business where only $1/80^{th}$ of its characteristics for success are intelligence-based? A factor of 10 seems more likely to approach prudence. The progressive income disassociation with IQ as maldistribution advances is plainly unwise and destructive.[54]

At its core, economics is about allocation of resources. Is it an economic objective to have an intelligent society? Rewards for intelligence most certainly come under the allocation umbrella. Maldistribution devalues the single trait that distinguishes us from lower life forms. The most obvious breach of economic responsibility is to fail to reward, in proper measure, our most valuable resource – human intelligence.

Maldistribution distorts the essential relationships necessary for people and nations to thrive for the narrow purpose of benefitting a tiny few (at most, 3% of the population). We distinguish ourselves from tomatoes and such goods that can be valued and distributed exclusively according to supply and demand curves, because we are the purchasing, working, and creating engine that makes the whole enterprise workable, interesting, and useful. To keep the allocation focus on key ingredients – humans and life forms upon which they depend – would seem to be far more important than pandering to the "not-IQ" parochial interests at the top.

The instinct of the economist is to put all decision-making and value at the instant of the transaction – a paycheck. Nothing could be less appropriate. When you compensate a human, you are paying for the past (education, experiences, training, et cetera) and buying the future (the capacity to raise the next generation and care for the elders). In contrast to most animals, from infancy to adulthood, humans are exceptionally vulnerable and require a huge investment in time and resources for them to thrive. Examination of brain development during this period confirms the obvious. If compensation is reduced to a mean action to keep worker pay at the lowest achievable point, the past cannot be paid for, nor the future bought.

In its young state, the "not-IQ" factor seems to provide a standard that gives us a more accurate assessment than most of us currently have. This standard alone appears sufficient for the benchmark, especially since from the 18th to 94th percentile, it so closely matches the shape of MAJ49 and the demonstrated compensations for intelligence. So it will be included in the spreadsheets. Should it need revision, it can be revised there. Given its capacities to set a consistent standard through the wide range of MAJs and income levels that we have seen in the above graphs (#100-#104), it is hard to imagine a standard that would offer large improvements.

Return to the tribe.

The 72% of the population without a 4-year college education and the 60% majority, to which much of our discussion has been directed, are at the lower end of the scale.

As elsewhere, characteristics other than intelligence measurements play a dominant role. Responsibility, dedication, conscientiousness, study, practice, ability to put in a good day's work, and the list goes on … . These are not only of great value, they are often of preeminent value. They make more difference in many work situations than does raw initial intelligence.

I work with my hands frequently – carpentry and the like – and have a complete metal-working machine shop in my basement for prototype design (industrial lathe and computer controlled milling machine, together weighing more than most cars). Constantly good ideas come from a wide variety of people. A completely illiterate friend is a reliable source for many of them. I have been fortunate to know people of breathtaking intelligence and equally fortunate to work with ordinary folk, who on a good day, keep observations and ideas flowing.

When looking at a table or graph with 60% of the people having an IQ of 104 or lower, experience tells me that many fine decent folk can be found there. We have no reason to criticize them. They may be at 104 or lower. That is what humanity is about. Don't minimize it. It is central. When we talk about the MAJ, this fact implicitly resides in the background.

Keep in mind, though, that there is not an exact correspondence between percentile rankings and workers' IQ, especially at the lower percentiles. Highest IQ people in a household are often key income earners. Those with less marketable skills or a lower IQ may draw a lower paycheck than the key income earner, or attend to necessary duties at the home, garden, or on the farm, which may or may not generate income. A household working together, each to his or her abilities. A nice picture it is. We all have our place and our importance.

The MAJ needs sufficient opportunities. They have built, and will continue to build, great nations if they are given half a chance. They do, and can do, an honest day's work. Often they stretch beyond their God-given abilities to do exceptionally well. They may be star performers in a particular area. But they require jobs generally in line with their abilities. The MAJ should never be chastised for failing to work in heavily abstract thought of the kind you can hear listening in on graduate courses at a university. Nor should the MAJ be held hostage to vision which falls in line with some ill-conceived dreamed-up policy objectives that have little likelihood of materializing.

As shown in *Henry J. Kaiser Western Colossus*, at the shipyards, "they were a strange host, not only the healthy but the half-sick, the half-alive, the halt, the maimed, the partially blind. Thousands were 4-Fs, rejects from the draft. Thousands were women not used to heavy work they were called upon to do. Many were old, really too old to work at all, but this was war time and everyone's services were needed in one way or another. Dr. Cecil Cutting described them as a 'walking pathological museum.'"[55]

No one ever before had built a ship in fewer than twenty-four days. September 1942, Kaiser's people built one in ten days. Two months later, they did it in four days.

Back in November 1940, Kaiser had never built even one ship. His "shipyard" in 1940 was a mudflat, nothing more. From 1941 to 1945, his people built 1,490 ocean going ships – merchant ships and warships. That would be more than one ship a day, on average. Peak employment was 197,000. If you ever have any doubt about the capacity of the ordinary person, think again.

Not only could the workers be described as average, Henry J. Kaiser was a short, fat guy, who himself said "I am certain that I was less than an average boy to everyone but my mother." He left school after the 8th grade. He started off in business as a photographer. He was honest. He prohibited corruption and bribes of any kind. He hired people he had faith in, who were unproven, and who often had no prior experience in managing the jobs for which they were responsible (and these were huge jobs).

It was Kaiser's conviction, stated in the *Western Colossus*, "that every person has something to offer if given a fair chance, and if treated with proper respect. It was a microcosm of America itself – where the blending of different races and different levels of skills produces a strong and balanced economy."

Kaiser 1928: "... you can't get fine talent into your organization by simply offering high salaries. You and the men who work with you have to build yourselves up to the capacity to tackle bigger and bigger jobs,"

Kaiser 1944: "I know I speak for countless thousands when I say that both labor and management want to build. When we generalize our hopes in the thought that we want to build a better America, we really mean that we want to build a more abundant life for every American. And this, again is a Christian precept, preserved in the immortal words: 'I am come that ye might have life, and that ye might have it more abundantly.' ... The only approach is the humanitarian one: the 'give and take' between men of good will; the wholehearted desire to agree; the will to work together."

As the *Western Colossus* put it, "Liking people came naturally to him. He automatically accepted people for what they were. He believed in their intrinsic goodness. He had instinctive confidence in their potential. ... He accepted the role of unions wholeheartedly. ... Some of his best and most lasting friendships were with union leaders ..."

Dr Sidney Garfield graduated from medical school in 1933 at the depths of the Great Depression and within a few years had a small hospital. He found insurance companies haggling and challenging his fees. For non-industrial illnesses and diseases, he charged a flat $1.50 per month per company employee [about $27/month in current dollars]. Garfield found that employees were coming in early enough so that their illnesses could be controlled, instead of waiting until they were desperately ill as they had formerly done.

Kaiser questioned Garfield extensively about his preventative care program and came straight to the point, "Young man, if your idea is half as good as you say it is, it's not only good for this project, it's good for the entire country." Dr. Garfield was opposed by organized interests and Kaiser was again on point: "Nothing new or good has ever been achieved without strong opposition. If you were not opposed, it would be because you are not contributing anything worthwhile."[56]

The result: Kaiser Permanente Medical Care Program was built. His other jobs: Bonneville Dam, one year ahead of schedule and profitable, Boulder Dam, 2 years 2 months ahead of schedule and under budget; Grand Coulee Dam, a year and a half ahead of schedule and under budget.

The Schadenfruede School of Economics will always lose to the Kaiser School. It is the true and accurate belief and faith in people. It is the capacity to get your hands dirty to get the job done. It is the capacity to sacrifice to achieve an ever more noble position. These will succeed. Honor begets honor; trust begets trust; faith begets faith; and hope is the mainspring of life. The only deadly sin is cynicism.[57]

Agriculture, manufacturing, and construction made the nation great and gave us jobs populated, in large part, by the MAJ. I have done all of these manually for extended periods and loved it. Look there, and in similar areas for your MAJ to thrive.

Though many economists are fascinated with making conjectures about those at the high end of the income scale, there is need to pause and reconsider. Look around at the components that make your own life happy and at the components necessary for the perpetuation of the species.

The best portions of your home, city and town were made and put together by those of us of at the moderate scarcity range – we who did a good job.

The dose of ability and technology originating from the Top1% is indispensible, but bringing on the show usually requires the work of the ordinary guy or girl. Think about the things that bring pleasure to your life. It is often the ordinary person who was the motor behind it. Call it sophomoric, unworthy of academic consideration, and far beneath your status if you like, but calling it human and what makes the whole enterprise work is my preference.

When reduced to practicality, it takes a huge amount of time, effort, and conscientiousness to get things done. Consider how many hands-on hours it takes you to do a job well, whether it be tending a vegetable garden to feed your family, or improving or building a section of your home.

To get things right at home is a lot of work. So too, is it a lot of work in the public sphere. Walk room to room in your home; drive down each street in your town or city; you can see the job that needs to be done. The vast majority of unattended tasks in our lives and in our nation require work of the ordinary person.

The things that make a nation interesting usually involve the convergence of work and dedication coming squarely from the mainstream person of normal ability. When a nation works and is vital, it is because the game is being played well and sensibly at the middle. If this is not done, the nation is not taking care of the tribe.

When I was a child there was a beautiful phrase, the then de facto motto of the United States: "Out of many, One" (E Pluribus Unum). What a lovely way to express greatness.

The presumption in a large business or society that when 99% of the people work and deliver the end product, a preponderance of the bonus for a job well done should go to the Top1% ... perhaps it's worth pondering.

In the Mayan culture, kings claimed supernatural power to deliver rain and prosperity. In return, the peasants provided lavish lifestyles replete with palaces, corn, and venison. That promise was broken when drought and climatic changes occurred. In Copán, Honduras, the royal palace was burned around 850 AD (presumably a revolt). Deforestation, periodic droughts, overpopulation, and limited food supply were key players. There were no archeological signs of anyone in the valley 400 years later.[58] Now it's a nice river valley with a small town. I have been there.

Our current economic kings claim supernatural powers to deliver a working economy. Like their Mayan predecessors, they enjoy lavish life styles. Have they got the story right? Have they got the theory right? *Are they taking care of the tribe?*

Your high school class.

In your high school class there were perhaps a few people, say one-in-a-hundred, who in your mind stood out as possessing qualities that you particularly admired. You may have felt they would be especially useful to their community, business, nation, or the world. And, deservedly they should end up in the Top1%. There was also the vast number of lower status. Perhaps the players, their abilities, and their circumstances change so greatly later that the high school assessment was perilous from the outset.

But we think back on high school because, except for the approximate one out of 7 who will not graduate from high school, it may have been the last time in our lives that we daily had visceral contact with such a wide cross section of our economy. In the economy, we are all in this enterprise together – seen and unseen. The economy must deal not only with us and people of our status, but all of us. It cannot be Gown versus Town.

The word fair. It is such a short word. And such a difficult one.

But that is what an economy must seek to be. The economy must take your high school class and those that did not graduate, and do the best job reasonably possible. Our survival and happiness depend on it. About 72% of the U.S. population do not have a four-year college degree or higher. The clear majority reside there.

The Kaiser people are of the same fiber as your high school class.

Perhaps one of the greatest advantages of equitable distributions is that people tend to be rewarded for characteristics that are valuable for society, even when they do not directly correspond to some a workplace-assessed value, or some particular intelligence or performance measurement.

Every instant of the day I am reminded that the things of great beauty and importance come from work that is not well compensated. Here at home there are numerous handmade items that required great ability to make. None of these are valuable as far as the marketplace is concerned. The majority were from eBay and cheap: Shirazi and Qashqia Persian carpets, marble murals from Lebanon, hand-painted Talavera tile from Mexico, hand-crafted leather from Oaxaca, suzanis from Uzbekistan, textiles from Guatemala, handmade wooden pens from Texas, and, when in China, a silk business suit in a style I chose, hand tailored to fit me.

With Wikipedia, Google, and the Internet, it also seems likely that many contributors are not necessarily at the high reaches on the economic ladder. At least so far, the plain message is that the contributions from a wide swath of the income scale are intellectually valuable – priceless would more accurately state it.

The message is clear. We get things of great personal value from the handwork and original contributions of others. Too frequently, there is an inverse relationship between how well such people are paid and the quality of their work. In the U.S. and throughout the world, people make huge contributions that enhance the lives of others via numerous circuitous routes. The hope of leveling unfairness to which they are subject is found in equitable distribution.

Albeit that business may be blind to it, it benefits circuitously by fair compensation because fair pay provides income used to purchase products. An equitable distribution fosters the very social vitality that makes it possible to do business.

It seems unlikely that there ever can be an exact standard for measuring the value of an individual or the capacity to contribute. At the peak, Leonardo da Vinci's remark, "men of lofty genius sometimes accomplish the most when they work the least," comes to mind.

Far more ordinarily, one of the most beneficial friendships I had in my childhood was with a tenant farmer who usually would not receive passing notice. The friendship made me a better person.

Do the powerful and beneficial relationships in your life correspond to wealth? Doesn't something about what it means to be human, something having to do with love and affection, play a larger role? The answer may suggest that it is wiser to spread the bounty widely enough to make the capacity to thrive possible.

These are not soft points. They are points that make life worth living. To unnecessarily remove the dignity to contribute from anyone removes a bit of vitality from all who come in contact with that person. To remove it from an entire class is crassly destructive – approaching insanity.

Riches to rags and ...

I feel compelled to pause here and mention a perspective that drives me in these writings. For the past 40 years, I have not mentioned the following and hope it will not appear to be name dropping or posturing.

My great grandfather was a highly successful Quaker businessman in the mid-1800s. Consistent with Quaker tradition, he was noted for absolute honesty and integrity. For my family, his good fortune and financial ability benefited subsequent generations to this date. That status in my youth, albeit not extreme wealth, gave me access to circumstances that many others would not have had.

My Uncle Walter – a Member of Parliament, knighted by the queen – had a large manor home the public would visit. The family "dressed for dinner," which is to say that when a boy, I would wear everyday either a white dinner jacket or tuxedo to dinner when visiting them.

The British side of the family moved in high circles. When Chip Bohlen was ambassador to France, we were invited to the embassy to see his wife Avis, a dear friend of my aunt from the time they were children, and I might add a very interesting person, as were most of my Aunt Lenette's friends.

Notwithstanding the comfortable circumstances of the British side of the family, I liked all of them immensely, especially my cousin Minnie, who died entirely too young. So this book is not written as a diatribe against wealth. There are many fine wealthy people. There are instances where wealth is used maliciously and selfishly. There are instances where it is not.

As these words go to paper, the Internet shows that 18-year old Samantha Garvey, now living in a homeless shelter, is a semifinalist in a prestigious Intel national science competition. Her words are not those of defeatism or crying in a bucket: "There are other people out there. People my age going through the same exact thing. If I can do it, so can they. They can do just as much, if not more, than I can do."[59] I certainly wish her well. She is very interesting. If you listen to all of what she has to say in context, you also hear her words of intelligence, kindness, and acknowledgement of the deep difficulties her family is going through.

She has a fine, kind family and an enthusiastic science teacher. Of the reported 1.6 million U.S. homeless children, many are not so fortunate. If you have ever been in great poverty, you know what this means without seeing the words now in front of you. You attempt to retain pride alongside poverty – a difficult undertaking. We are so tuned to the culture of money that prudence compels myth. Myth, which at my peril, I dispel in the following.

During a particularly rough financial period slightly more than a decade ago, I worked at minimum wage for two years for two competing fast food restaurants, at times working both jobs simultaneously. It was no willful experiment with the objective of writing about it. The object was to put food on the table, to survive, and to keep and stay in my home.

A few scruffy characters work fast food. Usually they don't last. The work is demanding and difficult. Most who stick around do it well. Work often starts long before the break of day when most people are in REM sleep and it may continue to an hour that is equally inconvenient. You hardly have enough money to survive. If you work fast food, you are schooled in the art of living under extreme unremitting adversity. I do not wish that on anyone.

One of the most able people I have known worked at one of the restaurants. Chinese, at age 50, she learned English. Her daughter, of similar ability, is now a physician. Another coworker is now a math professor. To my embarrassment, a Game Theory book, borrowed from him, has yet to be returned.

Those who speak dismissively of the low-class worker are ignorant. I would pay money for the privilege of seeing them stick to the job and live off the wage it provides.

It would make a great documentary to take a 100 such cases of the decriers of the poor working person and make a film of them attempting to do the job, unremittingly day after day. Let one of them alone make 2,000+ biscuits from scratch on a busy morning, as some of us have done. I would try to edit out most of their whining. It would detract from the comedy of watching them trying to keep up with the common worker. I would, however, want to film their families now living under the bounty of a minimum wage alone. That might be instructive. Heck, look at the budgets for many of the mega-bust films. At least this one would draw a large and amused audience. And no celebrity actors or special effects would eat up the budget. Reality alone would be quite enough.

Low and underclass, closer than you expect.

We are all part of the curve. Right to the bottom.

Since 1938, the minimum wage in the U.S. has set a floor on the income for the working man that translated up the wage scale. In the following graph-115, we see that the 1938-2010 minimum wage income produced an average annual inflation-adjusted income equivalent to about $14,500 annually. The income in graph-115 results from multiplying the minimum wage rate times the customary number of annual labor hours. This annual minimum wage income reached its peak in approximately 1968. It fell to its lowest point since 1950 in 2006 – $10,200 annually.

#115

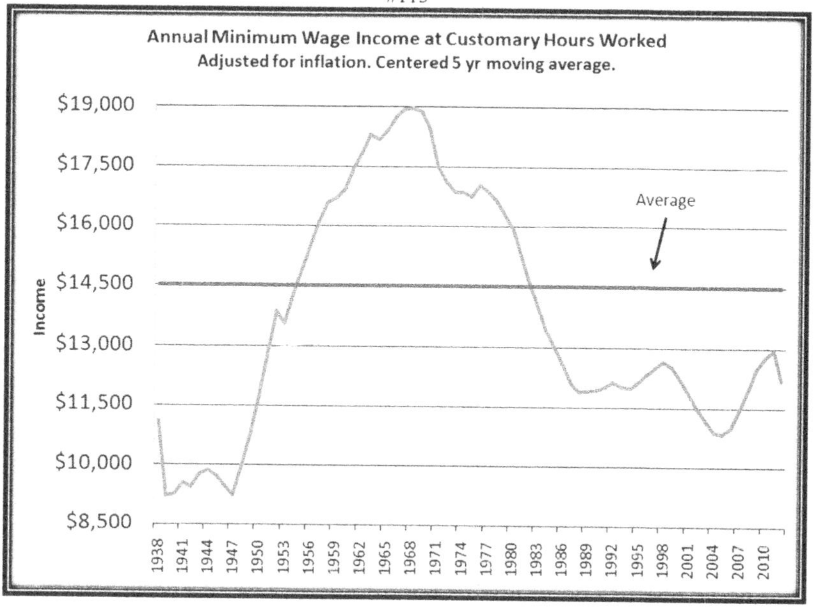

In the real world, the minimum wage worker's income is often reduced beneath the shown levels by seasonal work, unemployment, et cetera. In the year 2010, 6% of hourly workers were paid at or beneath the minimum wage (2.5% at the minimum wage, 3.5% beneath the minimum wage).[60] The restaurant and hospitality industry have many workers beneath the minimum wage.

The minimum wage is a valuable aid to fair compensation for all workers, particularly those not represented by labor unions.[61] Its floor rate defines the wage culture. The floor dropping subsequent to the 1970s severely damaged the MAJ and non-union workers above them. They no longer had the power of government working on their behalf to keep their inflation-adjusted wage at traditional levels.

As can be seen in the lookup-table file, X$ curves often have similar shapes. If the region which most directly pertains to the minimum wage worker drops (while higher incomes do not drop), the curve is bent downward to accommodate this change. Classically and unavoidably, when a downward bend occurs in the region favorably influenced by minimum wage, an upward bend at some higher point must occur, for the plain reason that all the percentages must sum to 100%. By this logic, a drop in minimum wage income abets maldistribution.

#116

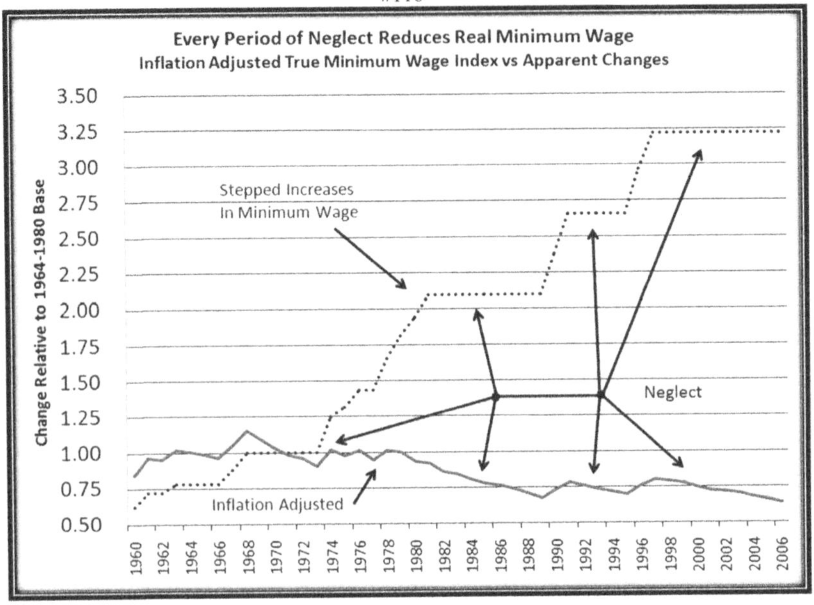

The mechanism for reducing the real inflation-adjusted minimum wage can be summarized in one word: ***Neglect!***

Look at those periods in graph-116 where the neglect arrows point. You will see a consistent repeated process that reduces the inflation-adjusted minimum wage: long lags without changes in the minimum wage. During these lags, inflation is left to eat into the worker's income. In the period 1964-1980, there had been deliberate and regular attention to adjusting the minimum wage so that the working person was protected. This process was breached in the 1969-1973 interval, but not so much so that it could not be restored.

The 1982-1989 breach was more serious and became the unrevoked trend setter. It pulled the inflation-adjusted minimum wage down 32%. From this point onward, the real minimum wage hovered in the neighborhood of being 25% lower than the 1964-1980 median. Three subsequent periods of neglect (1992-1995; 1998-2006; and 2010-2012) kept the worker down. The most devastating in 2006 pulled the worker down 37% from the base median.

All of these occurred because of lack of attention to prevent the adverse impact that inflation would otherwise wreak on the working person. Regular inflation adjustments had been the known standard of attentiveness required to prevent the gutting of the working man's wage. The failures to adjust were deliberate.

The process of periodic adjustments in the minimum wage is fraught with difficulties – neglect being just one of them. There are also instances where periodic adjustments create an excessively high minimum wage. From 1961 to 1971 the minimum wage occasionally exceeded the base line median, as can be seen in the humps in the above two graphs (#115 and #116). This was unwise.

#117

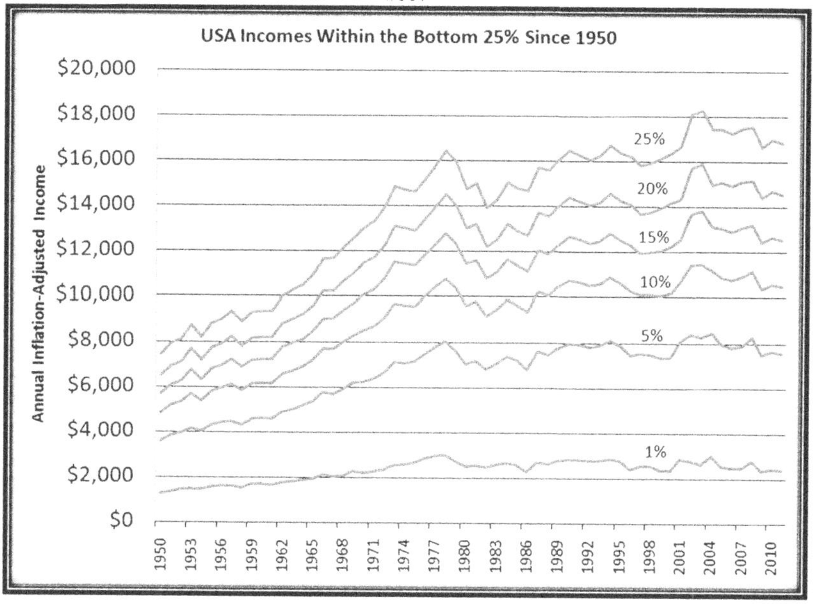

The only protection for consistent fairness for the working person and the nation at large is to have the minimum wage automatically indexed annually to inflation. To prudently return to the average $14,500 minimum wage annual income would require an inflation indexed increase plus 1.36% for ten years [1.36%= ($14,503/ $12,673)^(1/10)-1].

In the previous graph-117 we see people directly influenced by the minimum wage. Each line represents the inflation-adjusted income of the person at the designated percentile. The quick summary might well be: From 1950 to 1978, the incomes of those in the bottom quarter rose rapidly. But by 2010, their incomes were often less than their 1978 income. This summary, however, does not tell the story. To get that, you need to dig.

From 1950 through the 1970s, there was an implicit contract between the people and the government. "You, the government, lay down the rules for the economy and oversee its fairness, and we, the people, will be your productive and willing partner." Both sides took the deal seriously. It was subject to some variations and interpretations, but both parties held up to the agreement. From about 1952 to 1969, income distribution remained equitable; in some instances it was nearly constant. From 1970-1978 the lower classes received an historically increased share, after which the bumpy but sustained downward slide smashed the contract.

This slide did not occur because of latter-day theories trotted out about new information economies or other recently contrived think-tank phrases. It occurred for the same reason that downward moving income-distribution trend lines have always taken shape at the low end.

The message to the low and underclass is this: "*There is plenty of GDP, income, and wealth, and it is growing, but from this point on, you get a smaller share of it.* You had better like it and behave well or we will trash on you to a greater extent than you have ever dreamed possible. So suck up and take it."

The low and underclass are not nitwits. They don't need a crystal ball to see who is getting a larger share and who is getting a smaller one. The following graph-119 shows that their income share was worse than in the 1950s. If you prefer the explicit: In the six shown graph lines, from the 25th to the 1st percentile graph lines, the loss of income for each group was respectively 18.5%, 19.2%, 21.2%, 22.8%, 25.5%, and 35.1% relative to the moderate 1952 to 1969 median. And relative to the equitable 1978 year, the drops looked like this: 25.2%, 26.6%, 28.1%, 28.8%, 30.9%, and 41.9%. Take your pick. In either case, the game had new rules completely different from those of the 1950s, 1960s, and 1970s. Those rules moved from civilized behavior to the uncivilized.

#119

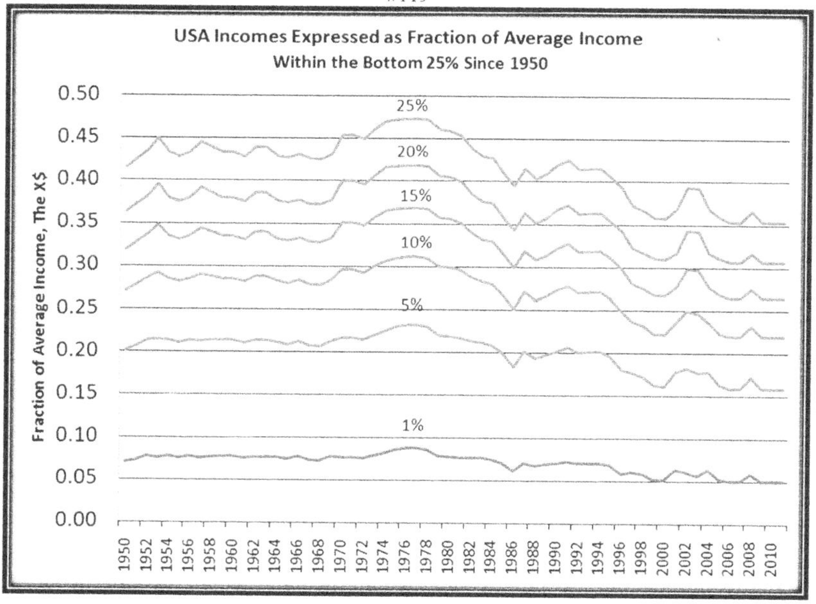

One out of four people walking down the street are in the bottom 25%. These two graphs (#117 and #119) show the consequences for this group. The group is 25 times larger than the Top1%. I repeat it: *The bottom 25% of the population has 25 times more people in it than does the Top1%.*

You trash us regardless of our actions. If we draw welfare benefits we are singled out. At least that contains a rational logic associated with free-loading. But when we do get jobs, you go out of your way to ensure that the minimum wage is far beneath levels of compensation deemed appropriate since the 1950s. By doing so, aren't you removing the very incentives necessary for us to pull ourselves up by the bootstraps? Aren't you removing the role models within our own class who we can respect for good and honorable reasons?

Are we, our families, our children, and our friends so despicable in your eyes (and you so superior) that meanness and condescension needs to be applied to us? How, by deliberately making conditions worse for us, even when we work and do our part, do you expect us, our children and our class to rise to higher levels? Has it not always been hard times for those of us in the pits? What advantage is gained by making it yet more difficult? Won't we instead adapt to the meaner prospects guaranteed by maldistribution and become more brutish and yet more recalcitrant? Aren't there enough brutes already down here? How can the evolution to a meaner and more desperate lower order benefit a great nation? Won't your actions reverse the great historical swing that all of us, as a nation, rich and poor, made marching out of the depths of the Great Depression?

Minimum wage and social spending on the poor.

The previous graphs (#117 and #119) of the bottom 25% segue into an understanding of the minimum wage and social spending on the poor.

Let's take a fixed case assumption that a $14,500 annual income from the minimum wage (as was a historical average) is appropriate in a nation having a $48,000 average income. This assumption translates into a specific threshold: a 0.3 fraction of the average income being the point at which minimum-wage protection is deemed necessary [0.3= $14,500/48,000]. This threshold would lay down an understanding that if your wage income is slightly less than ⅓ of the average income for the nation, then the nation offers you protection in law, prohibiting an employer from driving your wage further south. It also implies that we as a nation recognize that financial difficulties and distress beneath this point are likely. In the U.S. in 2010, the threshold for poverty was approximately the 0.264 X$ point.[62]

#120

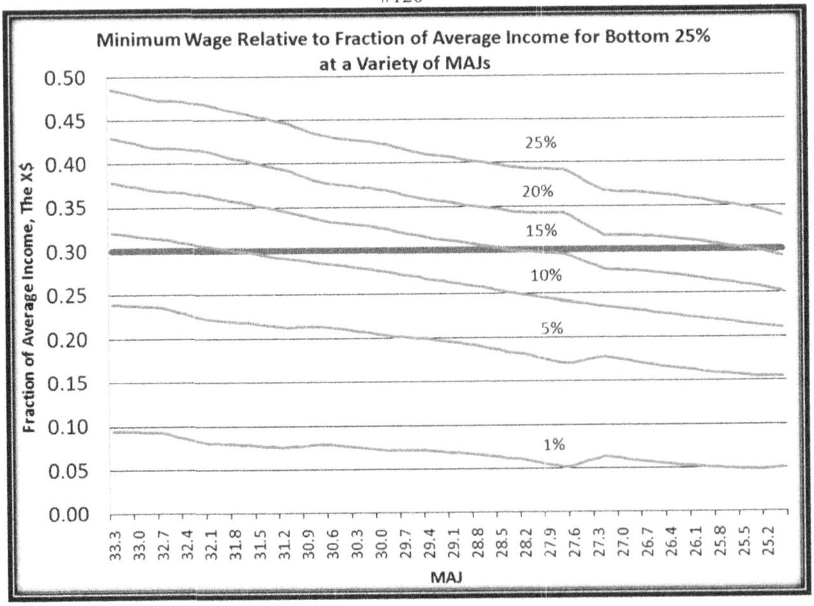

Look at the bottom 25% in above graph-120 as it would exist from MAJ33 to the maldistributed MAJ25 in the lookup table. Direct your attention to the point where the curves intersect the 0.3 horizontal line. These intersections show the point in the 0.3 scenario at which the minimum wage would start taking effect.

From this we see in constant increasing fashion that protection would be required for 10% of the population at MAJ31.8, 15% of the population at MAJ28.4, and 20% of the population at MAJ25.4. The graph is awkwardly trying to tell us a story. As maldistribution increases, social programs encompass ever-larger proportions of the nation that are unable to rise above the 0.3 threshold. This is the threshold for living a life with an income above the minimum wage – explicitly a life providing sufficient income for an honorable and fair living via normal market forces alone, without government intervention.

#121

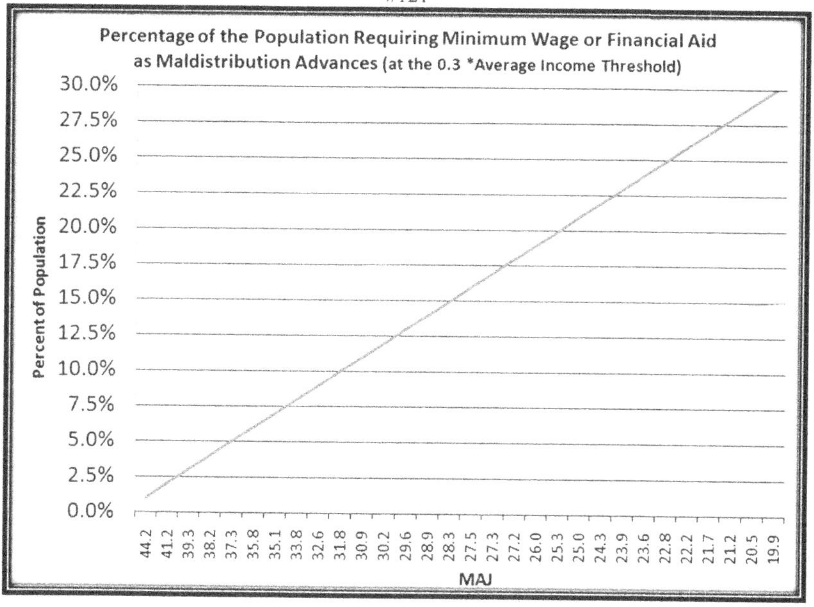

The above graph-121* more precisely shows that the number of people who come under protection of the minimum wage balloons as maldistribution advances. At MAJ33, 8.5% of the population fall beneath the 0.3 average income threshold. At MAJ25, it expands to 21% – an increase of 12.5%. In a population of 313 million, the move to MAJ25 places 39.1 million people in unnecessarily difficult financial conditions. [39.1= 313*12.5%.]

* Despite the appearances, the relationship in the graph is not purely linear, because the shown MAJ values do not increase exactly linearly.

The lookup table makes it easy to see the percent of GDP that would be required to support compensatory benefits to the lower class that fell beneath the 0.3 threshold [it is the sum of the negative values of 0.3 less the X$ for each MAJ; the X$ is a fraction of the GDP].

Maldistribution increasingly removes lower classes from the normal market economy. As such, it stands in *direct opposition to an effective market economy at the low end.* The impact is huge. While perhaps the Top3% of the nation enjoys the main market benefits from maldistribution, the market-based economy is, in large part, denied to a much larger group, the bottom 25%. By not having access to a minimum wage income sufficiently large to significantly elevate them above poverty, the twin evils of maldistribution and an inadequate minimum wage kill the vibrancy that a strong market economy would otherwise produce within the lower social orders. We see a cost of this outcome for the rest of us in the following graph-122.

#122

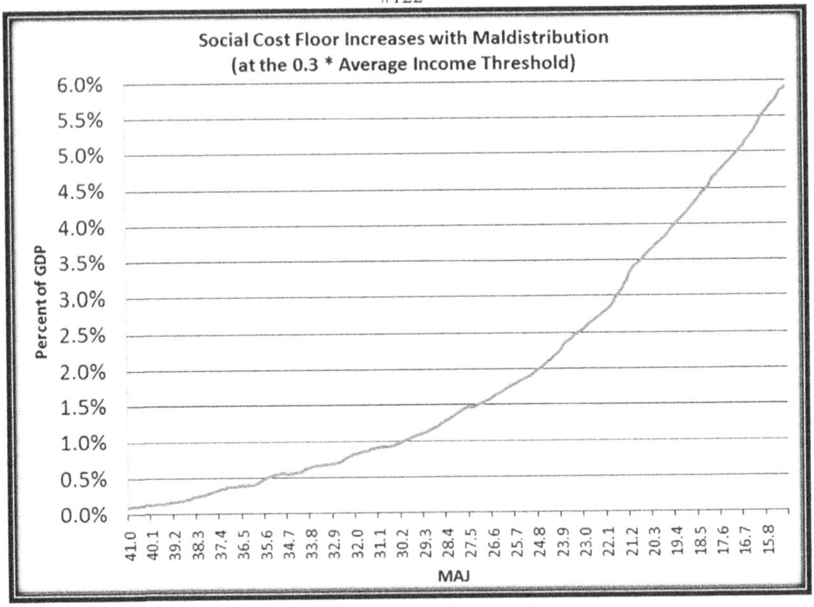

Maldistribution incrementally removes the lower classes from the income stream. Their life support then becomes increasing governmental. Income misery as a consequence of maldistribution comes at a price, not only for those that experience it, but for the citizenry who must cover the cost of the financial aid transfer, usually by higher taxes plus accumulated interest costs on any debt run up in years when the national debt is not paid down. Though the upper reaches on the income ladder are the primary beneficiary and cause of this maldistribution cost, everyone must pay for the social ills it creates. At MAJ33, the cost would have been 0.67%; at MAJ25, it shoots up to 1.93% – the difference: 1.26%, about an additional $184+ billion taxes annually on a GDP of 14.58 trillion.[63]

Each man, woman, and child in the USA appears to be paying about $587 annually to support this portion of the maldistribution program – an amount they would not be paying at MAJ33 [$586.96= $183,853,800,000/ 313,232,044]. Though these calculations are of a back-of-the-napkin character and rank no better than a first approximation, they seem to err on the low side, especially because of the zero transaction cost. The more brutal social order that accompanies maldistribution also presents additional costs in the social services infrastructure, prison costs, police force, et cetera, which in a real world analysis would need to be added in. The adverse effects come in stunning variety of areas, as Wilkinson and Pickett show in their book *The Spirit Level: Why Equality is Better for Everyone*.[64]

As you can surmise from the above graph-122, when maldistribution reaches ever more acute levels, social service expenses zoom upward. In a poor, underdeveloped, maldistributed country, the social costs can be so high that government would be unable to provide adequate assistance at the low end.

The terrible contradiction: employment or fair wage.

In the following graph-124, we see that in the U.S., minimum wage income (expressed as an X$) from its inception through the 1970s was in the range of incomes earned at the 50th and 30th percentile. Once it dropped from these levels, it transitioned to incomes approaching the 15th percentile, often dropping beneath the poverty threshold.

By 2011, incomes at the 50th, 30th, and 15th percentile were at low percentage shares not experienced since the Great Depression. It is abundantly clear that by 1987, the minimum wage played no significant role to counter maldistribution. By the year 2000, it played no role in keeping the minimum wage worker significantly above the poverty threshold.

Economists often argue that the minimum wage reduces employment. From a view of economic theory, I am sympathetic to this argument. The argument takes this form: If you set a minimum wage that exceeds the value of the work contributed by the worker, then the incentive to hire that person is reduced or extinguished. The clear underlying assumption is that the market correctly prices the worth of the worker – often called "price discovery" in efficient-market economic theory.[65] To set a minimum wage value above this point would require the employer to act contrary to economic reasoning and to pay more for the worker than he or she is worth.

#124

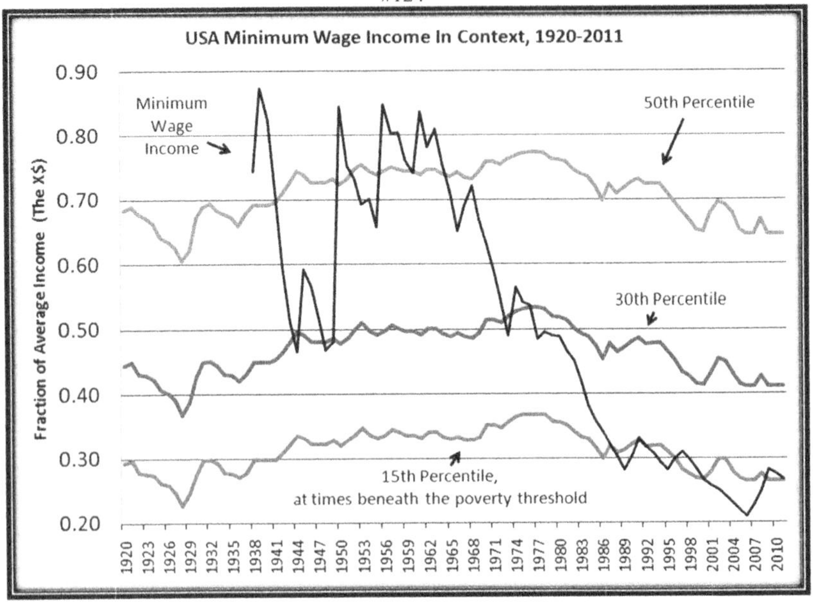

But the prices paid for labor, for management, and for the CEO are not reliably and exclusively determined by market forces. They are determined largely by culture. You can pick and choose between a huge variety of compensation curves that different nations have used – such as in the X$ curves in the lookup table – and find a wide variety of curves that can deliver a market economy which runs very well. The preference in this book has been for a MAJ33, but there are other curves in this same neighborhood that do quite nicely for the market economy and its citizens.

When an employer is acting in a maldistributed economy, his worldview is that the market-determined distribution curve is sacrosanct. The curve has determined his compensation correctly, and it determines the laborers compensation correctly too. Wrong on both points.

The plain case is that the market economy does not have the capacity within its workings to reverse maldistribution. And, except for the dramatic reversal from the Great Depression through the 1970s, there have been few instances where government has played a leading role to turn it around. Instead, Adam Smith's observation in the *Wealth of Nations* has dominated: "Civil government ... is in reality instituted for the defense of the rich against the poor, or those who have some property against those who have none at all." Only when culture diverges from the maldistribution ethic does it vanish.

The curves that the employer sees and acts on vary greatly. Consider employers acting in two different worlds: the MAJ33 world and the MAJ25 world.

If he acts in the MAJ25 world, and labor is protected by the 0.3 minimum wage standard, the employer will start feeling put upon whenever hiring beneath the 21st percentile. By contrast, the employer in the MAJ33 world will not feel he is disadvantaged until he is dipping into workers beneath the 8.5th percentile, as indicated by the intersection with the horizontal 1.0 line in the following graph-125.

#125

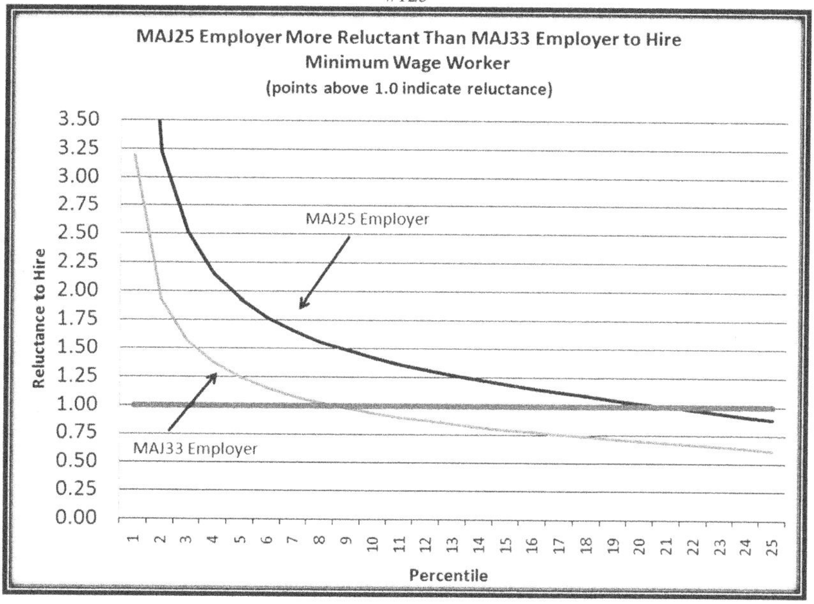

The values you see in graph-125 represent dividing 0.3 by the X$. For example, at a 1.5 value, the employer will feel he is paying 1.5 times more than he should for the worker. The emotion of the MAJ25 and MAJ33 employers are apt to be identical at the 8th and 3rd percentiles respectively. They will both feel they are paying about 1.5 times too much. Whether that 5 point percentile difference will cause the MAJ25 employer to hire, say 5%, fewer workers is a rational concern, but it is difficult to know how it will play out in practice.

The central conflict is that the minimum wage is attempting to bend the distribution curve upward at the low end, and thereby bend the upper portion of the curve down. If the employer says no to this process, then additional unemployment results. But if the minimum wage is within culturally acceptable ranges, such as it can be with inflation indexing, the impact on the employment rate may be insignificant.

Too frequently abandoning or excessively lowering minimum wage produces a Tragedy of the Markets, wherein individual firms rationally lowering wages to reduce costs and seeking to thereby increase profits destructively impact the market as a whole by spoiling revenues and thus profits that all firms together would otherwise have received.

We will touch on this later, but I suggest that the employer calculate the percentage of wage cuts saving *actually passed on in consumer price* (not your selling price). Calculate the inverse of it. Keep that number in mind. It is closely related to product price elasticity of demand, and more often than not suggests that minimum wage reductions tend to be detrimental, as you will see soon enough.

U.S. history appears to contradict the finely argued economic position that the minimum wage will increase unemployment. The inflation-adjusted minimum wage at inception was $4.04. The median since year 2000 has been $6.59. The median since 1950 has been $7.32. These respectively correspond to X$ thresholds of 0.744, 0.25, and 0.48.

The historical record in the following graph-127 shows that GDP per capita tended to grow year-to-year at faster rates when minimum wage income was high. In years when the minimum wage was less than 0.3 times average income, GDP growth slowed greatly, hovering around 1%. The minimum wage is often successful because it increases demand. It increases demand by placing money in the hands of consumers with exceptionally high propensity to consume, by properties associated with product price elasticity of demand, by increased velocity of money, by raising floor incomes throughout the wage scale, and by having lower classes that socially and economically have greater opportunities. Since GDP is another way of saying aggregate demand, the empirical evidence seems to suggest that a chief failing of the anti-minimum wage stance is that it neglects to adequately account for wage-earner consumer-generated demand created by the minimum wage.

#127

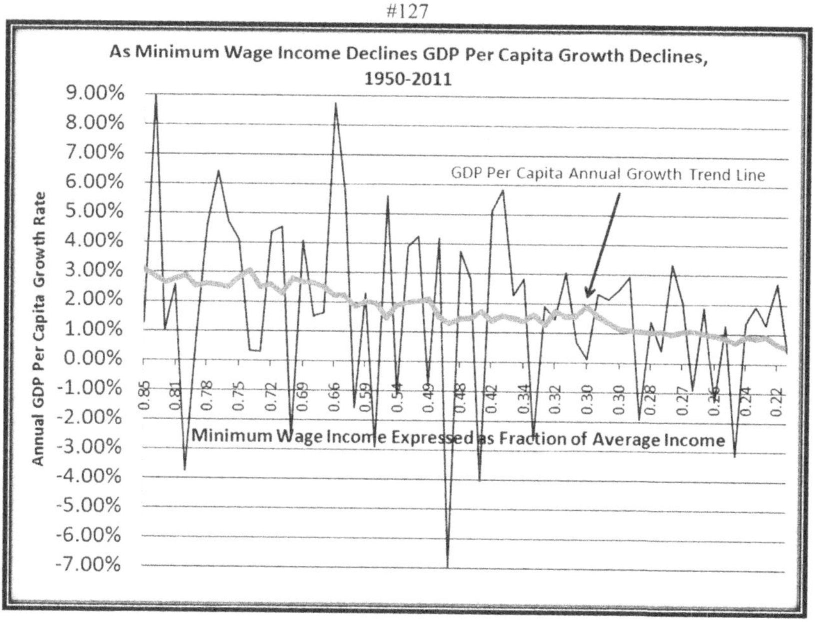

Other components – such as economic growth, long standing economic vitality, and corporate predilections – have dominant influence on employment rates. It is usually a stretch when we hear anti-minimum wage arguments trotted out at the time of accelerating maldistribution. The prime objective then usually is to bring the low class worker closer a desired point on a maldistribution curve.

Rich for unwholesome reasons.

Superficial charm
Cunning, Manipulative
Callous, Lack of empathy
Lack of remorse or guilt
Without Conscience
Abusive treatment of others
Grandiosity, Egocentricity
Emotionally shallow
Pathological lying
Anti-Social behavior
Parasitic lifestyle
Criminal versatility

"Moral Imbecile" was the ancient term used to describe a person having many such characteristics. It remains my preference. Some use the term sociopath. Wikipedia under the heading "Psychopathy" gives you a finely-honed synopsis. Do not confuse the word psychopath with the word psychotic. Both words begin with a "Psych." Their similarity ends there. Please look up the words on the Internet or other reliable source to be sure you understand the difference. They are *vastly different.*[*]

What the psychopath can do in the criminal sense is chilling. The worst of them are so far from the norm that even within prisons, they are a minority. The literature seems to indicate that no treatments reverse the psychopathic personality, but that some nations do have low occurrences of psychopaths.

I have great difficulty in writing the following because the Adam Smith business model of a firm acting to improve the lives of others strikes me as being the appropriate and usually the dominant business force. However, the freedom of the unfettered market also makes it possible for a parasitic person to thrive.

When amorality triumphs, moral disengagement and ultimately immorality prosper. Too frequently, we see moral imbecility coming out of business and economic decisions. Compensation committees seem to look upon many of the characteristics in the psychopathy checklist as being suitable, if not prerequisites, for executives. Academic attention given to the topic can be found with a Google search: "Hare corporate psychopathy." Had not a culture of corporate moral imbecility existed, it seems to me that corporations would have weeded out the CEOs that have brought too frequent disasters to their firms and to the nation.

Frank psychopaths are estimated to occur at the rate of 1% of the population in the United States.[66] Psychopaths are not delusional. They do not, as a class, suffer from lack of intelligence. They know what they are doing.

Assuming that psychopaths are evenly represented throughout the current U.S. population (including the Top1%) would imply the following: Starting U.S. 2012 population= 316,265,537; 3,162,655 psychopaths (one-in-a-hundred); 31,627 psychopaths in the Top1% (one-in-a-hundred); 15,813 psychopaths in the Upper½%. (half of the Top1%)

---

[*] I trust you get the drift. I am not an expert in the area. You can get information about it elsewhere that is far more reliable than what would come from me. Also by using those sources, we don't stray from the topic at hand.

If you wanted to crudely estimate the income of the highest income USA psychopath, consider that there are probably 3,162,655 psychopaths in the United States. Thus the highest income psychopath may well be at the one-in-3,162,655 income scarcity level. In the spreadsheets we see one-in-2-million and one-in-four-million columns. Taking the average of the two should yield a first approximation in the neighborhood of the one-in-3-million-scarcity level. By such logic, the highest income USA psychopath would tend to have an annual income of about $52,000,000 in 2011 (1,092.3X$); the wealthiest would have a net worth of about $2,463,776,000.

For many excellent reasons, pro and con, these figures can be disputed. It is open to conjecture whether the psychopathic personality could conserve such wealth for an extended period. On the other hand, the logic may under-represent the number of psychopaths in the Top1%. Because they completely lack altruistic motives, psychopaths tend to employ their energies elsewhere. Logically, the Top1% would seem to be the honey pot to disproportionately draw them. They would employ all their skills to get there and profit from it.

I know the following graph-130 is a stretch. The starting data is thin. But look, it was a kick putting it together. And perhaps it will entertain you.

But in the process of having a little fun, something more serious occurred. Assume that the dominant group within the Top1% and society as a whole normally has honorable and decent intentions and is powerful enough to exercise them.[67] Under such circumstances, it becomes likely that the equitably distributed market economy has a surprisingly powerful capacity to weed out malefactors of any kind (psychopaths or not) that otherwise would proliferate with a profligate maldistribution. That cheaters don't prosper is a boon to capitalism and the free market.

We have seen earlier at 20X$ and 15X$ earnings, via the Selectivity Ratio, that about nine out of ten were weeded out by returning to an equitable distribution. In the case of the high-income psychopath, we are presented with a person with an income equal to a 1,092X$. This is huge. Far different than the previous case of incomes of a million dollars or less.

#130

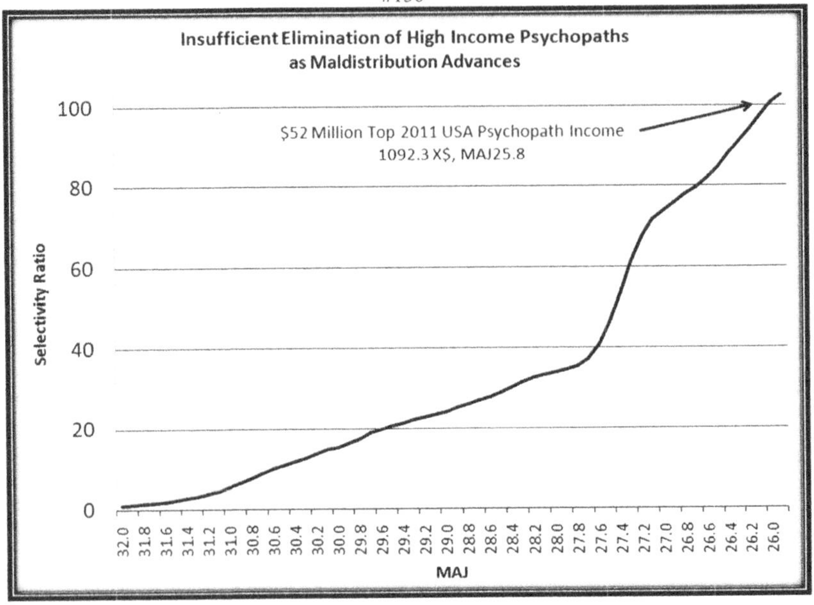

When we look at the graph-130, we see the selectivity curve for a 1092X$ income. The floodgates at MAJ25.8 (the current U.S. maldistribution) were wide open. They were letting in more than 100 times as many people to earn this extraordinarily high income than would have earned it with an equitable distribution. They were letting in so many that it became highly likely that one of them would be a psychopath.

By letting 100 times more people into this group, the policing of it by law enforcement would have become increasingly difficult and ineffective.[68] This is a direct consequence of compensation decisions in a maldistributed society. An equitable distribution would have weeded out 99 of the 100 that would have existed at the one-in-3-million level with a MAJ25.8 maldistribution.

This suggests to me that, given equitable distributions, criminality and anti-social behavior at high levels can experience a powerful self-policing performed by normal market forces, long before law enforcement needs to come into the picture. Graph-130 strongly suggests that criminality in high places is apt to be promoted by maldistribution and abated by equitable distributions. With maldistribution, the Selectivity Ratio is too high and its rise too sharp, other than to suggest serious consequences.

When I was a youngster reading economics in high school, one of the articles was entitled "The Methodology of Positive Economics" – too many syllables and too abstract. But at the core, the 1950s article sought to raise a body of systemized knowledge (alluding to science) over criteria of what ought to be (morals). This was the era of the space race, the cure for polio, and vast scientific advances that improved everyone's lives. To place economics in the category of great seriousness where equilibrium graphs and functions might reign was to align economics with science as opposed to something so quaint and old-fashioned as morals and norms.

As can be found on the Internet, the same eminent economist cloaks corporate life in the amoral:

> ...[S]hould it [the corporation] spend the stockholders' money
> for purposes which it regards as socially responsible
> but which it cannot connect to its bottom line?
> The answer I would say is no. ...
>
> The corporation is amoral
> but the people who run the
> corporation are not amoral. ...
>
> Can a building have moral opinions?
> Can a building have social responsibility?
> If a building can't have social responsibility, what does it
> mean to say that a corporation can't? A corporation is simply
> an artificial legal structure. It doesn't have any;
> it's neither moral nor immoral. It's simply what it is.
> But the people who are engaged in it, whether the stockholders, whether the
> executives in it, whether the employees
> they all have moral responsibilities.[69]

The notion of the corporation being a legal structure analogous to a building is wrong. Corporations have responsibilities, as witnessed by the capacity to sue them. You can't sue a building. But picking an argument there is misleading. There are bigger fish.

The psychological wellbeing of those who work in the corporate culture is injured by the carving of morality, as indicated above. And more broadly, far greater damage is done by disassociating fiduciary responsibility and corporate culture from moral frameworks required for the economy, the society, and the nation to survive and prosper.

Ethical conduct:

> Right speech
> Right action
> Right livelihood

Ghandi:

> A person cannot do right in one department
> whilst attempting to do wrong in another department.
> Life is one indivisible whole.

Adam Smith saw economics as a branch of moral philosophy. Quaint, but right.[70]

CH. 5

THE WORLD

Since antiquity the rich have lived in splendor. Today nations may have trophy buildings and the like. These biceps of achievement are fine, inspiring, and perhaps necessary. But a nation has little distinction if it serves only the rich. For distinction, one must look elsewhere.

The Modernity Timeline.

We need to know how the MAJ is doing in each nation, but GDP per capita does not account for income distribution. For this reason, GDP per capita fails to give a reliable picture of the incomes of the majority in each nation. The methods we have been using here, however, make it trivially easy to see how successfully each nation provides incomes for its majority.

We can easily find the position on the Modernity Timeline using the following method: Match the MAJ income for any nation with the last year in U.S. MAJ income history when that nation's MAJ income was at least as great as the U.S. MAJ income [MAJ income= MAJ/60*GDP per capita]. Doing so gives the Modernity Year that you see in the following table. Table-134 provides one of the most reliable methods for gauging a nation's economic success.

#134

The Modernity Timeline

MAJ Income Rank	Percentile Income Rank	Nation	Modernity Year	Years Relative to USA	MAJ Income Rank	Percentile Income Rank	Nation	Modernity Year	Years Relative to USA
1	1%	Qatar	2091	79	57	36%	Azerbaijan	1940	-72
2	1%	Luxembourg	2060	48	58	37%	Seychelles	1939	-73
3	2%	Norway	2043	31	59	38%	Mexico	1939	-73
4	3%	Sweden	2025	13	60	38%	Panama	1938	-74
5	3%	Singapore	2024	12	61	39%	Iran	1938	-74
6	4%	Austria	2023	11	62	39%	Tunisia	1938	-74
7	4%	Switzerland	2021	9	63	40%	Albania	1938	-74
8	5%	Netherlands	2021	9	64	41%	CostaRica	1937	-75
9	6%	Iceland	2021	9	65	41%	Macedonia	1937	-75
10	6%	Canada	2018	6	66	42%	Ukraine	1937	-75
11	7%	Denmark	2018	6	67	43%	Algeria	1936	-76
12	8%	Germany	2018	6	68	43%	Kosovo	1936	-76
13	8%	Finland	2018	6	69	44%	Peru	1935	-77
14	9%	Australia	2017	5	70	45%	China	1934	-78
15	10%	Belgium	2015	3	71	45%	Maldives	1934	-78
16	10%	Ireland	2013	1	72	46%	Botswana	1933	-79
17	11%	Taiwan	2013	1	73	46%	Jamaica	1933	-79
18	**11%**	**UnitedStates**	2012	**0**	74	47%	Turkmenista	1933	-79
19	12%	France	2008	-4	75	48%	Suriname	1932	-80
20	13%	UnitedKingdc	2004	-8	76	48%	Bosnia and H	1932	-80
21	13%	Japan	1999	-13	77	49%	Dominican R	1931	-81
22	14%	Korea,South	1998	-14	**78**	**50%**	**Brazil**	**1930**	**-82**
23	15%	Slovenia	1989	-23	79	50%	Egypt	1919	-93
24	15%	Greece	1988	-24	80	51%	Guyana	1918	-94
25	16%	CzechRepubli	1988	-24	81	52%	Thailand	1913	-99
26	17%	Malta	1988	-24	82	52%	Ecuador	1907	-105
27	17%	HongKong	1986	-26	83	53%	Armenia	1906	-106
28	18%	Spain	1986	-26	84	54%	Colombia	1903	-109
29	18%	Italy	1975	-37	85	54%	Belize	1901	-111
30	19%	Israel	1973	-39	86	55%	Jordan	1896	-116
31	20%	NewZealand	1973	-39	87	55%	SouthAfrica	1895	-117
32	20%	Slovakia	1971	-41	88	56%	ElSalvador	1895	-117
33	21%	Cyprus	1968	-44	89	57%	SyrianArabR	1894	-118
34	22%	Portugal	1965	-47	90	57%	Angola	1891	-121
35	22%	Hungary	1964	-48	91	58%	Bhutan	1889	-123
36	23%	TrinidadandT	1962	-50	92	59%	Georgia	1889	-123
37	24%	Estonia	1961	-51	93	59%	Morocco	1888	-124
38	24%	Poland	1961	-51	94	60%	Indonesia	1886	-126
39	**25%**	**Croatia**	**1959**	**-53**	95	61%	SriLanka	1882	-130
40	25%	Belarus	1953	-59	96	61%	Paraguay	1880	-132
41	26%	Lithuania	1952	-60	97	62%	Mongolia	1880	-132
42	27%	Latvia	1948	-64	98	62%	India	1879	-133
43	27%	Russia	1945	-67	99	63%	Guatemala	1877	-135
44	28%	Kazakhstan	1945	-67	100	64%	Swaziland	1877	-135
45	29%	Gabon	1943	-69	101	64%	Congo,Rep.	1877	-135
46	29%	Mauritius	1943	-69	102	65%	Uzbekistan	1876	-136
47	30%	Serbia	1943	-69	103	66%	Vietnam	1875	-137
48	31%	Romania	1942	-70	104	66%	Philippines	1874	-138
49	31%	Uruguay	1941	-71	105	67%	Bolivia	1867	-145
50	32%	Malaysia	1941	-71	106	68%	CapeVerde	1866	-146
51	32%	Argentina	1941	-71	107	68%	Pakistan	1866	-146
52	33%	Montenegro	1941	-71	108	69%	Djibouti	1864	-148
53	34%	Chile	1940	-72	109	69%	Yemen	1864	-148
54	34%	Bulgaria	1940	-72	110	70%	Timor-Leste	1863	-149
55	35%	Venezuela	1940	-72	111	71%	Moldova	1862	-150
56	36%	Turkey	1940	-72	112	71%	Laos	1861	-151

An IMF report shows that more than 75% of major economic powers have worsened their income distributions in the Mid-1980s to Mid-2000s interval. Only a quarter of the nations in the study remained substantially constant or became more equitable.[71] With the maldistribution contagion in progress, measuring nations using MAJ income becomes increasingly important.[72] The Modernity Timeline tells us how we are doing.

The Modernity Timeline (continued)

	MAJ Income Rank	Percentile Income Rank	Nation	Modernity Year	Years Relative to USA
113	113	72%	Honduras	1860	-152
114	114	73%	Kyrgyzstan	1858	-154
115	115	73%	Ghana	1855	-157
116	116	74%	Nicaragua	1854	-158
117	117	75%	Nigeria	1852	-160
118	**118**	**75%**	**Tajikistan**	**1852**	**-160**
119	119	76%	Mauritania	1848	-164
120	120	76%	Cameroon	1847	-165
121	121	77%	Namibia	1846	-166
122	122	78%	Bangladesh	1843	-169
123	123	78%	PapuaNewGu	1842	-170
124	124	79%	Cambodia	1842	-170
125	125	80%	Senegal	1842	-170
126	126	80%	Chad	1835	-177
127	127	81%	Coted'Ivoire	1832	-180
128	128	82%	Benin	1832	-180
129	129	82%	Gambia,The	1831	-181
130	130	83%	Tanzania	1828	-184
131	131	83%	SaoTomeand	1825	-187
132	132	84%	Kenya	1824	-188
133	133	85%	Micronesia,Fe	1820	-192
134	134	85%	Guinea-Bissau	1820	-192

MAJ Income Rank	Percentile Income Rank	Nation	Modernity Year	Years Relative to USA
135	86%	BurkinaFaso	1818	-194
136	87%	Mali	1817	-195
137	87%	Ethiopia	1817	-195
138	88%	Afghanistan	1815	-197
139	89%	Zambia	1814	-198
140	89%	Uganda	1812	-200
141	90%	Nepal	1810	-202
142	90%	Guinea	1810	-202
143	91%	Togo	1808	-204
144	92%	Lesotho	1802	-210
145	92%	Malawi	1798	-214
146	93%	Mozambique	1796	-216
147	94%	Rwanda	1794	-218
148	94%	Madagascar	1792	-220
149	95%	Haiti	1788	224
150	96%	Niger	1773	-239
151	96%	Comoros	1771	-241
152	97%	SierraLeone	1766	-246
153	97%	Liberia	1766	-246
154	98%	CentralAfrica	1756	-256
155	99%	Zimbabwe	1752	-260
156	99%	Burundi	1745	**-267**
157	100%	Congo,Dem.	1740	-272

Notwithstanding the simplicity of the method, you have crucial development information. You can see the current relative MAJ position of nations along a continuum of MAJ income growths that were historically achieved [and when necessary, by a trend line extending it into the future or distant past]. By doing so, you can see the number of years of growth required to raise the MAJ income for any nation to a designated higher level (if nations are destined to follow the growth path that the United States did). The timeline gives an appreciation of the true task of moving nations through history and into the future.

Affection throughout the timeline.

This Modernity Timeline section is a very difficult section for me to write. It can easily enflame emotions inappropriately. Hopefully, this will not occur. As I type these words I wrestle with how to say it.

I'll begin by mentioning a motorcycle trip I took to Mexico in 1965. ... Graduated from high school.... A dreadful Spanish student. ... Fearful of failing Spanish in college. ... I liked economics, so I struck out on my own to study economics and Spanish at the summer session of the National University in Mexico City. The trip was a coming-of-age eye opener. I flew from Virginia to Tennessee. Then on the cheap, took a bus to Houston. I was a naive farm boy who believed (as I still do) in stewardship, conservation of soil, and decency. Flying over Tennessee, I saw as far as the eye could see mountains strip-mined bare. It was a shock. I've yet to get over it. ... Never knew people could be so cruel to the land.

The plan was to buy a used Honda 305cc motorcycle in Houston, but none were to be found. A dealership had a new 160cc Honda. I had never ridden a motorcycle. The salesman took me for a test ride, flying through downtown Houston weaving through as many cars as he could find. Terrified, I screamed again and again: "I'll buy it. I'll buy it." It turned out to be an excellent bike for the trip. I saw Mexico at a slow pace, close up – so close that in my mind's eye, I still see individual grasshoppers as I rode along.

Edmundo Flores, my economics professor in Mexico, drove home a pivotal concept: "Underdevelopment is a Madison Avenue advertising phrase. There is no such thing as underdevelopment. It is poverty." He is right. It was poverty then. It is poverty now. Anyone who lives it knows it.

From that trip onward, I have loved Mexico. The people, the land – it is a close emotional bond. A similar feeling occasionally comes when visiting other countries of roughly the same economic status. I live in a working-class neighborhood in Appalachia, once in a while going elsewhere. The fancy bright lights of economic success are ok for an occasional visit, but plain and less troublesome ways are my preference. There are attributes to not living at the budding edge of modernity. Many people throughout the world know it.

I am reminded, when thinking back on my grandparents' home, how nice it was on the screen porch with neighbors coming in and out. That was the 1950s. Looking at the classic films from the 1920s and 1930s similarly shows fully developed lives and ways of living. Reading authors of the 1800s again provides a reminder that much of the old times were attractive and interesting. Ability, intelligence, and humor obviously are not newly born children of modernity.

Clearly as creatures of the present, we benefit greatly from modernity, but treasures of the past and other ways of living are plainly evident, often appealing. But if you are poor, your view is apt to be more conflicted because you can see modernity, but your nation and present income may compel you to live an entirely different life.

For each nation, we can see in the graph-137 how modernity (as measured by the income of the 60% majority) plays out. In half of the nations of the world, the majority of people live at an income level equal to or greater than their MAJ counterparts in the U.S. experienced in the year 1930.

In nearly all remaining nations, the MAJ is living at an income level lower than the U.S. MAJ income in year 1919. One quarter of nations are above year 1959. One quarter of nations are beneath year 1852. The range is huge and you can see it in graph-137.

#137

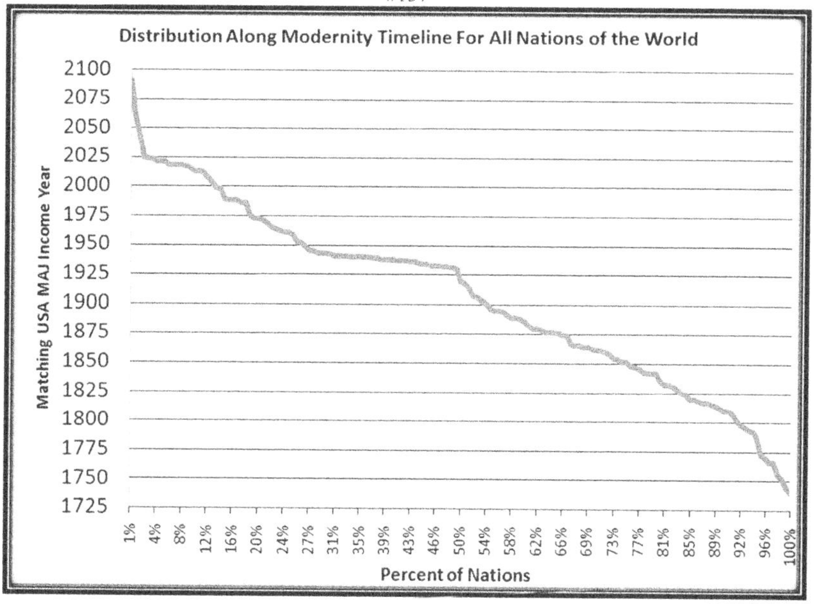

The timeline tends to define your life whether you are in the MAJ or above it. If maldistribution is acute and modernity primitive, an element of meanness, dismissiveness, and dominance too frequently is imbedded in the upper class's treatment of the MAJ.

Geography and the USA MAJ.

It is hardly the magic of economics alone that propels U.S. success. Contrary to extravagant economic claims, the U.S. advantage is, in large part, a blessing of geography and attitude.

O beautiful for spacious skies,
For amber waves of grain,
For purple mountain majesties
Above the fruited plain!

America! America!
God shed His grace on thee,
And crown thy good with brotherhood
From sea to shining sea! …

America! America!
God mend thine ev'ry flaw,
Confirm thy soul in self-control,
Thy liberty in law.[73]

The advantages of geography are implicit in the lyrics. By climate, by absence of tropical disease, by agricultural productivity, by access to oceans and by navigable waterways, geography confers enormous economic advantages on the United States. Should you doubt geography's influence on economics, think deeply. Worldwide regions within the temperate zone and within 60 miles (100 kilometers) of the seacoast or a navigable waterway constitute only 8.4% of the world's inhabitable area. Yet this tiny region contains 22.8% of the world's population and produces more than half of the world's GDP (52.9%).[74] It goes without saying that population and economic success would be more widely dispersed if geography and economic success were not so potently linked.

The U.S. has a variably shaped coastline on both the Atlantic and Pacific Ocean with good harbors. It has the Mississippi River and tributaries midway, and the Great Lakes to the north, all of these aiding water transportation and heavy shipments. With access to two oceans along much of its border, more than 50% of the U.S. population lives within 50 miles of the oceans or navigable waterways.[75] The many benefits provided by water are central to the economic workings of a nation.

The temperate zone in the U.S. reduces parasites and provides favorable climates for farms and for healthful living. Parasites are so severe in many poor, hot nations that intestinal worms and tropical diseases are major reasons that children do poorly in school. There, deworming children is often key to improving school success. The U.S. also once shared similar conditions. From 1910 onward, the Rockefeller Foundation fought hookworms in children in the American South.[76]

The U.S. also has vastly different regions, thus a setback in one area can often be offset by a favorable outcome in another. These are silent but persistent and substantial advantages. No nation in the world has the United States' great geographic advantages. It is a gift. Its long-standing economic can-do spirit is outstanding. Alexis De Tocqueville in his 1830s writing on the U.S. was also struck by it.

Even with its huge geographical advantages, the U.S. ranks 18th in the world on the MAJ Modernity Timeline. Since most nations do not possess the U.S. advantages, it is clear that their strategy must be economically smarter about economic development and ensuring that it indeed does benefit their MAJ. It is only by superior methods that they can advance quickly up the timeline. They do not have the luxury of error.

Even if U.S. MAJ income growth rates were grafted onto other nations, in more than half of the nations it would not be sufficient for them to reach current U.S. MAJ income levels within an 82-year lifetime, as can be seen in the prior table at the 50th percentile point. Twenty-five percent of the nations would not even be able to reach the current standard in 160 years at the historical U.S. MAJ growth rates.

It is mean-spirited and wrong to hold out hope that past U.S. growth rates and a market economy are alone the answer for people in desperately poor nations. Poor nations require greater wisdom to succeed – to live smart, to grow smart, and to avoid big mistakes.

Highest priority: population growth less than job growth.

If population growth greatly exceeds job growth, a moribund economy and a vast, idle population is the outcome.

#139

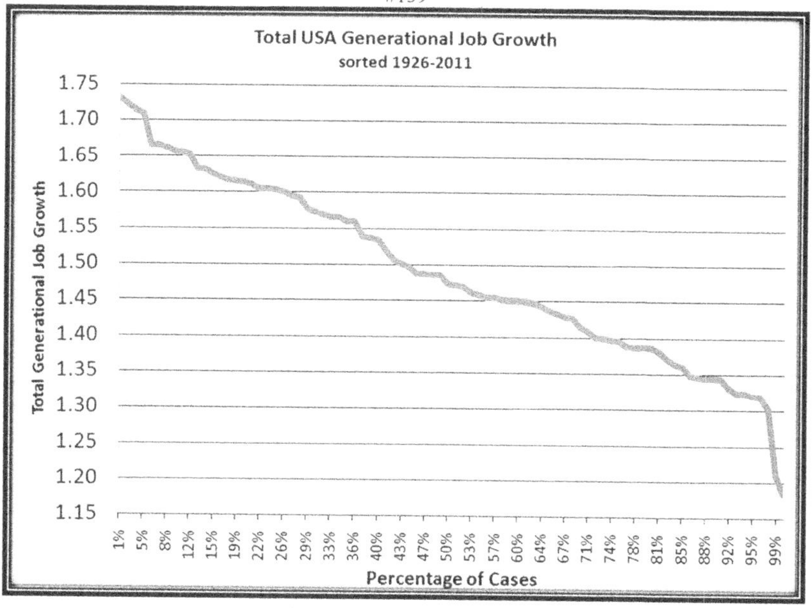

U.S. job growth history provides a ready standard for the number of jobs that can be created over a generation in a prosperous nation. At the median in all years since 1926, job growth in the U.S. has been slightly less than 1.5x over a generation as shown in the above graph-139. At this writing it is about 1.3x. *Long-term population growth should not exceed long-term job growth in any nation. Period.*

The ladies determine economic success.

Generational population growth provides a reference point from two perspectives. First, it encompasses a woman's primary child bearing years. Second, the period is long enough for analysis and yet young adults can still recall its approximate starting point (or know that it occurred no more than a few years before their birth).

If we consider three 26-year generations (total 78 yrs), each with a 2x growth rate in each generation, the outcome, at the end of the period, is a population 8x larger than it was at the time of our birth [8= 2^3]. Imagine the infrastructure: highways, traffic, and so on that might well be required under those conditions. This is untenable.

In several nations, average lifespan exceeds 78 years – three generations. In many instances, this means that our children and their children will be alive at the time of our death. At the end of the 78-year period, each woman having two children in each generation not only replenishes the population when she and her spouse are gone, but she produces a population growth considerably higher than most people would intuitively expect.

The graphic seeks to tell to tell a story. The ladies are the conduit for population growth. The graphic shows an exact 50% chance of a female birth in each generation, daughters being born at 26 year intervals,[77] and each lady in her generation giving birth to two children, who survive a full life. If this sequence persists into the indefinite future, population growth would be 3x every 78 years – the initial 2 parents dying soon after age 78 and leaving behind 6 descendants [3= 6/2] ... the male children marrying ladies from other families and being accounted for by a similar process there.

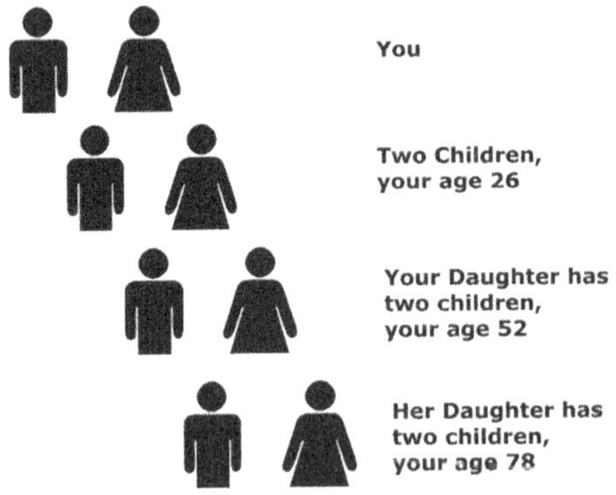

This 3x growth over 3 generations is equal to a 1.44x population growth per generation [1.44= 3^(1/3)]. A 1.44x generational population growth exceeds recent generational job growth capacity in the U.S. and in many other nations. *For each and every lady, two babies each is too many. By exceeding job growth capabilities, many children of average ability in adulthood will be idle, without jobs, and in economic distress.*

In the real world, the average interval between female births, the average number of children each lady has, average lifespan, and immigration and emigration and other components influence population growth. The way population growth transpires from generation to generation can vary greatly. But coincidentally, the population growth in the graphic did not differ greatly from the 78-year experience from 1933 onward, when world population grew 3.22 times larger, at a generational population growth averaging 1.48 [1.476= 3.22^(1/3)]. Yet you hear in the news: 4.6, 6.1, and 6.4 children per woman in Rwanda, the Congo, and Uganda. That won't work. National boundaries will burst; civilized life, fracture.

Except in a vanishingly few exceptionally rich nations such as Saudi Arabia, a generation population growth exceeding 2x clearly presents a huge obstacle to normal economic and social wellbeing. Consider all the problems of raising a family, having adequate schools for your children to flourish, and adequate jobs for decent incomes for parents.

As abundantly seen already, incomes are a function of scarcity. If population grows faster than jobs, those who are at low education and skill levels invariably suffer. And suffer greatly. It is doubly unfortunate that the poorest people and poorest regions in nearly all nations give birth to the most children. As overpopulation progresses, it cements them into poverty.

You can see in the following table (population in millions and growth rates over the previous 26 years) that seventeen nations exceeded 2x growth in 2010 and many others were not far behind. This creates a huge drag on per capita income. It requires that roughly 2.8% to 3.6% be subtracted from GDP growth to get per capita income growth [3.65%= 2.54^(1/26)-1; 2.8%= 2.0^ (1/26) -1]. That hobbling of per capita growth is, in many instances, sufficient to destroy a nation.

	Nation	Population 2010, Millions	Generation Population Growth 2010	Generation Population Growth 2030, est
1	Saudi Arabia	27.4	2.19	3.75
2	Yemen	24.1	2.57	2.48
3	Uganda	33.4	2.33	2.65
4	Niger	15.5	2.36	2.44
5	Congo Dem. Rep.	66.0	2.19	2.75
6	Malawi	14.9	2.14	2.55
7	Angola	19.1	2.17	2.48
8	Tanzania	44.8	2.12	2.43
9	Burkina Faso	16.5	2.07	2.27
10	Kenya	40.5	2.14	2.10
11	Senegal	12.4	2.05	2.23
12	Madagascar	20.7	2.17	1.93
13	Chad	11.2	2.24	1.78
14	Mali	15.4	1.95	2.34
15	Guinea	10.0	2.08	2.03
16	Iraq	32.0	2.10	1.95
17	Afghanistan	34.4	2.05	1.97
18	Ghana	24.4	1.96	1.97
19	Nigeria	158.4	1.89	2.06
20	Guatemala	14.4	1.85	2.04
21	Zambia	12.9	1.97	1.81
22	Syria	20.4	2.00	1.73
23	Sudan	43.6	1.90	1.87
24	Ethiopia	82.9	2.09	1.50
25	Cameroon	19.6	1.92	1.78
26	Cote d'Ivoire	19.7	1.96	1.27
27	Mozambique	23.4	1.77	1.52
28	Egypt	81.1	1.64	1.72
29	Algeria	35.5	1.65	1.66
30	Nepal	30.0	1.81	1.29
31	Philippines	93.3	1.77	1.35
32	Pakistan	173.6	1.88	1.13
33	Malaysia	28.4	1.85	1.17
34	Ecuador	14.5	1.63	1.57
35	Venezuela	28.8	1.70	1.42
36	Australia	22.3	1.44	1.85
37	Cambodia	14.1	1.87	0.98
38	Bolivia	9.9	1.70	1.29
39	Uzbekistan	28.2	1.59	1.45
40	Azerbaijan	9.0	1.38	1.79
41	Colombia	46.3	1.58	1.35
42	Dominican Repub.	9.9	1.57	1.37
43	Iran	74.0	1.65	1.14
44	Spain	46.1	1.20	2.02
45	Haiti	10.0	1.60	1.16
46	**India**	1170.9	1.56	1.23
47	Turkey	72.8	1.50	1.31
48	Sri Lanka	20.9	1.30	1.69
49	Bangladesh	148.7	1.66	0.97
50	Mexico	113.4	1.52	1.23
51	Vietnam	86.9	1.51	1.19
52	Indonesia	239.9	1.46	1.26
53	**Total World**	**6817.4**	**1.44**	**1.29**
54	Tunisia	10.5	1.50	1.17
55	Morocco	32.0	1.47	1.21
56	Peru	29.1	1.53	1.07
57	Canada	34.1	1.33	1.42
58	Chile	17.1	1.44	1.16
59	Brazil	194.9	1.46	1.06
60	Somalia	9.3	1.45	1.06
61	Argentina	40.4	1.35	1.14
62	Thailand	69.1	1.35	1.08
63	Italy	60.5	1.07	1.62
64	**United States**	309.1	1.31	1.13

High population growth is how you can be poor and stay poor, and how your children can be poor and stay poor without remedy. There is little reason to expect job growth to exceed about 1.5x per generation even under very favorable circumstances. It is apt to be far lower. A nation with population growth higher than job growth produces an increasingly large number of unemployed and concomitant problems that come with them – often called failed states.[78]

Population growth is not an ancillary consideration. It is central, often beyond the reach of prudent national economic management. Once on the slippery slope of excessive population growth, circumstances rule, not man. The lives of many kind and decent people are defined by the central failure of the society to control population. The distribution of lives hits them hard and with a grasp that does not release.

The first 25 nations listed in the table have acute population growth now and their population growth trends since 1995 are insufficiently corrective, as can be seen in the 2030 column.[79] Many other nations further down on the list have prospects that are not much better.

The table ranks nations in a systematic order that roughly suggests the degree to which they need to be

	Nation	Population 2010, Millions	Generation Population Growth 2010	Generation Population Growth 2030, est
65	North Korea	24.3	1.32	0.99
66	Belgium	10.9	1.10	1.40
67	**China**	1338.3	1.29	1.01
68	France	64.9	1.15	1.27
69	Myanmar	48.0	1.35	0.87
70	United Kingdom	62.2	1.10	1.32
71	Greece	11.3	1.14	1.07
72	South Korea	48.9	1.21	0.83
73	Netherlands	16.6	1.15	0.91
74	Cuba	11.3	1.13	0.93
75	Poland	38.2	1.03	1.11
76	Portugal	10.6	1.07	0.97
77	Romania	21.4	0.95	1.18
78	Japan	127.5	1.06	0.90
79	Germany	81.7	1.05	0.86
80	Russia	141.8	0.99	0.95
81	Ukraine	45.9	0.90	1.08
82	Hungary	10.0	0.94	0.97

attentive to population growth. Ninety-four percent of the world's population resides on this list. Most nations with a population exceeding 9 million are included.

The first 30 listed nations together have a population of one billion; the first 49 have a population of three billion. Nearly all of these have serious population growth problems. The 60% majority in the first 49 nations comprise 1.8 billion people, who in the main live under difficult conditions. The magnitude of the population growth problem is huge.

The combined population of Europe and the U.S. is 1.14 billion – far fewer than the distressed majority in nations with dangerous population growth. These are people, not just numbers. They need a chance for full and productive lives. Excessive population growth cripples them.

White's Law.

An adult male can deliver about 75 watts of muscle energy.[80] Not much more than a light bulb – about 1/10 of a horsepower. All other energy that makes our culture possible must come from elsewhere. Energy use separates us from primitive conditions. Culture is defined by it.

For most of our time on earth, we humans lived in Stone Age conditions without harnessing much energy except a fire to warm us and to cook our food. Later we also used energy supplied by domesticated animals for farming and transportation – the donkey, ox, horse, and other beasts of burden. Reportedly sailboats harnessed the wind as early as 3000 BC. Watermills began about the 2nd century BC. Windmills started appearing in Europe in the 1300s. All of these used small amounts of energy compared to the First Industrial Revolution (1750) and the age of steam that came with it. It then became plainly clear that energy defined culture. For the first time in history, the living standards of the masses underwent sustained growth. By 1870, the work done by steam exceeded that done by animal and human power together.[81]

The above snippet is intended to draw attention to the degree to which energy use has defined the culture we now take for granted. Without energy we return to near Stone Age conditions. However competent a people may be, when energy sources or access to them are removed or lessened, culture becomes more primitive, ever-closer to the human-muscle-power and beast-of-burden eras of the past.

White's Law, as follows, focuses on the relationship between culture, energy, and population:

> [C]ulture evolves as the amount of energy harnessed ***per capita*** per year is increased, or as the efficiency … of putting the energy to work is increased. [emphasis added][82]

Consistent with White's Law, when energy sources are finite or declining (as are fossil fuels), increasing population reverses culture. Nations with insufficient energy efficiency, insufficient energy sources, inappropriate population size, or inappropriate population growth reverse culture.

Richard Duncan indicates that world energy per capita from 1945 to 1973 grew at 3.45% per year; from 1973 to 1979 it grew at 0.64% per year; from 1979 to 1999 it declined 0.33% per year.[83] To mismanage energy production, energy efficiency, or population endangers a nation. This is territory ripe for pessimists, but it is also ripe for solutions and sensibility – little of which unfortunately is in evidence so far.

If you would like to reduce the relationship to a formula, it looks something like this:

Energy_Induced_Culture = Energy_Source x Efficiency / Population

High population damages culture. It has the potential to obliterate it.

Low on Modernity Timeline & high in population growth.

The great concern is that many nations with acute population growth have population growth patterns that are not significantly changing for the better. To the contrary, many nations are so far off track that their prospects are alarmingly bad. Especially in nations low on the modernity timeline, the higher the rank on the list, the greater the chance of serious economic and social disruptions resulting from excessive population growth.

Table-145 ranks fifty nations and attempts to show where, at greatest intensity, the twin problems of excessive population growth and low income for the MAJ can be found.* There are one billion people in the first 27 nations; 2.6 billion in the first 36, and 3.5 billion in the first 50. The table should not be used as a scorecard because it is not that precise and because many moderately smaller nations were not included. But you can be confident that those nations listed near the top do require immediate attention to the twin evils of low modernity ranking and excessive population growth – the latter being especially tenacious.

Population Growth & Modernity Rank Combined

1	Congo Dem. Rep.
2	Uganda
3	Malawi
4	Madagascar
5	Guinea
6	Burkina Faso
7	Tanzania
8	Kenya
9	Mali
10	Yemen
11	Afghanistan
12	Senegal
13	Chad
14	Zambia
15	Mozambique
16	Ethiopia
17	Nepal
18	Nigeria
19	Ghana
20	Angola
21	Cote d'Ivoire
22	Cameroon
23	Haiti
24	Guatemala
25	Cambodia
26	Pakistan
27	Philippines
28	Syria
29	Bolivia
30	Niger
31	Uzbekistan
32	Egypt
33	Bangladesh
34	Ecuador
35	Algeria
36	India
37	Colombia
38	Vietnam
39	Sri Lanka
40	Dominican Repub.
41	Venezuela
42	Indonesia
43	Malaysia
44	Morocco
45	Iran
46	Azerbaijan
47	Mexico
48	Turkey
49	Brazil
50	Peru

Catholic Church.

Colombia ranks #37 in the table of acutely troubled nations (Table-145). During the 1967-68 school year, I studied economics at the National University of Colombia and took a course in social work where I worked in an exceptionally poor barrio with Catholic nuns, for whom I had great respect, and who I felt were doing a fine job. The poor folk I was working with were not only decent and kind, many were outstandingly intelligent, but only a thin few were able to get responsible jobs – electric company lineman, et cetera. On a personal level, I liked everyone I knew there. The majority were unable to get work of any kind and remained at the door of destitution. Colombia's population then was already large and barely capable of providing a living for its people.

All forms of birth control were quashed by the Catholic Church. In that era and reportedly up through the 1980s, Catholic authorities were even unwilling to distribute a Vatican pamphlet on the rhythm method. Such intransigence contributed to the Colombia population growing 2.5 times larger than it was in 1967. By way of comparison, in the same period the U.S. population grew 1.5 times larger – far, far less.

---

* The table was formed by using the average of the adverse ranks of modernity year and of population growth (including expected future growth) as the sort key.

As can be seen in Wikipedia's page on condoms, in the 1930s the Anglican Church and the Federal Council of Churches in the U.S. sanctioned the use of birth control by married couples. The Roman Catholic Church responded by issuing the encyclical Casti Connubi affirming its opposition to contraceptives, a stance it never reversed. At the time of its 1930 ruling, the world population was roughly 2 billion and growing at a generational rate of 1.22x, neither of which appeared to constitute a grave problem. *Population at that time was controlled by hazards of life: high child mortality and short life spans.*

If world population growth had continued at that rate, world population now would be 55% of its present size – 3.88 billion, not its present 7 billion. The Catholic hierarchy who made the decision were unable to foresee the population explosion that resulted because of their decision. *When hazards of life are mainly removed from the population equation, then willful human decisions must be inserted to provide needed control.* Without this, world population growth radically increases. That is precisely what happened, beyond what could have been known in 1930 when the Church initiated the decision to oppose contraception.

Remembering the apology of Pope John Paul II for the role of Christians in the Holocaust (an event rooted in roughly the same era as when the Catholic Church rejected contraception), we can see that rectification on this matter may be possible in the not too distant future.[84] As clearly vile and intentional as the Holocaust was, it seems inevitable that population growth (albeit not so obviously) wields a considerably more vicious hand – ever-growing billions of people repeatedly suffering and many dying into the infinitely distant future because of unquelled and excessive population growth.

The Church could now play a positive role to improve the spiritual wellbeing of its flock by removing the damage that its stance on contraception has already caused. Today there are about one billion Catholics worldwide. Many of them are in Latin America, where excessive population growth results in vicious poverty and social disorder, as is evident from the above lists.

Population growth & Modernity Timeline linked.

We can see in the following smoothed graph-147 that high generational population growth rates – such as 1.6x and greater – are a spoiler. With them, the economic wellbeing of the 60% majority tends to be equivalent to a life spent in the 1870s or earlier. Not until 1.58x growth rates and lower does the MAJ enter an economic wellbeing consistent with the 1900s. And not until 1.4x are they into the 1950s.

#147

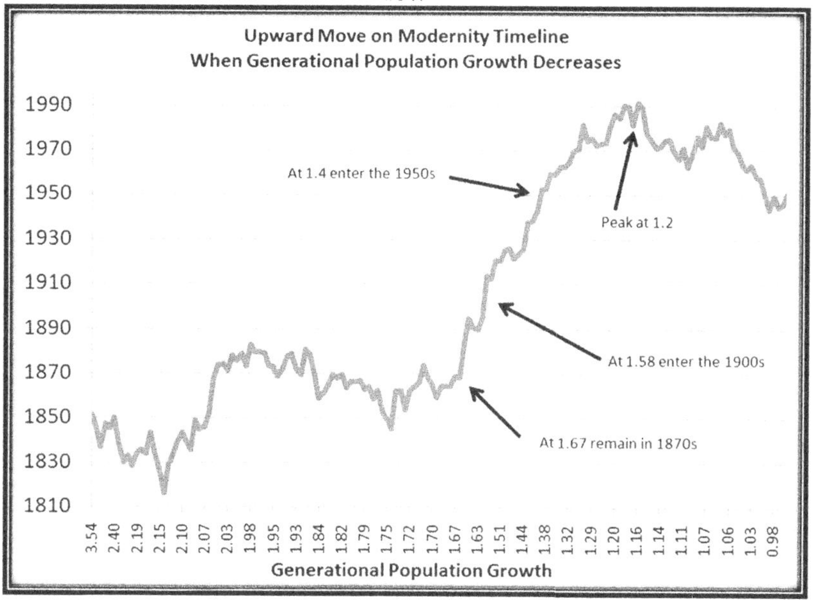

These are not ironclad points of transformation (there is huge variability in the data). The central inescapable point, though, is that the majority suffer when population growth rates are disproportionately high. It takes a sharp reduction in high population growth rates to help propel the majority wellbeing upward – often far sharper than commonly appreciated. Societal and economic structures have large enough difficulties adapting to modest changes, but huge accelerations in population simply outstrip resources, abilities, and social norms.

The Modernity Timeline and the "Successful States Index."

The Modernity Timeline is a method that ranks nations according to their MAJ income. It accounts for both economic vitality and income distribution. As shown in graph-148, the ranking performs much like the well-developed and reputable Failed States Index (2012) published by the magazine *Foreign Policy* and the Fund for Peace.[85] The Success Rank here is formed by inverting Failed States Ranks so that successful nations are ranked first.

The Failed States Index is developed by evaluating the following categories in each nation: Demographic Pressures, Refugees and Internally

Displaced People, Uneven Economic Development (including distribution of income), Group Grievance, Human Flight and Brain Drain, Poverty and Economic Decline, State Legitimacy, Public Services, Human Rights and Rule of Law, Security Apparatus, Factionalized Elites, and External Intervention. These categories can be best understood by evaluating the original report. But to give examples: The Factionalized Elites category would include Power Struggles, Defectors, Flawed Elections, and Political Competition. The Public Services category would include Policing, Criminality, Education Provision, Literacy, Water & Sanitation, Infrastructure, Quality Healthcare, Telephony, Internet Access, Energy Reliability, and Roads. As confirmed here, the conduct of elites and basic public services are crucial to success.

Generally corresponding to the Failed-States nomenclature, the Success Rank uses the following rank categories: 1-12 are Most Stable/Sustainable; 13-23 are Stable; 24-45 are Moderate/Borderline; 46-126 are Warning/In danger; and 127-151 are Critical/Alert. These categories are marked on the vertical rank axis in the graph. As you can see, many nations are under significant stress. Few nations are deemed stable.

#148

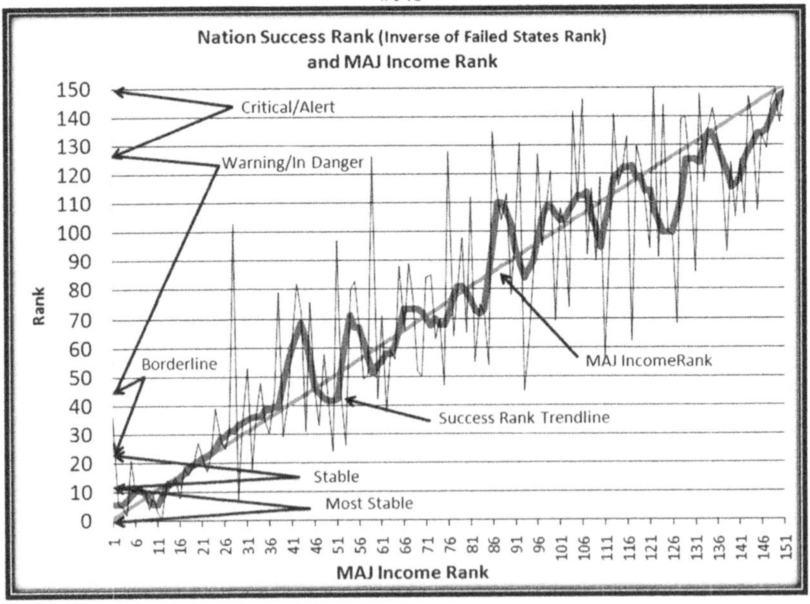

The MAJ Income Rank (and thus the Modernity Timeline Rank) are shown on the diagonal in graph-148. The Failed States Index is sophisticatedly developed. It was of interest that the simple MAJ income ranking also tended to follow its same path. The valuable features that distinguish successful nations seem to be closely intertwined with MAJ income.

#149

Nation	Modernity Timeline Year	MAJ Income Rank	Success Rank	Success Rank Diff.	Nation	Modernity Timeline Year	MAJ Income Rank	Success Rank	Success Rank Diff.	Nation	Modernity Timeline Year	MAJ Income Rank	Success Rank	Success Rank Diff.
Qatar	2091	1	36	-35	Azerbaijan	1940	51	97	-46	Philippines	1874	101	108	-7
Luxembourg	2060	2	6	-4	Bulgaria	1940	52	43	9	Bolivia	1867	102	102	0
Norway	2043	3	5	-2	Chile	1940	53	26	27	CapeVerde	1866	103	74	29
Sweden	2025	4	2	2	Turkey	1940	54	80	-26	Pakistan	1866	104	142	-38
Singapore	2024	5	21	-16	Venezuela	1940	55	83	-28	Djibouti	1864	105	111	-6
Austria	2023	6	10	-4	Mexico	1939	56	67	-11	Yemen	1864	106	146	-40
Iceland	2021	7	12	-5	Seychelles	1939	57	49	8	Moldova	1862	107	92	15
Netherlands	2021	8	11	-3	Albania	1938	58	51	7	Laos	1861	108	115	-7
Switzerland	2021	9	4	5	Iran	1938	59	126	-67	Honduras	1860	109	90	19
Canada	2018	10	9	1	Panama	1938	60	42	18	Kyrgyzstan	1858	110	119	-9
Denmark	2018	11	3	8	Tunisia	1938	61	71	-10	Ghana	1855	111	57	54
Finland	2018	12	1	11	CostaRica	1937	62	38	24	Nicaragua	1854	112	96	16
Germany	2018	13	14	-1	Macedonia	1937	63	59	4	Nigeria	1852	113	141	-28
Australia	2017	14	13	1	Ukraine	1937	64	56	8	Tajikistan	1852	114	116	-2
Belgium	2015	15	15	0	Algeria	1936	65	88	-23	Mauritania	1848	115	122	-7
Ireland	2013	16	8	8	Peru	1935	66	66	0	Cameroon	1847	116	133	-17
UnitedStates	2012	17	19	-2	China	1934	67	89	-22	Namibia	1846	117	62	55
France	2008	18	16	2	Maldives	1934	68	77	-9	Bangladesh	1843	118	130	-12
UnitedKingdc	2004	19	20	-1	Botswana	1933	69	52	17	Cambodia	1842	119	123	-4
Japan	1999	20	27	-7	Jamaica	1933	70	50	20	PapuaNewGu	1842	120	110	10
Korea,South	1998	21	22	-1	Turkmenistar	1933	71	84	-13	Senegal	1842	121	94	27
Slovenia	1989	22	17	5	Bosnia and H	1932	72	85	-13	Chad	1835	122	150	-28
CzechRepubli	1988	23	23	0	Suriname	1932	73	63	10	Benin	1832	123	91	32
Greece	1988	24	39	-15	Dominican Re	1931	74	70	4	Coted'Ivoire	1832	124	144	-20
Malta	1988	25	28	-3	Brazil	1930	75	47	28	Gambia,The	1831	125	100	25
Spain	1986	26	25	1	Egypt	1919	76	128	-52	Tanzania	1828	126	99	27
Italy	1975	27	32	-5	Guyana	1918	77	64	13	SaoTomeand	1825	127	68	59
Israel	1973	28	103	-75	Thailand	1913	78	81	-3	Kenya	1824	128	139	-11
NewZealand	1973	29	7	22	Ecuador	1907	79	98	-19	Guinea-Bissa	1820	129	140	-11
Slovakia	1971	30	34	-4	Armenia	1906	80	65	15	BurkinaFaso	1818	130	118	12
Cyprus	1968	31	53	-22	Colombia	1903	81	112	-31	Mali	1817	131	86	45
Portugal	1965	32	18	14	Belize	1901	82	55	27	Afghanistan	1815	132	148	-16
Hungary	1964	33	37	-4	Jordan	1896	83	75	8	Zambia	1814	133	117	16
TrinidadandT	1962	34	48	-14	ElSalvador	1895	84	72	12	Uganda	1812	134	136	-2
Estonia	1961	35	35	0	SouthAfrica	1895	85	54	31	Guinea	1810	135	143	-8
Poland	1961	36	30	6	SyrianArabRe	1894	86	135	-49	Nepal	1810	136	132	4
Croatia	1959	37	44	-7	Angola	1891	87	114	-27	Togo	1808	137	120	17
Belarus	1953	38	79	-41	Bhutan	1889	88	104	-16	Lesotho	1802	138	93	45
Lithuania	1952	39	29	10	Georgia	1889	89	113	-24	Malawi	1798	139	124	15
Latvia	1948	40	40	0	Morocco	1888	90	78	12	Mozambique	1796	140	105	35
Kazakhstan	1945	41	60	-19	Indonesia	1886	91	101	-10	Rwanda	1794	141	125	16
Russia	1945	42	82	-40	SriLanka	1882	92	131	-39	Madagascar	1792	142	106	36
Gabon	1943	43	73	-30	Mongolia	1880	93	45	48	Haiti	1788	143	147	-4
Mauritius	1943	44	31	13	Paraguay	1880	94	61	33	Niger	1773	144	137	7
Serbia	1943	45	76	-31	India	1879	95	87	8	Comoros	1771	145	107	38
Romania	1942	46	46	0	Congo,Rep.	1877	96	127	-31	Liberia	1766	146	134	12
Argentina	1941	47	33	14	Guatemala	1877	97	95	2	SierraLeone	1766	147	129	18
Malaysia	1941	48	58	-10	Swaziland	1877	98	109	-11	CentralAfrica	1756	148	145	3
Montenegro	1941	49	41	8	Uzbekistan	1876	99	121	-22	Zimbabwe	1752	149	149	0
Uruguay	1941	50	24	26	Vietnam	1875	100	69	31	Burundi	1745	150	138	12
										Congo,Dem.I	1740	151	151	0

Table-149 includes nation names, the Modernity Timeline, the Success Rank Difference, and data shown in the graph. Whenever the Success Rank is of higher status than the MAJ Income Rank (i.e., Success Rank Difference being positive), those nations based on Failed-State criteria are delivering a higher quality of life than other nations with similar MAJ economic strength, and they must be vigilant not to slip backwards. On the other hand, when the Success Rank Difference is negative in the table, those nations are advised that they have the economic strength to deliver a higher quality of life to their citizens than they are doing. If they were doing as well as they should, their rank among nations would be raised by the absolute value of the indicated Success Rank Difference. And since quality of life and national well-being grow in conjunction with MAJ income, all nations are well advised to focus on advancing the MAJ. Nations that inhibit MAJ income do so at their peril.

As in the table, graph-148 also indicates when nations are delivering a higher quality of life than other nations with similar MAJ incomes. Whenever a nation is beneath the diagonal, it is delivering a higher quality of life than commonly associated with its MAJ income. Conversely, whenever a nation is above the diagonal, it is delivering a lower quality of life than it should, given the strength of its MAJ income.

To those who are wedded to the unfettered free market: Your position more often than not is married to elites, not to the MAJ. Yet it is the market economy at the MAJ that advances nations. In many of these nations, elites are unconstrained. Look at the hundreds of nations listed here. Where do you find your success stories? There are numerous cases to choose from. I don't see the bright stories of success emanating from the unfettered elites. I do see them coming from the top dozen stable states and from equitable, mixed, capitalistic economies similar to those that existed in the USA during the 1950s, 1960s, and 1970s – all of which gave a fair shake to the MAJ. The ample and increasing freedoms and opportunities there are quite sufficient to produce successful nations. To free market buccaneers, your voice may charm others, but my preference remains with demonstrated performance. For the world at large, it is the MAJ and prudence that offer the greatest rewards.

Population growth too frequently high & staying there.

In its distant past, the U.S. also had high generational population growths (which included immigration) exceeding 2.0x (graph-151). It took 70 years (1870-1940) for it to go from a 2.0x to a 1.35x population growth. Nations now do not have the luxury of lethargy. Many are already on the precipice.

As a mantra, economists assert that with economic growth, population growth slows. Yes, it slows. But does it slow fast enough, and particularly does it slow fast enough in key nations? My answer is a resounding, "No." Sir David Attenborough refers to the failure to address population control as the "absurd taboo." He is right – brilliantly so – in his "People and Planet" speech available on YouTube.[86]

#151

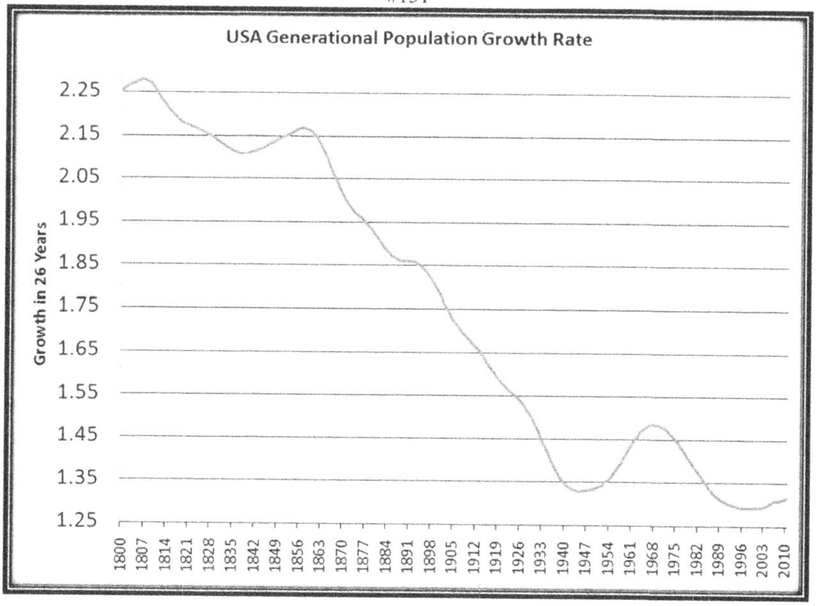

#151B

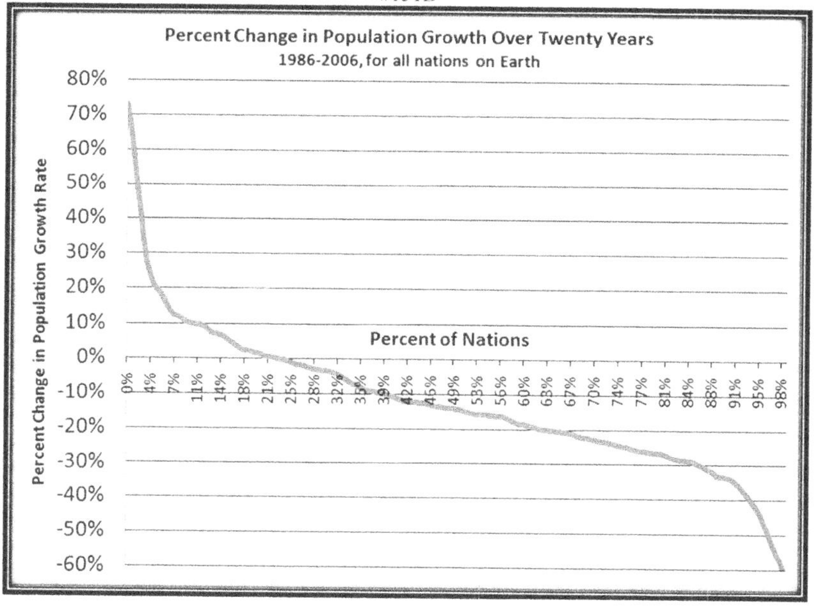

In the above graph-151B, looking at the 20-year (1986-2006) interval in generational growth rates for all nations, we see many of the worst offending nations' populations are growing at an unchanged rate or only slowing slightly [the 1986-2006 interval being more precisely median 1984-88 to median 2004-08 data points]. Graph-151D shows that generational population growth changed slowly. In 23% of nations, population growth increased. In 39% of nations, it has not even decreased 10%; in 63%, not even 20%; in 86%, not even 30%. Only in 6% has it decreased 40%. Only in 4% has it decreased more than 50%. But this summary does not tell us which nations are doing what. Since we are most concerned with problem population growth (nations at 1.35+ per generation), let's look at the following graph-152 of all of those nations worldwide.

#152

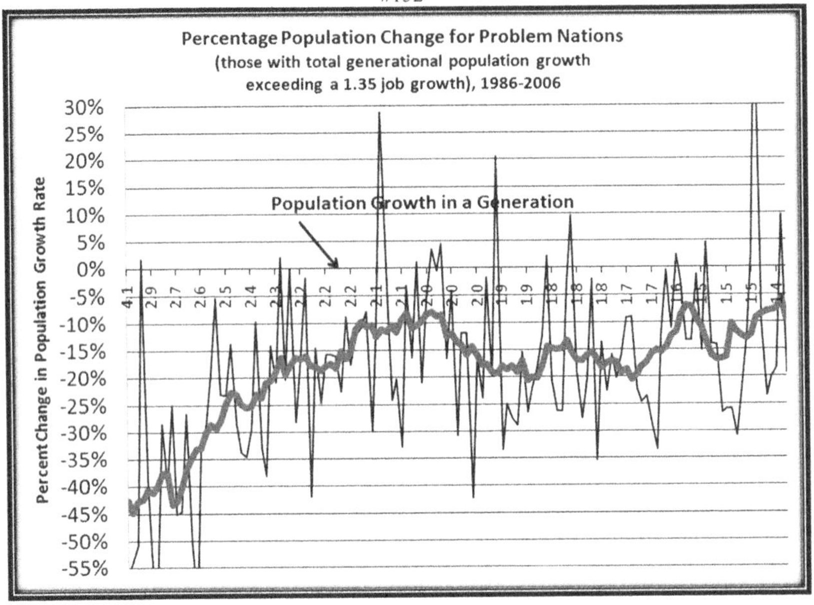

In the above graph-152, we see that the trend line only bent downward significantly at points exceeding a 2.3 growth. Even when population growth far outstripped reasonable expectations for job growth (explicitly 1.7 to 2.3), the general trend was not to reduce population growth more than 20% – leaving population growth rates that will continue to seriously harm the majority. The outcome is so vastly destructive that it makes you cry. These are decent people placed in untenable economic and social conditions by wildly inappropriate population growth rates.

As we can see in the following graph-153, in 1986 exactly 66% of nations had a generational population growth that exceeded reasonable expectations for job growth. Twenty years later in 2006, 57% of nations still remained over the 1.35 threshold. A 9% improvement, but an improvement coming too slowly and leaving numerous nations far above the job threshold. This is a core reason unemployment grows.

#153

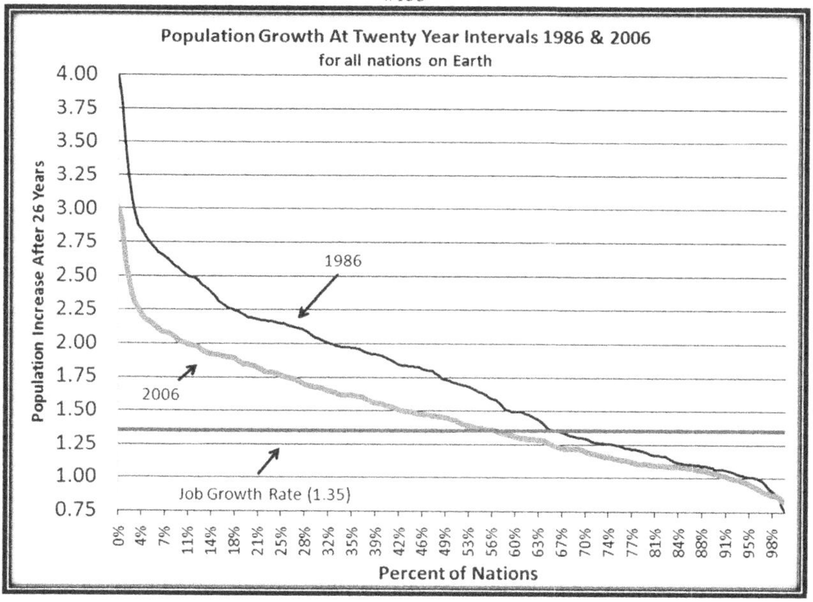

Idle population. Population growth vs. job creation.

Job creation adjusted for hours worked grew at 1.35x generationally (every 26 years) from 1900 through 2011 in the United States. Its slowing is caused by fewer hours worked. Yet further increasing efficiencies may slow it more. It is perilous and foolish for population to grow at a rate faster than potential job creation. To do so will certainly increase the number of idle people within a nation or force them to migrate to other nations.

It would be optimistic to assume that poor economies can produce the above 1.35x generational job growth that the U.S. did. U.S. growth was delivered under highly favorable conditions. The difference between the 1.35x generational job growth and the generational population growth will minimally equal the growth rate of the idle population not having jobs in adulthood. You can expect growth in the idle population to exceed this amount.

If present rates were to continue, within a generation forty-three nations could expect to produce an idle population in an amount greater than 20% of their present total population (43% at the median). That percentage is about 2.25x greater in two generations and about 3.75x greater in three generations. The number of idle people produced is simply huge in these nations. This is unfair to the people born and to the nation as a whole.

#154

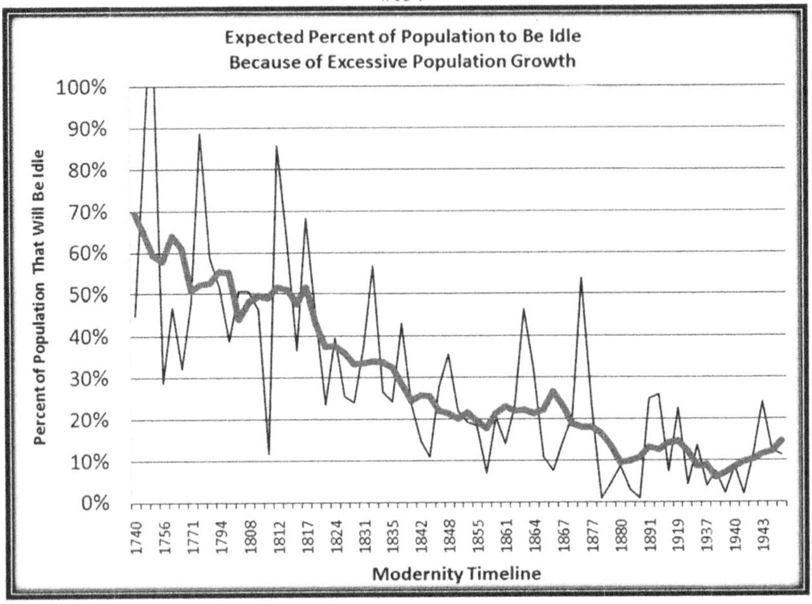

At the median, these forty-three nations are at year 1817 on the Modernity Timeline (125 years behind nations not reporting population growth exceeding 1.35x generationally). Their population growth has forced their people to live primitively and will continue to do so until they take effective population growth action.

The above graph-154 contains all nations where expected population growth exceeds 1.35x per generation. It shows the idle population produced within a generation and the nations' position on the Modernity Timeline. Nations low on the Modernity Timeline have too few resources to withstand a vastly increasing idle population. Yet they have them in greatest measure because of excessive population growth.

We began with a song.

God mend thine ev'ry flaw,
Confirm thy soul in self-control,
Thy liberty in law.[87]

Its line, "Confirm thy soul in self-control" is universal – success giving.

Flesh on the planet.

As Ian Roberts remarked: "[People] immediately focus on population. Actually, when it comes down to it, it's not how many mouths there are to feed, it is how much flesh there is on the planet."[88]

It is flesh and numbers that make up human biomass. BMI is a weight measurement that adjusts for height. Comparing two prosperous nations, the U.S. and Japan, we see that the U.S. BMI was 28.7 and Japan's was 22.9, which is to say that the average adult U.S. citizen, after adjusting for body height, is carrying 25% more weight than the average Japanese [25%= 28.7/22.9-1].[89]

Although nations that have rapidly increasing population are creating problems, those of us in the economically advanced nations, by increasing our size, are also placing disproportionate pressure on the land. Our increased size requires increased food to support it.

Biomass. 45% for humans after 3X growth.

There are numerous ways civilizations can collapse. Overpopulation is one of the most reliable.

Using a portion of the data in a table under Wikipedia's Biomass (ecology) heading, I put together this informal table to get a first approximation of some consequences of a 3x human population growth.

Species	Biomass by Weight in Million Tonnes, 2011	Percent Biomass, 2011	After 3x Human Population Growth, Biomass by Weight in Million Tonnes	After 3x Human Population Growth, Percent Biomass
Ants	1,000	20.63%	1,000	14.51%
Marine fish	1,000	20.63%	1,000	14.51%
Cyanobacteria (apicoplankton)	1,000	20.63%	1,000	14.51%
Cattle	520	**10.73%**	1,560	**22.63%**
Termites	445	9.18%	445	6.46%
Antarctic krill	379	7.82%	379	5.50%
Humans	350	**7.22%**	1,050	**15.23%**
Sheep and goats	105	**2.17%**	315	**4.57%**
Chickens	48	**0.99%**	144	**2.09%**
Blue whales	1	0.01%	1	0.01%
Total	4,848		6,894	
Percent of human related biomass		**21%**		**45%**

The table here lists key non-plant biomass. If cattle, sheep and goats, and chickens (which exist primarily to satisfy the human diet) were to grow at 3x in tandem with humans, then this group would comprise 45% of the listed biomass, in contrast to its present 21%. This optimistically assumes that the other listed species would remain at current levels.

Consider the plants on which humans and their livestock depend. The following are listed in ranked order according to their percentage of approximate total weight of food produced worldwide. The vast majority of them would seem to generally increase in response to population growth: sugarcane 24.5%, wheat 11.6%, rice 11.6%, maize (corn) 10.8%, potato 6.0%, sugarbeet 5.6%, cassava 3.4%, barley 3.0%, sweet potato 2.9%, soybean 2.6%, banana/plantain 1.8%, tomato 1.8%, cottonseed 1.2%, orange 1.2%, grape 1.2%, sorghum 1.1%, apple 1.1%, coconut 1.0%, cabbage 1.0%, watermelon 0.8%, onion 0.8%, rapeseed/canola 0.7%, yam 0.7%,

Population Per Square Football Field of Arable Land

Rank	Nation	Football Field Number
1	Djibouti	657.7
2	Seychelles	69.6
3	Maldives	61.3
4	Qatar	49.2
5	TrinidadandT	43.1
6	Malta	41.0
7	Iceland	35.2
8	Japan	24.4
9	Korea,South	24.4
10	Jordan	24.4
11	Egypt	21.8
12	PapuaNewGu	21.5
13	Israel	18.5
14	CostaRica	17.5
15	SriLanka	17.0
16	Jamaica	16.9
17	Colombia	16.7
18	Switzerland	15.2
19	SaoTomeand	14.7
20	Bangladesh	14.4
21	Philippines	14.1
22	Netherlands	13.0
23	Yemen	13.0
24	Malaysia	12.0
25	Mauritius	11.1
26	Vietnam	10.7
27	Belgium	10.4
28	Slovenia	9.6
29	Nepal	9.6
30	Dominican Re	9.4
31	China	9.2
32	Chile	9.2
33	Indonesia	8.7
34	Ecuador	8.7
35	UnitedKingdo	8.6
36	Venezuela	8.4
37	Haiti	8.2
38	Suriname	8.1
39	Cyprus	8.1
40	NewZealand	8.0
41	Georgia	7.7
42	CapeVerde	7.5
43	ElSalvador	7.4
44	Congo,Dem.R	7.1
45	Guatemala	7.0
46	Tajikistan	7.0
47	Liberia	6.9
48	Rwanda	6.7
49	Comoros	6.6
50	Botswana	6.6

oats 0.6%, peanuts 0.6%, millet 0.6%, sunflower 0.6%, rye 0.5%, mango 0.4%, and beans 0.4%.[90] And although not listed, cotton accounts for 2.5% of arable land (land used for growing crops).[91]

Arable land.

There is only a limited amount of arable land. The number of nations whose population far outstrip the capacity of the soil is stunning. Picture in your mind an American football playing field: 100 yards long (almost 100 meters). Mark off land that is approximately one square football playing field (100 yds. x 100 yds.).[92] The table you see here lists nations in rank order of population intensity per square football field of arable land based on 2000-2009 median World Bank data.

The top dozen on the list would require the square football field to feed more than 20 people. Perhaps you have grown a garden that you relied on to feed your family. We have something in common. I would hazard a guess that, you too, would find it inconceivable to expect a square football field garden, with some livestock and a few chickens to reliably feed that many people. Without food imports, it is obvious that people would starve in a heartbeat. Wealthy nations can import; poor nations less so. Jared Diamond attributed Rwanda's genocide to population competition over land.[93] Rwanda is now 48th on the list with 6.7 people per square football field. In the worst of times it was at 7.5. Points above this exceed the threshold of danger. As you see, this is not an issue of population growth leading to untenable conditions. It is a question of already untenable conditions becoming yet more untenable.

#157

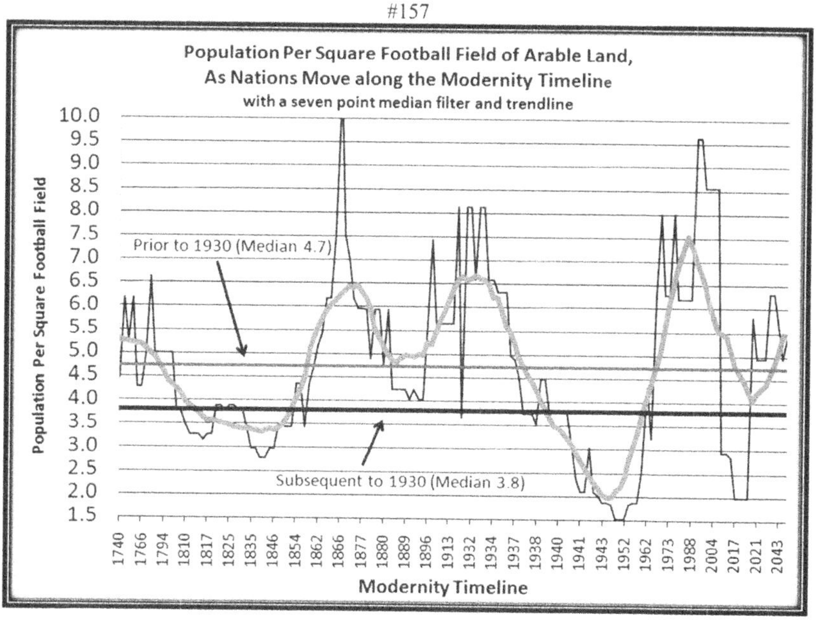

The pressure that nations place on arable land, as shown in above graph-157, assumes variable shapes about which it is risky to draw conclusions. There are obviously both rich and poor nations that put high pressure on the land. However, using the original data, we find that the football field median was 4.4 for all nations, but prior to a 1930 Modernity Timeline position, it was 4.7, and for the nations above 1930 on the Timeline, it was 3.8; thus suggesting that poor nations are putting about 25% more pressure on the land [25%= 4.7/3.8-1]. Poor nations are at the mercy of this pressure because they have less buying power to acquire food internationally when their own crops become insufficient.

Arable land, what's left of it.

David Montgomery's splendid book *Dirt: The Erosion of Civilizations* tells the story of civilizations rising and falling according to the health of their soil. It is an ancient and predictable process that applied to the Romans, the Greeks, and the Mayans, just as much as it does today.

Since 1945, erosion worldwide has degraded an amount of agricultural land equal to the combined size of China and India. Today about a third of China's cultivated land is being seriously eroded. I have seen it. Montgomery indicates that arable land is declining at a rate of about 1% a year.[94] In fairness to the topic, there are a variety of opinions out there. But for brevity, the following graph-158 summarizes only the consequence of an uninterrupted 1% continuous decline.

#158

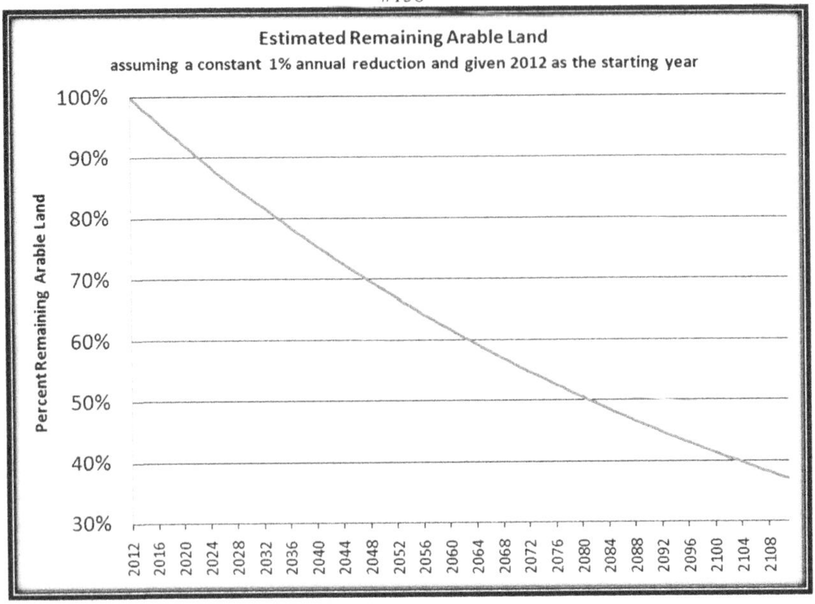

Table-159 attempts to show where, at greatest intensity, the twin problems of high pressure on arable land and low income for the MAJ can be found.* However, $farmland_1$ is not equal to $farmland_2$, which is to say there is a huge variety of soil and farm quality. To lump them all under a single phrase "arable land" is at best misleading and often frankly inaccurate. Much of the land being farmed is already marginal land of poor quality and low yields.[95]

Further, if farmland is created by deforestation, as it is in many places, the health of the land is degraded. While that land may be deemed "arable" for a short while, usually it will soon be worthless for farming. The value of trees is inescapable, whether in agriculture or in urban settings.

Trees are a marker for income inequality. Wealthy neighborhoods have them in abundance. Poor neighborhoods do not. Satellite images from Google Earth bear this out.[96] One of the smartest transitions from poverty to wealth is to plant and maintain trees.

---

* Table-159was formed by using the average of the adverse ranks of modernity year and square football field number as the sort key.

General trends through history take two forms: A civilization first populates fertile river valleys. As population expands, it moves into increasingly marginal land, ultimately into sloping land prone to erosion. With the expanding population, excessive pressure is placed on the land to produce food. Land is cleared of trees. The soil becomes depleted. Erosion intensifies especially on the sloping land. Unable to produce sufficient food, the civilization crashes or fails.[97]

Another sequence is for farmers to ruin the land, soon abandoning it to move onward onto new land. Even at the founding of the United States, George Washington and others sharply criticized this land destruction practice, which was massive especially in the South. As Montgomery relates, "After five years of tobacco cultivation the ground was too depleted in nutrients to grow much of anything. … [F]armers just kept on clearing new fields."[98] Even without modern mechanization, the destruction was massive. To this date, damage remains in many regions.[99]

Albeit serious, in these scenarios (civilizations failing or farmers moving on to deplete new land), the damage was regionally confined. The distinction now is that the population pressure is global, not regional – thus consequences are global, not just regional.

For 129 of the nations on the Modernity Timeline, sufficient World-Bank arable land data was available to draw the following conclusions.[100] For the 1960-1969 period, the median for the nations represented in the following graph-160 was 2.4 people per square football field. By 2000-2009, it had increased to 4.9 –

Pressure on Arable Land and Modernity Year Combined

Rank	Nation	Modernity Year	Football Field Number
1	Congo,Dem.F	1740	7.1
2	Nepal	1810	9.6
3	Haiti	1788	8.2
4	PapuaNewGι	1842	21.5
5	SaoTomeand	1825	14.7
6	Djibouti	1864	657.7
7	Liberia	1766	6.9
8	Bangladesh	1843	14.4
9	Comoros	1771	6.6
10	Burundi	1745	6.2
11	Rwanda	1794	6.7
12	Yemen	1864	13.0
13	Philippines	1874	14.1
14	Madagascar	1792	5.0
15	SriLanka	1882	17.0
16	Lesotho	1802	5.4
17	Vietnam	1875	10.7
18	Jordan	1896	24.4
19	SierraLeone	1766	4.3
20	Tajikistan	1852	7.0
21	Kenya	1824	5.6
22	Maldives	1934	61.3
23	Egypt	1919	21.8
24	Colombia	1903	16.7
25	Ethiopia	1817	4.9
26	Mauritania	1848	6.3
27	Coted'Ivoire	1832	5.4
28	CapeVerde	1866	7.5
29	Mozambique	1796	3.8
30	Indonesia	1886	8.7
31	Seychelles	1939	69.6
32	Uganda	1812	3.9
33	Jamaica	1933	16.9
34	Guatemala	1877	7.0
35	Georgia	1889	7.7
36	Malawi	1798	3.5
37	CostaRica	1937	17.5
38	Guinea-Bissa	1820	3.9
39	Honduras	1860	5.4
40	Pakistan	1866	6.2
41	Ecuador	1907	8.7
42	Dominican R	1931	9.4
43	ElSalvador	1895	7.4
44	Timor-Leste	1863	5.1
45	Gambia,The	1831	3.8
46	Congo,Rep.	1877	6.0
47	Zimbabwe	1752	2.7
48	Zambia	1814	3.3
49	China	1934	9.2
50	India	1879	5.9

twice as many people per unit of land. By 2000-2009, 81% of nations exceeded the previous 2.4 median.

#160

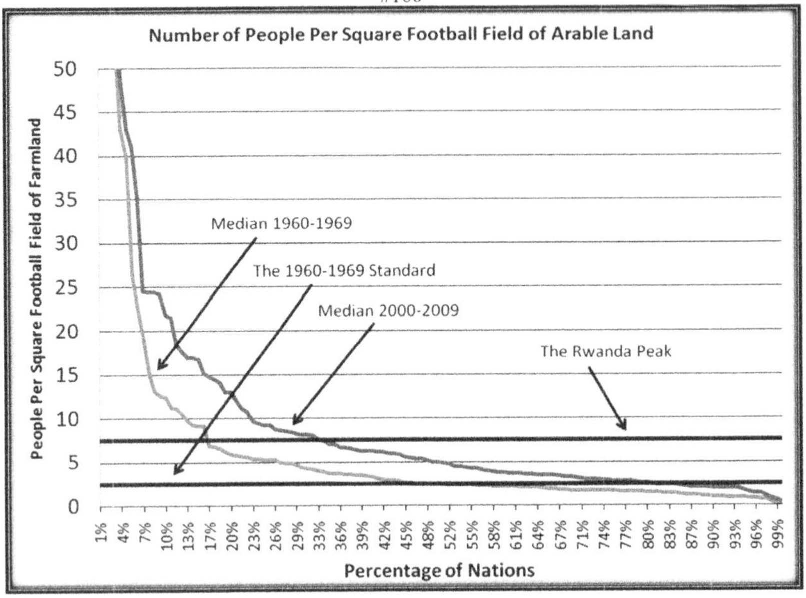

Over 40 years, the pressure on the land increased at a rate of 1.8% per year [2.024= 4.92/2.43; 1.78%= 2.024^(1/40)-1]. Eleven percent of nations were above 20. As Jared Diamond indicated, land disputes, genocide, and Rwanda were a nasty brew. At its worst, Rwanda had 7.5 people on each arable square football field. In 1960-69, only 16% of nations put this much pressure on the land. By 2000-2009, 33% of nations were at this testy point. Some were rich enough that they could import food with ease. Many were not.

Farming by extraction: soil and oil.

I come with prejudice. I grew up and worked on a farm. If it had been profitable, my preference would have been to remain there. The work is satisfying. Not great, just a nice way of living. A farming orientation fosters a sharp attention to the care of the land. I cannot describe the depth of revulsion when seeing eroded land. It is the first job of stewardship to care for the land, and, when the soil is out of repair, to do all in one's power restore it. In many nations this job is simply unattended to.

Look to the stars and planets above – then the earth below. The earth beneath your feet surpasses all treasures. It gives the life found nowhere else. Michael Wood's visit to Uruk in "The Cradle of Civilization" (on

YouTube and DVD) dramatically and clearly shows the path that was taken there.[101] From once being the verdant giver of life for our long-ago ancestors, the literal cradle of civilization has made the full run to an endpoint of being a blasted landscape. We too risk the same journey.

There is nothing in the entire known universe which brings and supports the life that the subsoil beneath our feet provides. We are tied to soil. Being remote from it does not remove our dependence on it. When it is lost, so too is life.

I am uncertain how to begin. In an attempt to convey it, I have cut a hair from my head and measured it with a micrometer. It's three thousandths of an inch thick. My waist circumference is 33 inches. I have checked to see the diameter of the earth. It is approximately 7,926 miles. Topsoil, what plants predominately live in, is usually 2 to 8 inches thick. For ease of example, I am going to call it a foot. If we were to consider the topsoil to be the skin of the earth, which we and substantially all creatures rely on for life, how should we think of it? After doing the calculations, it would be as if the skin around my waist was 12,000 times thinner than a human hair – that is the narrow skin of the earth. Our civilization, our life, is held together by this very fragile and thin integument – extractable, yet irreplaceable.

Topsoil loss is so great that the U.S. Department of Agriculture has a poster to illustrate the extent of topsoil loss in the State of Missouri. In it they give an example that for every 100 bushels of corn that are produced, the equivalent of 100 bushels of topsoil are lost. They also state, "It takes about 500 years for nature to create one inch of topsoil."[102] But at an erosion rate of 5.6 tons per acre annually, one inch of topsoil is lost within 30 years. Not a comforting picture. A bushel of topsoil gone for each bushel of corn sold; topsoil lost in 30 years that takes 500 years to create. Those underling properties stand in opposition to the bucolic notion of farming. Instead now at the core, farming too frequently is a process of extraction, slowly mining the land – removing its life and its capacity to give life.

When population increases indefinitely and the resource topsoil is finite, there is a pause for consideration. Food comes from topsoil. That applies whether we are urban or rural. No distance from it is sufficient to remove us from our dependence on it. It lets us live, or alternatively, if we ignore it, it lets us die. If you have any doubt about its importance worldwide, go to a barren desert. Look around. Or, reconsider Haiti and other examples of deforestation. Such devastation is too easily achieved. It does not feed people.

Rigoberta Menchú made a comment about her Mayan tradition, which I translate as: "We cultivate corn and a few beans. Before beginning to plant we have a ceremony for the seeds and the land. We ask for permission from our mother earth for the wound that we are going to inflict on her by planting the corn."[103] That tradition and wisdom of honoring the soil strikes me as appropriate. As Wendell Berry says, we must grow like a tree, not like a fire.[104]

Albeit indirectly, farming is now an exercise in extraction – first extracting topsoil as we have seen, and second extracting fossil fuels, as we will now see.

Calories are energy. Each calorie of food that we eat is literally the energy that makes it possible to live. Less obviously, each calorie that we consume also requires energy consumption to grow the food source, and take it through all of the steps that bring it to our table. In today's mechanized world, that energy is enormous. Since 1974, it has been estimated that approximately 9.5 calories are expended to produce one food calorie.[105] These industrial calories come principally from fossil fuels. For every calorie we ingest, we effectively consume about 8+ calories of fossil fuels.

Though we intellectually assume that the farm, with its natural process of plant and animal growth, is the source of our food, the reality now is that oil extraction is what delivers food production. One estimate suggests that in the United States, each person is effectively "eating" the equivalent of about 1.1 gallons of oil a day, 400 gallons a year.[106] It took about 20 to 650 million years to create the fossil fuels that we now use at a furious rate to drive modern agriculture.

Those fuels seems to be expended in roughly the following proportions: 31% for manufacturing fertilizer, 16% for transportation, 13% for irrigation, 10% for operating farm machinery, with the balance going to raising livestock (not including feed), crop drying, pesticide, et cetera. In part, these heavy energy expenditures arise from the Green Revolution (1950-1984). Worldwide, it is estimated to have increased grain production about 250%, but its methods necessitate high fossil fuel use.[107] Thirty percent of oil consumption goes to agriculture. [108] The revolution in food production staved off famine, but adversely, it also made huge population increases possible. Having food production dependent on topsoil and fossil fuel extraction in great quantities warns us that population at current levels is already perilous. To yet grow population further would seem to bring only vast misery.

How much population growth can the earth absorb before human growth completely overreaches earth's capabilities? The impact on plant kingdoms on which our food-source animals depend would even be more massive than our present non-plant biomass consumption. The prospect of new food sources technologically created from fungus, genetic modification, and other yet to be imagined sources to meet the food needs of humans swarming the earth ... This would not seem to represent progress. It would not seem to conform to our spiritual, intellectual, or religious purpose for being on this earth in the first place. A human species transformed into an instrument of thorough and complete predation and extraction – doesn't that stand in stark opposition to the very meaning of the word Civilization?

Ozymandian Economics

In the desert, on the sands, a pedestal stands.
And on the pedestal these words appear:
'My name is Ozymandias, king of kings:
Look on my works, ye Mighty and despair!'
Nothing beside remains. Round the decay
Of that colossal wreck, boundless and bare
The lone and level sands stretch far away.
Percy Bysshe Shelley, 1817, modified and abridged

Farming can work. Decency can work.

I have visited various organic farms, Polyface Farms of *Omnivore's Dilemma* fame, and of course, with my own farm background numerous others, many of which had great merit.[109] However, the standout I stumbled on in 2007, not even knowing it was a farm when I arrived, and certainly not anticipating the sensational job it did.

Environmentally, Selva Negra in Matagalpa, Nicaragua is the soundest farming operation I have seen. Nicaragua, despite its many fine characteristics, presents formidable geographic difficulties of dry weather and soil depletion. Selva Negra distinguishes itself because it thrives in precisely such a setting. It is a 300-acre farm and nature reserve. Its forests were carefully planted with plants and a variety of trees with different root structures. Grasslands and forest work together – one must have the other.

The result over time is that Selva Negra has developed its own microclimate with numerous flowing springs in an otherwise dry region. The forest is stunningly beautiful, unlike much of the rough land leading up to it. The forest brings the climate and water on which the farm thrives. The Selva Negra cabins, lodge, and layout are an architectural dreamland, not so much for their novelty, but for how comfortably they and their plantings fit into the setting. You would be perfectly happy if you saw no more than this. At least that is how I felt when I arrived.

Walking further down the hill, I saw the school house and homes of the people who worked on the farm; and further down, the dairy cows. Every day, without exception, the cows are rotated into a small new field. This vastly increases the productivity of the land because the grazed field has time to heal, the new grown grass grows quickly and new grass is also preferred by the cattle. That single innovation made it possible to literally double herd size using the same amount of land. And the land was in better ecological shape because of it. The farm had far more lessons to teach than I could properly relate. I do not hold it out as utopia. But to my eyes it provides encouragement that the sensible marriage of forest with smart farming can work, and work well, even under adverse conditions. I was also encouraged that it had been a long-term endeavor stretching back to the early 1900s. It had achieved its outcome, not through a shot-in-the-pan academic dream, but by continuous trial and error, shepherded by the hand of intelligence, creativity, and persistence.

There are a few instances of sustained successful agriculture: some sections of China, 4,000+ years;[110] Egypt prior to the damming of the Nile, 7,000 years;[111] *terra preta* in the Amazon, 2,000 years;[112] Colca Valley, Peru, 1,500 years;[113] the island Tikopia, 1,000+ years;[114] Tsangpo valley, Tibet, 1,000+ years.[115] These isolated stories of success are matched by the success of the Dutch after catastrophic medieval famines and plague. As David Montgomery relates:

> [T]he Netherlands are covered by quartz-rich dirt ill suited for agriculture. ... [T]he Dutch began mixing manure, leaves, and other organic waste into their dirt. ... [O]ver time they built up dark, organic-rich soils to as much as three feet thick. Lacking land they made soil.[116]

Successful land management is labor intensive and personal. From what I have seen of it, absentee decision-making and ownership do not work. Geographical and human considerations are regional. They are best addressed with that in mind, explicitly favoring the hand of caution. The marriage of forest, farm, dedication, and intelligence that Selva Negra showed is an example of the elements which in combination are potent. Not perfect, but good enough.

(In the real world, what is ever perfect? Except you, dear reader.)

(Dear perfect reader, My praises to you are infinite. Don't let anyone tell you otherwise. Ok, this chatter ends. You can let your eyes move down the page.)

On a more levelheaded note, please observe that income-distribution spreadsheets for nearly all of the nations of the world are available at Dillives.com (as in Di$_{\text{stribution of}}$Lives).

CH. 6

PROGRESSIVE? Not Hardly.

Always a difficult word, the presumption is that taxation should be **fair.** It is especially difficult if fairness is to rest on profound income-distribution ignorance. As I believe you have seen, we have known too little about income distribution. Citizens and governments need to have a precise understanding of income distribution before there can be any hope of constructing a system of fair taxation.

Even the knowledge we now have has been insufficiently implemented. In the old USA, taxation schemes were constructed far more wisely than they are today. Let's see what has happened and why.

The notion of the "margin" has permeated income tax construction since 1913. Economists have a predilection for looking at the marginal. The origin, I believe, can be traced to primitive economics. To give a little background, the "Marginal Revolution" in economics appeared in the 1860s and 1870s, and was given a huge boost by Alfred Marshall's publication of *Principles of Economics* in 1890.[117] All of this, for economists, gave rise to the "margin" having great academic importance. Our marginal tax rate structure retains those vestiges of academia that give "the margin" pretensions of importance.

However, the margin is of little use in taxation. A list of average taxation at each point would do just as well and would be far easier to understand. Using a marginal structure too readily hides the true form of taxation. The margin is subject to manipulation, demagoguery, and chicanery.

Worst of all, we citizens cannot grasp the income tax picture with such a confusing presentation.

By contrast, average taxation lets you see exactly how much people are being taxed at every point. As you will see, these pages will soon enough distance themselves from the margin. But before doing so, we need to understand how the marginal tax has been applied to the top income bracket. We need a clear picture of how those at the high economic strata now benefit relative to past periods of taxation.

The tax code has several points of philosophical change. The initial philosophy was to have gradations of taxation all the way up to very scarce incomes. In about 70% of the years from 1913 to 1941, the threshold for applying the top bracket exceeded one in a million; and in 20% of the years, the scarcity threshold was so high that it was unlikely that any taxpayer would attain such a high income. Population was 134 million in 1942, so few, if any, taxpayers were actually taxed at the highest bracket rate. The particulars can be seen in Table-170. In this 1913-1941 period, which I call Stage I, there seems to have been a bona fide effort to distinguish between high-income taxpayers all the way up to the very top.

"Tax at the Threshold" refers to the Top-Bracket income tax threshold above which further marginal tax rate increases don't occur. For the rich, this causes a flattening of tax above this point. The measurement is handy because it cuts across time and conditions; and by stating this flat-tax threshold in X$s, it simultaneously accounts for tax rate, inflation, and changes in income distribution.*

	Period	Median Tax at the Threshold in X$s	Median Scarcity
Stage I	1913-1941	1,499	8,293,482
Stage II	1942-1964	132.5	150,364
Stage III	1965-1981	32.0	11,981
Stage IV	1982-2011	8.2	144

The short story of the past century of income taxes can be understood by looking at the 4 stages of income-tax top-bracket philosophy. As shown in the table here, Stage I (1913-1941) is a period in which the taxation

* "Tax at the Threshold in X$s" is equal to the "Top Bracket Income Threshold in X$s" multiplied by "Top Tax Rate." It is not a tax rate that is paid, but it is a marker for how Top Income Bracket taxing is structured, because it illustrates the level of taxation upon entering the Top Bracket. And as indicated previously, please keep in mind that scarcity is based on full population, not number of tax filers. For example, one-in-4,000 would refer to one person in a town of 4,000, not one tax filer in 4,000.

gradients reached very high levels well in excess of one million (8.2 million at the median). In all subsequent stages, the gradations significantly dropped, as did tax at the threshold. Notwithstanding, Stage II (1942-1964) was sufficient to prevent maldistribution from gaining a foothold.

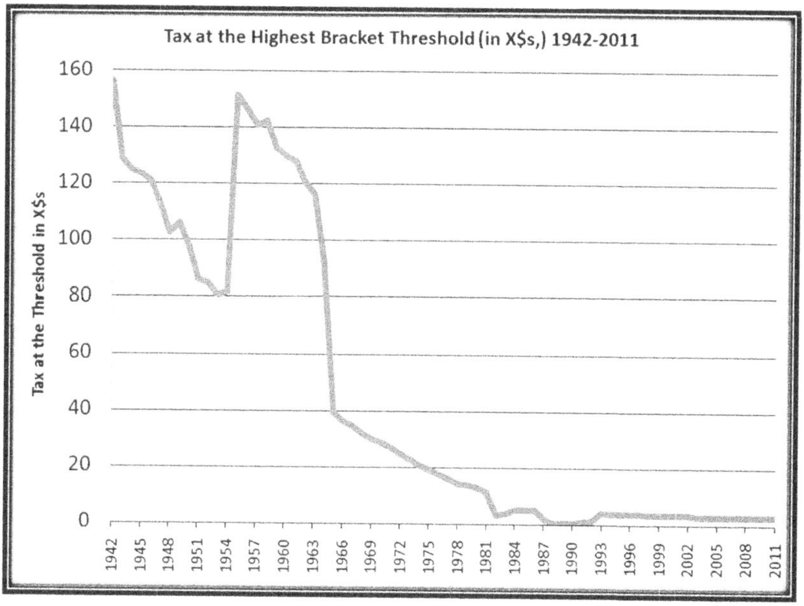

#169

I never thought I would be writing this, but what we now need is a bald guy about 5' 10.5" tall, who weighs somewhere between 175-185 pounds, and who plays golf at every opportunity he can get, specifically: Eisenhower. Look at his Presidential term 1953-1961 within graph-169 and the tables here. His median threshold tax was 145.8 and his median gradations reached up to the one-in-225,160 scarcity level (see Table-170). As shown in graph-169, that was one of the last times in the post WWII era that taxation greatly impeded the accumulation of vast income and wealth at the top. From then on, it was a downward slide.

Stage IV (1981-2012) completely opened the flood gates. The top tax rate dropped to the lowest it had been since 1931. There was no taxation impediment to maldistribution whatsoever. The tax rates for those at the pinnacle were trivially low and maldistribution came apace.

#170

Ninety-nine Years of USA Top Tax Rates

year	Top Tax Rate	Bracket Income Thresh-old in X$s	Tax at the Thresh-old in X$s	Scarcity
1913	7%	1,390	97	6,236,945
1914	7%	1,499	105	6,860,184
1915	7%	1,452	102	4,929,279
1916	15%	4,729	709	29,207,839
1917	67%	3,989	2,673	35,083,928
1918	77%	1,586	1,221	8,293,482
1919	73%	1,435	1,048	7,337,321
1920	73%	1,293	944	11,712,122
1921	73%	1,530	1,117	19,806,234
1922	58%	317	184	293,665
1923	58%	279	162	217,097
1924	46%	683	314	1,344,178
1925	25%	134	33	31,595
1926	25%	127	32	25,705
1927	25%	130	32	20,272
1928	25%	130	33	15,069
1929	25%	123	31	17,756
1930	25%	139	35	46,062
1931	25%	167	42	123,488
1932	63%	2,172	1,368	45,099,223
1933	63%	2,318	1,460	44,054,715
1934	63%	2,026	1,276	16,949,361
1935	63%	1,829	1,152	13,167,606
1936	79%	8,068	6,374	268,309,351
1937	79%	7,376	5,827	285,819,935
1938	79%	7,829	6,185	853,704,982
1939	79%	7,453	5,888	762,506,518
1940	79%	6,856	5,416	629,521,082
1941	81%	5,599	4,535	414,561,519
1942	88%	178	156	181,529
1943	88%	146	129	140,071
1944	94%	133	125	187,076
1945	94%	131	123	150,364
1946	91%	133	121	111,365
1947	91%	124	113	94,039
1948	91%	113	102	75,340
1949	91%	117	106	96,612
1950	91%	107	98	65,161
1951	91%	95	86	58,585
1952	92%	92	85	84,432
1953	92%	88	81	131,837
1954	91%	90	82	65,790
1955	91%	166	151	268,562
1956	91%	161	147	303,558
1957	91%	155	141	455,780
1958	91%	156	142	316,367
1959	91%	146	133	218,126
1960	91%	143	130	225,160
1961	91%	140	128	177,869
1962	91%	132	121	209,206
1963	91%	127	116	189,992
1964	77%	120	93	127,891
1965	70%	56.4	39	18,271
1966	70%	52.0	36	17,127
1967	70%	49.9	35	12,953
1968	70%	45.8	32	10,151
1969	70%	42.8	30	10,551
1970	70%	41.0	29	21,245
1971	70%	38.3	27	17,699
1972	70%	35.3	25	11,981
1973	70%	32.0	22	14,154
1974	70%	29.7	21	15,412
1975	70%	27.4	19	12,381
1976	70%	24.9	17	9,465
1977	70%	22.8	16	7,406
1978	70%	20.4	14	5,348
1979	70%	19.6	14	3,689
1980	70%	18.5	13	2,889
1981	70%	16.4	11	1,802
1982	50%	6.3	3.2	144
1983	50%	7.5	3.8	201
1984	50%	10.1	5.1	258
1985	50%	9.9	5.0	201
1986	50%	9.8	4.9	201
1987	39%	4.8	1.8	144
1988	28%	1.5	0.4	30
1989	28%	1.5	0.4	30
1990	28%	1.5	0.4	30
1991	31%	3.6	1.1	87
1992	31%	3.6	1.1	87
1993	40%	10.1	4.0	258
1994	40%	9.6	3.8	201
1995	40%	9.5	3.8	201
1996	40%	9.3	3.7	201
1997	40%	9.1	3.6	201
1998	40%	8.9	3.5	144
1999	40%	8.6	3.4	144
2000	40%	8.3	3.3	144
2001	39%	8.4	3.3	144
2002	39%	8.5	3.3	201
2003	35%	8.3	2.9	201
2004	35%	8.1	2.8	144
2005	35%	7.9	2.7	144
2006	35%	7.7	2.7	144
2007	35%	7.7	2.7	144
2008	35%	7.8	2.7	144
2009	35%	8.4	2.9	144
2010	35%	8.1	2.8	144
2011	35%	8.0	2.8	144

I am tired of saying X$. It is too formal. Instead I will say this guy is earning a 1,000 people (or whatever other X$ applies). You have turned enough pages in this book to get the drift. And I rather like saying "He earned a 1,000 people." I can easily picture such an income kingdom and can have some fun saying it.

By Stage IV, a guy with a 1,000 people income, would be facing a substantially flat tax subsequent to the 8th or 9th person. The Upper½% begins at the one-in-200 level. Thus, the Stage IV median scarcity at 144 served to flatten the tax for the entire Upper½%. As we have seen, this is where the greatest maldistributions occurred (e.g., graph-30). Yet the stopping point for high bracket increases occurred before it even reached the Upper½%.

If you were to cherry-pick years of iniquity,[118] the prize winners are 1988-1990 at 0.4 on Tax at the Threshold as seen in Table-170. We did not even reach a full person on that one (0.4). It was also insufficient to fund government.

Stage IV is how you transform a democracy into an oligarchy. It is the lesson plan. Nowhere in USA tax history has there been anything like it. Every day now, the news and our own eyes witness its impact.

It built incomes for the profligately rich. It built governmental debt for the rest of us.

The booby prize: It lowered our standard of living. The anti-tax brigade won the battle. The super rich were safe to grow. And that is what they did.

Preventing maldistribution before it gets a foothold.

Explicitly, high taxes at pinnacle incomes are ***not about redistribution***. They are about setting tax levels that prevent maldistribution from occurring in the first place. Few people were ever taxed at the 91% margins that existed in the 1950s. These taxes were a preventative measure that guaranteed that excessive income and wealth were not widely accumulated at the top.

By taxation setting those ceilings, corporations were advised in advance that inappropriately high compensation was pointless because it would go into taxes anyway. So they moderated their pay packages. Similarly, a private business person was advised by taxation that beyond a certain point, his or her after-tax income would not increase greatly if activities were disproportionately remunerative. High tax bracket rates thus ensured that a winner-take-all ethic did not pervade. It gave everybody a fair shot at getting a good (even a high) after-tax income, but it prevented oligarchy. It prevented plutocracy. It prevented monopoly incomes.

We need not look as far back as our founders for wisdom. Just looking back to FDR, Truman, and Eisenhower is enough. They built and maintained a culture of taxation and compensation wisdom that was the foundation of a capitalism that thrived as never before.[119] When you remove that ethic, you increasingly have oligarchy, plutocracy, and monopoly. You also impoverish the MAJ and reduce the incomes of 92% of the population. FDR, Truman, and Eisenhower saw to it that we prospered together. The incremental chipping away at their ethic reversed that destiny.

Looking at the stages.

#172

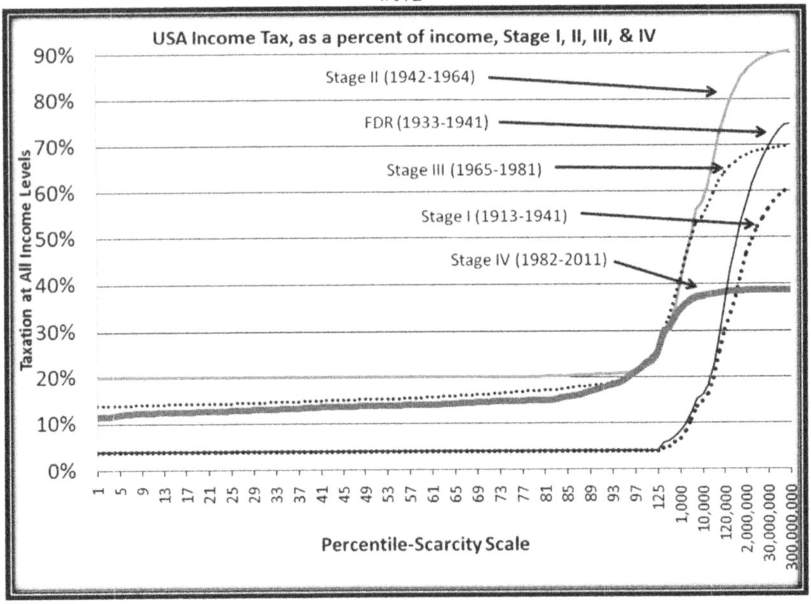

As indicated, Stage IV (1982-2011) is vastly different from all other previous forms of U.S. taxation. Graph-172 provides the full picture from bottom to top, showing median curves for each of the four Stages. As you can see, there was a profound flattening in Stage IV that became pronounced at about the one-in-4,000 scarcity level. At this level and higher, taxation provided no impediment to maldistribution. A person at the one-in-4,000 level would be earning about 50 people a year (approximately $2.3 million). A small town with a population of about 4,000 people might have one person at this level. Stage IV taxation exists to benefit these people and those of higher rank.

By contrast, within the Top1%, Stage IV taxation did not reduce taxes by more than 2.2% for people lower than the one-in-250 level. Many pages back (graph-30) we saw the sharp increase in Upper½% incomes as maldistribution advanced, but a far more moderate increase in Lower½% incomes. The dividing line between the Upper½% and the Lower½% is the one-in-200 point. Stage IV was designed for the Upper½%, not the Lower½%.

In the early years of Stage IV (1985), the Americans for Tax Reform was founded. It developed the Taxpayer Protection Pledge that binds its signers to ***never support a tax increase.*** As of this writing, it has been signed by 238 of the 242 House Republicans (98%) and 41 of the 47 GOP senators (87%).[120] So if you like Stage IV, you know where you can get more of it. Just give them a call. Send them a few million dollars. And we can run a Stone Age economy backed by Stone Age logic. There are enough of them. They are well funded. They are sufficiently enthusiastic that they can preserve oligarchy until its last quivering pulse. It now appears that this crowd has greater power than the President to determine our destiny.

The take and give.

#173

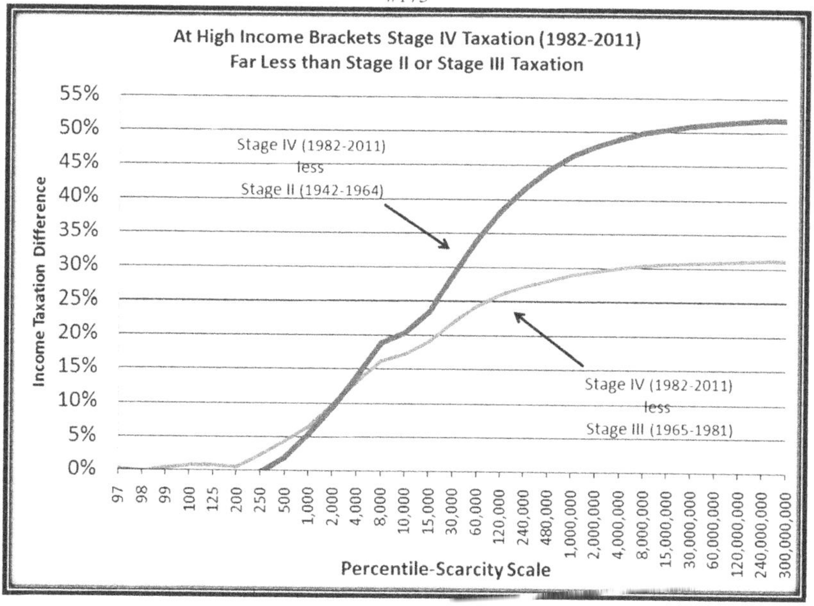

We have spent a great deal of time in this book on the maldistribution transition which took 25% of the income from the MAJ [-¼= (25/33.3333)-1]. That taking took 30 years to perfect.

But with the stroke of a pen, a giving of 25%+ took place. It did not go to the MAJ. It went precisely in the opposite direction – to the already wealthy, specifically to those at the one-in-120,000 scarcity level and above. And this giving has occurred once a year for 30 years now. Since the tax gift occurs to those who are already feverishly wealthy (earning 250+ people per year, $11.6+ million), there is no need for them to spend it on necessities. They can sock it away in investments, becoming ever-richer as those investments grow.

For this small elite, the gift is a wealth and power-creating machine. An additional 25%+ each year for 30 years provides a spectacular boost. This is the consequence of replacing Stage III tax policy (Johnson, Nixon, Ford, Carter) with Stage IV tax policy (Reagan, Bush1, Clinton, Bush2, Obama). It can be seen in graph-173.

If we were to look further back to compare Stage II (FDR, Truman, Eisenhower, Kennedy) with Stage IV, the scenario is transformed into a 38%+ yearly advantage at the one-in-120,000 level and above, as can be seen in graph-173. Not only did Stage IV fail to collect enough taxes to fund government (thus enormous deficits and debt), it developed elite-driven values in contrast to the nation-building values that existed during Stage II and Stage III. Its greatest damage was done there.

Practical. Then ruminating.

If you ran your own business prior to Stage IV taxation, you knew that high taxation at the upper income reaches was beneficial to lower earning employees. When you, as the owner, knew that you were going to be taxed like crazy on high profits, you had a strong incentive to pay subordinates more (better an expense than more profit now). Money which otherwise would flow into governmental tax collector hands now could benefit and strengthen your own firm by paying workers well, starting a new project, hiring quality people, and purchasing needed machinery. You could focus on developing high quality output instead of being tempted to hoard and divert profits for your own benefit alone. Though running a business is genuinely tough, and it is often difficult to turn a profit, once things get rolling it is amusing how desperate you can become to moderate profits as the end of the tax year rolls around.

High bracket taxation also keeps the demon within in check. If you are earning at the one-in-120,000 level, you are earning about 250 people a year. Do you really think you are that good? If so, do you think the question might be open for debate, say if 10 unbiased people who knew you best were to silently vote their opinion without adverse repercussions?

The fierce battle to preserve the Stage IV tax perks for the elite is amusing. If their logic had been plainly incorporated into the first sentence of the Declaration of Independence, how many soldiers would have appeared at Valley Forge? How many people would have widely supported such perks of wealth? As I understood it, there was some objection to a monarchy at the time. I don't see that substituting distant monarchy for a de facto local monarchy of wealth would have been all that appealing. But then I have been surprised at the enthusiasm for Stage IV goings on for some time and may have underestimated the capacity for economic self-flagellation.

I don't get it. Show me what's progressive.

Framing the debate: Almost exclusively, opposition to higher tax at the income pinnacle is stated relative to a person's income, not his or her capacity to pay. If you are vastly wealthy, you know that income is only a small reflection of your capacity to pay income tax. Your wealth is so much greater than your income that dipping into it to pay income taxes is often only a modest inconvenience.

We can chuckle in harmony as the super-rich cast the story of taxation as if their interests and those of the common man were aligned. Those of us at the low end are more hard-pressed to pay income tax than the wealthy.

Graph-176 shows the sharp decline in the income tax burden as one becomes ever more wealthy. For us common folk, it may be difficult to grasp, but when one is vastly wealthy, income fluctuations in a day or a week are often immense. For each million dollars invested, the stock market going up or down 5 percentage points means a ±$50,000 change, more than the average person makes in a year. And when a person is vastly rich, they have many millions of dollars invested in various assets. Most of their conversation about these big numbers they don't make public. They are used to vast changes and are fine-tuned to minimizing the ones that are adverse to them.

If you are at the 80th wealth percentile, your income taxes may be about 5% of your wealth (graph-176). But at the one-in-120,000 scarcity level, it may be closer to 1.3% of that person's wealth. You are more hard put upon to pay income tax than the highly wealthy person. It is a burden about 3.75 times as great for you to pay income tax than it is for the high earner [3.8= 5%/1.3%].

#176

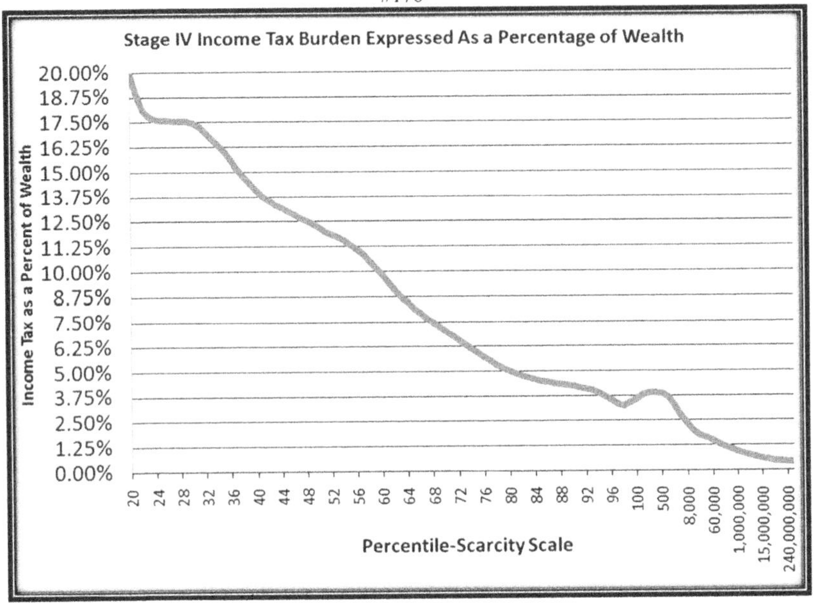

The high earner is an expert at winning arguments. He will hammer home that he paid $4.2 million in taxes. He will repeat this until he sees tears coming to your eyes. Then he will stop. He knows when to stop. For example, he will stop before getting around to mentioning that his net worth is about $312 million. So long as he sees those tears in your eyes, he knows you will argue on his behalf to lower income taxes yet further. The one thing he prefers above all else is an agent acting freely on his behalf. He hates to pay his servants.

Education.

> The fact is that income inequality is real; it's been rising for more than 25 years. The reason is clear: We have an economy that increasingly rewards education, and skills because of that education.[121]
>
> – George W. Bush, 2007

One of the favorite ploys of the elite is to focus on the deplorable state of education in all classes lower than their own. This old saw has played its tune for centuries. Since childhood I can recall complaints about education, the majority of which were valid. The truth be told, many of us, when children, went to schools that were flawed in one aspect or another, and too often we did not do as well as we should have because of our own failings, as much as those of the schools.

The rich, though, have another motive for focusing on the sorry state of education, unrelated to the welfare of the lower classes. They can claim educational differences are the cause of low incomes at the bottom and conversely, in view of their superior education, the cause of super high incomes at the top.

On that point it is they, not us, that need the education. So for those of you who purchased the gold-plated, diamond-studded edition of this book, I urge you to look closely at the following graphs and experience the bliss of education. We will start by looking at differences between the Top4% in 1979 and 2007, using Congressional Budget Office (CBO) data subjected to my computer programs (as discussed in the Appendix). You will observe in graph-177 that when matched for people of equal status, very high incomes in 2006 were far greater than in 1979 but at the lower end of the scale, they were much closer together.

#177

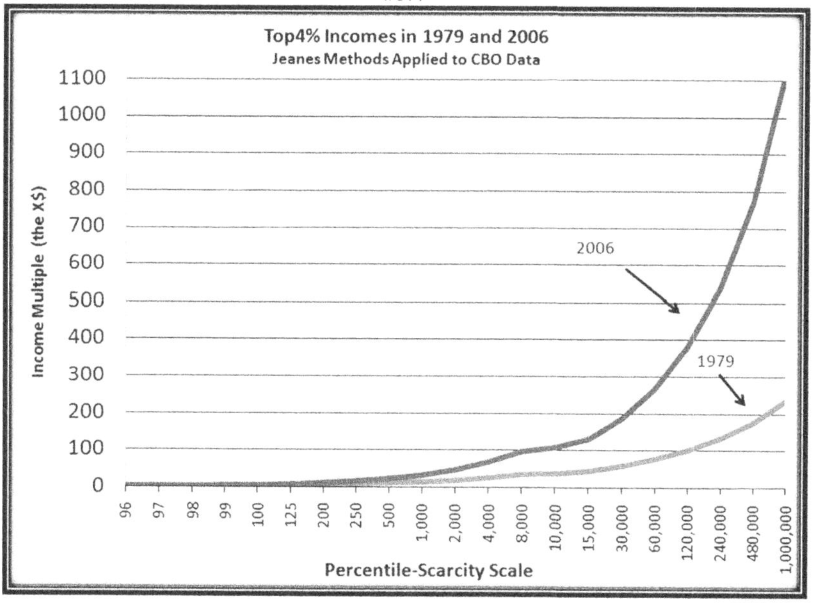

To be specific, the point that escapes me in the elite's maldistribution-because-of-education argument is that at the one in 240,000 scarcity level, what was so deficient about folks at that level in 1979 in contrast to the new 2006 elite at the identical scarcity level? What was the education-on-steroids program that produced the sensational difference? The old education saw does not seem to explain the difference at this point on the scale or the differences elsewhere within the Upper½% which we see in graph-177.

I offer the thesis that favorable tax treatment, not educational difference, was the reason that the super-rich advanced so spectacularly. And that it is disingenuous to assert that education was responsible for their spectacular rise vis-à-vis their 1979 peers.

With that out of the way, we now can crack the nut.

Cracking the nut.

The shape of the tax advantage curve in graph-179 appears much like the one in the Stage III-to-Stage IV transition that we saw earlier in graph-173. But unlike prior comparison of philosophies, here we focus on the specific changes from 1979 to 2006.

Using the modified Congressional Budget Office (CBO) data, the Top4% of the population, above the teeter point is the group that benefited from maldistribution. Graph-179 shows the 1979-2008 tax advantage at all levels within this group. The advantage was calculated by subtracting the 2008 tax rate from the 1979 tax rate (based on average income tax paid at each level). The tax advantage was less than 6.7% for those at points lower than the one-in-200 scarcity point (the threshold point for entering the Upper½%). At higher points on the scale, the advantage was spectacular. And it was an advantage received annually. At the one-in-10,000 point, it reached a 25% tax advantage. And the tax advantage continued to grow the higher you went, as can be seen in graph-179. To have your tax bill 25% lower than was customary is indeed a sweet deal. But it was too sweet to spread widely; so those at the one-in-10,000 and above were the few to get it.

From the data in the graph-177, we can calculate the fractional income change caused by maldistribution alone that occurred at each point from 1979 to 2006. Similarly, WealthX$ data is also available. With the two, we can get a picture of the degree to which favorable tax treatment at the high end of the scale contributed to maldistribution. We can do this by calculating the average annual increases in the two X$ measurements [average annual change=fraction^(1/(2006-1979))-1] and charting them in graph-179.

At the one-in-240,000 scarcity level, because of maldistribution transition alone, income grew an additional 5.3% annually; and wealth, an additional 3.5%. Graph-179B exists for those of you who might be making a first approximation of what fraction of the Tax Advantage translated into income and wealth growth. So far at the median it's about 18%.

#179

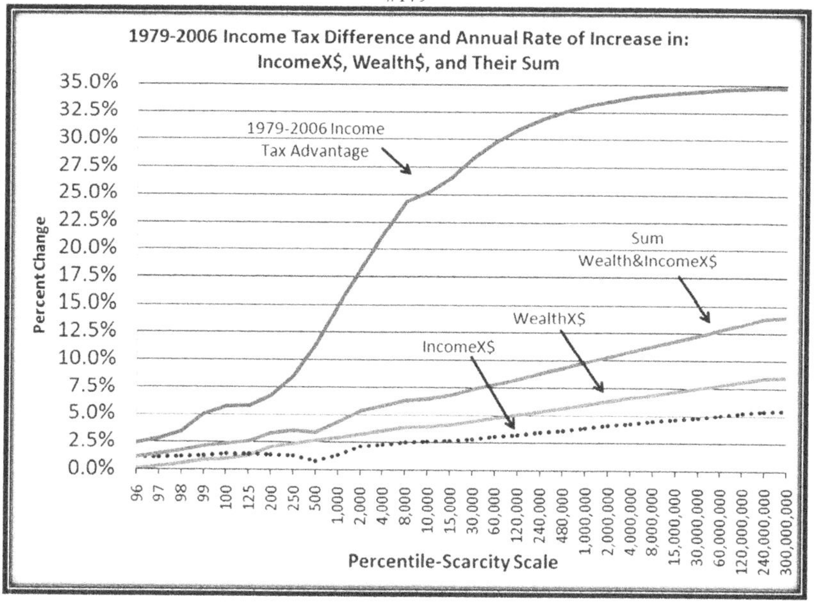

#179B

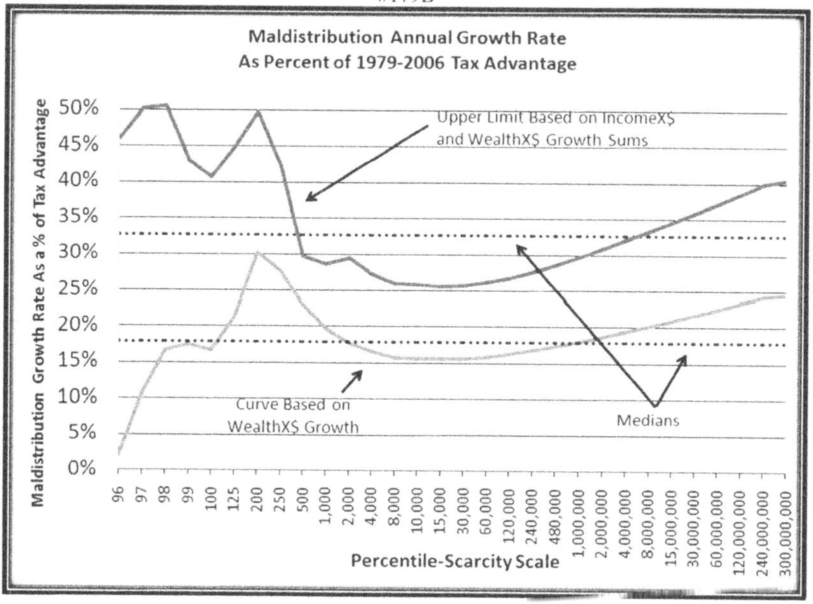

A word of caution: I believe the relationship in graph-179B is more complex than a simple multiplier. The numbers there just describe potential tax-induced wealth increases during the 1979-2006 period. Summing wealth and income in the graphs was done only to define an upper limit estimate. Some portion of income is included in wealth; thus, we can be reasonably confident that the total income and wealth tax-induced maldistribution would have been less than this figure.

The huge tax advantage and its concomitant pressure to increase maldistribution stands in opposition to the central point that neither the IncomeX$ nor the WealthX$ should have been growing in the first place. A competent manager seeking to preserve an appropriate income distribution will closely monitor the rate of change in the IncomeX$ and WealthX$, especially at all levels above the one-in-4,000 point. He knows that it is undesirable that an equitable income distribution perish. Over the long-term, the average change at these high levels should not exceed 0%. If it does, he knows that taxation at the high levels is insufficient to quell maldistribution. That taxation at the high levels is then ratcheted upwards until the equitability of wealth and income distribution is assured.

The Madison mish mash.

I am going to pause because I think it is wise to. We can get too deeply into numbers, forgetting the essence. The essence is the democracy. The democracy which from the outset was never certain to survive, or to use Lincoln's nice choice of words: to endure.

In its first decade, the nation did not yet have the Constitution on which the whole enterprise now rests. In 1787, the proposed Constitution had been drafted, but not yet ratified by the states. There were arguments about whether it should be adopted. To strengthen the argument for the Constitution, a series of articles were published now known as the *Federalist Papers*. The tenth of which, used here, was penned by James Madison anonymously. It concerned itself with the danger of mob rule and argued that the representative government embodied in the Constitution was the best available option in an imperfect world. Madison, as a proponent of the Constitution, was keenly aware of the imperfectability of man.

He was writing at a time when the horse was the quickest form of transportation. The nation was predominantly agricultural. Manufacturing was advancing in New England. And income distribution in New England was highly equitable (about a MAJ35). Through the 1830s, as De Tocqueville observed, equality among freemen was the nation's defining characteristic. Madison's writings do not seem oriented toward changing circumstances so much as seeking to set a stage where wisdom in government would have the greatest chance of success.

In the following, I will be unfair to Madison because his original argument without my tampering is the best representation of his thoughts. Here, however, I reorder his language to shorten and draw attention to issues that he considered, many of which today, we also address, using a slightly different vernacular.

> "... By a faction, I understand a number of citizens, whether amounting to a majority or a minority of the whole, who are united and actuated by some common impulse of passion, or of interest, adverse to the rights of other citizens, or to the permanent and aggregate interests of the community.
>
> "... the most common and durable source of factions has been the various and unequal distribution of property. Those who hold and those who are without property have ever formed distinct interests in society. Those who are creditors, and those who are debtors, fall under a like discrimination.
>
> "...The regulation of these various and interfering interests forms the principal task of modern legislation, and involves the spirit of party and faction in the necessary and ordinary operations of the government.
>
> "... The apportionment of taxes on the various descriptions of property is an act which seems to require the most exact impartiality; yet there is, perhaps, no legislative act in which greater opportunity and temptation are given to a predominant party to trample on the rules of justice. Every shilling with which they overburden the inferior number, is a shilling saved to their own pockets.
>
> "... the public good is disregarded in the conflicts of rival parties, and that measures are too often decided ... by the superior force of an interested and overbearing majority.
>
> "... A republic, by ... representation takes place, opens a different prospect, and promises the cure ... in controlling the effects of faction.
>
> "... the delegation of the government ... to a small number of citizens elected by the rest... to refine and enlarge the public views, by passing

> them through the medium of a chosen body of citizens, whose wisdom may best discern the true interest of their country, and whose patriotism and love of justice will be least likely to sacrifice it to temporary or partial considerations. ... On the other hand, the effect may be inverted. Men of factious tempers, of local prejudices, or of sinister designs, may, by intrigue, by corruption, or by other means ... betray the interests, of the people. ... Besides other impediments, it may be remarked that, where there is a consciousness of unjust or dishonorable purposes, communication is always checked by distrust in proportion to the number whose concurrence is necessary.
>
> "... Does it, in fine, consist in the greater obstacles opposed to the concert and accomplishment of the secret wishes of an unjust and interested majority?
>
> "The influence of factious leaders may kindle a flame ... but will be unable to spread a general conflagration... A rage for ... any ... improper or wicked project, will be less apt to pervade the whole body of the Union than a particular member of it..." [122]

It would be possible to call attention to numerous passages that relate to the present. The one I would like to draw attention to is "taxes ... which seems to require the most exact impartiality."

Please keep "the most exact impartiality" in mind. That is where we will try to go.

The rich were too heavily taxed. Yes, I mean it.

The singular message is that the long throw of USA tax history has provided no consistent standard for taxes at the high end. This can be seen in graph-183. In summary, Stage I, II, and FDR in the main provided taxes that were commendably within ±5% of the equitable standard up until the one-in-15,000 point. But at the higher levels, they tended to overtax the rich a median 10%.

Stage III and IV are bipolar. Starting at the one-in-200 point, Stage III overtaxed a wide swath of the Upper½%, a median 12.8%. The most egregious of all USA tax history remains Stage IV taxation, which did not kick in its main benefits for the elite until the one-in-1,000 point at 7.5%, after which the advantages came with a vengeance, peaking at about 42%. From the 91st percentile to one-in-125 point, Stage IV provided no tax advantage in order to achieve the boon for those at the top.

#183

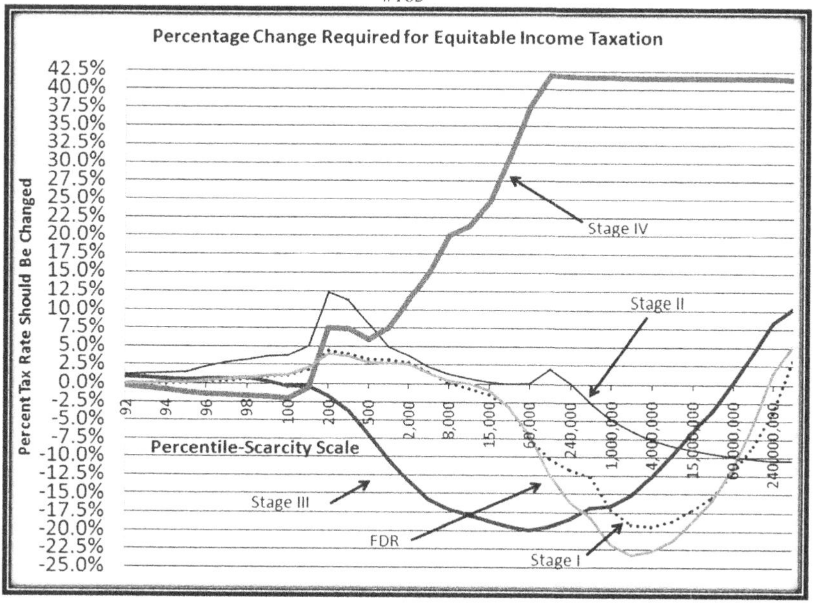

#183B

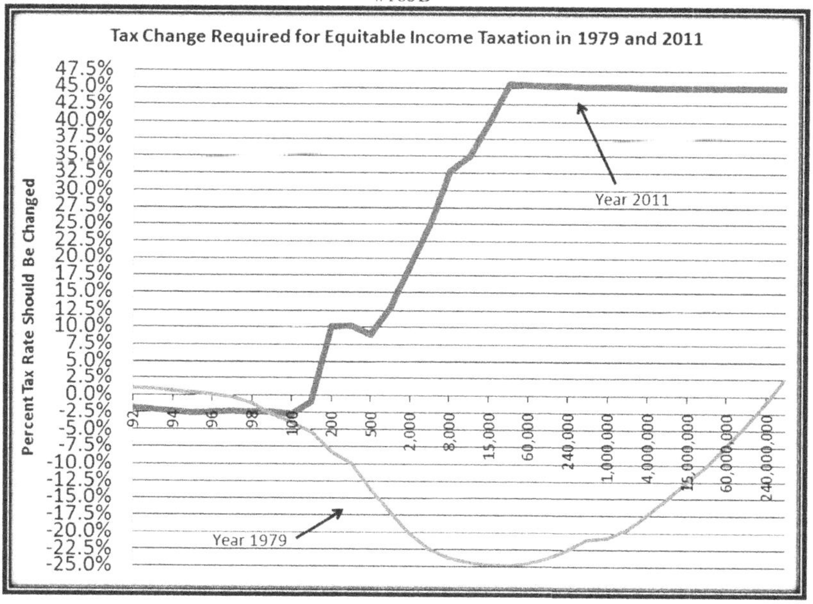

More specifically, we look at two years in the Stage III-to-Stage IV transition: 1979 and 2011 in graph-183B. Income taxation in 1979 over-taxed the Top2% a median 17%. A broad swath of the Top2% were over-taxed, often approaching 25%. This was too much for the rich to stomach. In revenge, they saw to it that the elites prospered. Income taxation in 2011 provided an 8.9% advantage at the one-in-500 point that shot up rapidly from there to a 45.5% tax advantage.

#184

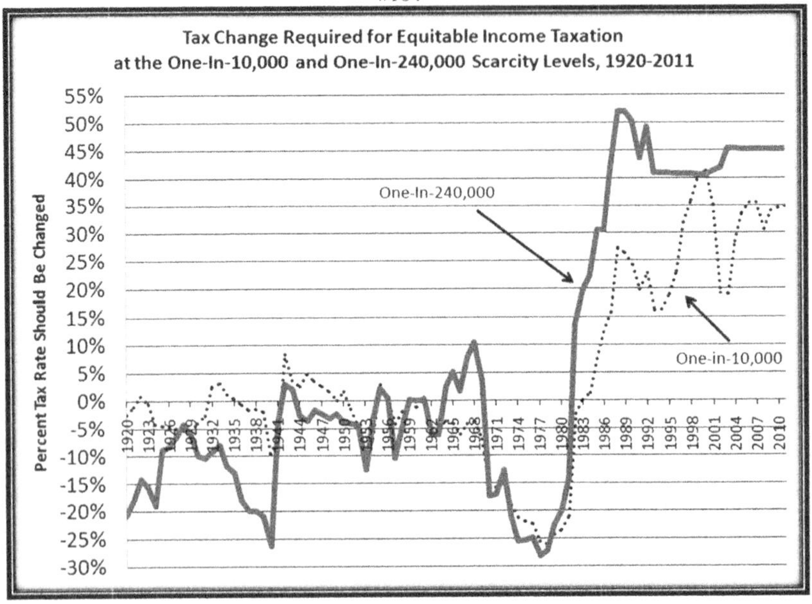

Graph-184 tells a story similar to the former graphs, except it focuses on people at the one-in-10,000 and one-in-240,000 income levels from 1920 to 2011. Within these groups from 1920 to 1970, most of the variation occurred within the range of a 5% under-taxation to a 10% overtaxation. And occasionally the two groups found themselves on opposite sides of the line in the same year, for example 3.1% and -7.9% in 1933. For these two groups, the two great taxing errors were a median 21.5% overtaxing from 1970 to 1981 and the median 40.4% under-taxing from 1986 to 2011.

The lesson is plain. Once an appropriate income distribution is achieved, such as in the 1970s, those who promote a fair or liberal agenda need to be careful above all else that they do not wrongly overtax the rich. The message from 1979 and Stage III taxation is that the rich were being overtaxed. It was suicidal to overtax them because they had the money, power, and ultimately vengeance to respond. The Stage III-to-Stage IV transition and the 1979-2011 case are evidence of it.

Given the favorable income distributions for the MAJ, the rich in 1979 were overtaxed. The rich responded by reducing their taxes to a point about 45% beneath where they should have been. Not only did they get disproportionately favorable tax treatment by this move, they dragged into place an oligarchy of the kind the USA has not seen previously. Along with it came the concomitant ills for all those beneath the teeter point. For that taxation error in the 1970s, the nation paid deeply. In good times and bad, a democracy requires attentive tax management at the high end of the scale. Without it, the MAJ is imperiled. The nation is imperiled. The democracy is imperiled.

The most exact impartiality.

Too frequently, tax discussions devolve into a zeal for different opinions, mutual animosities, frivolous or fanciful distinctions, factious tempers, prejudices, sinister designs, and various mischiefs more disposed to vex and oppress rather than to cooperate. Yet taxation is the instrument that makes government possible. It is beneficial – no, necessary – to be enlightened statesmen and citizens to ensure this great enterprise that we call democracy works, and works for all of us. Taxation is at the heart of it.

My family's farm is within 5 miles of President Madison's home and within 30 miles of President Jefferson's home. From childhood onward it was impressed upon me that government was a serious and beneficial exercise; and public service, noble. I believe those lessons were correct and worthy of aspiring to. Please turn the page to consider a technique for implementing Madison's "most exact impartiality" in our modern democracy.

CH. 7

BIG ROCKS: adaptive taxation.

Long ago I had a conversation with Dietrich Fischer. Through the filter of memory, the story he told goes much like the following. I will call it the Big Rocks Story:

You are given two piles of rocks: big rocks and small pebbles. You are given a jar in which to put them. There are enough big rocks that they alone would fill the jar to the brim.

How can you most effectively fill the jar?

Try starting with the pebbles. Try starting with the big rocks.

If you start with pebbles, the big rocks will not fit into the jar.

Starting with big rocks is the most effective way to fill the jar. The pebbles can be fitted around them.[123]

Similarly, this applies to big issues. If we consistently address the great non-issues of our time and trivial details (the pebbles), the outcome is likely to be disappointing, because the important issues (the big rocks) never find their way into the jar.

Our democracy was built on getting the big rocks into place. We were fortunate that it happened at the outset and that, when later required, at great decision points, the big rocks were properly attended to. Our less glorious moments were spent with the pebbles.

This author is drawing to a close. The work is now in the citizen's hand. We have trekked through many pages. You may well have anticipated we would land here and may also have anticipated the remaining pages. As you moved through the book up to this point, you have seen that we really knew very little about income distribution and that its principal measures, such as Ginis, quintiles, and the like, were useless for arriving at solutions or for letting us understand our place in this great enterprise that we call an economy.

Most particularly, a subset of that economy, taxation, has been hobbled by our lack of knowledge about income distribution and its effect. Even with the best intensions at exceptionally high incomes, taxation drifted away from appropriate standards. At best it was hit and miss. Sometimes getting it right; more often, not.

Fair taxation and income distribution are inexorably linked. We intuitively grasp this when we visit polar-opposite nations, say one nation that is unusually equitable (at MAJ36 for example) and another nation, which is oppressively cruel (at MAJ8).* In a heartbeat, we would join hands to say that the rich in the cruelly oppressive nation should be placed under a heavier tax burden than the rich in a patently fair nation, whose income already comprises a far smaller share of national wealth.

Even if we were unmoved by ethics, the exigencies of pragmatism would motivate us to give the wealthy in any nation ample incentive to ensure that the nation would naturally move to a position that was as equitable as was reasonably practicable within a well functioning capitalistic system.

Adaptive taxation.

Graph-189 (overall 16% average tax) and graph-189B (overall 20% average tax) illustrate adaptive taxation. The only difference in the graphs is that the latter is designed to produce about 4% more tax revenue. In both graphs, as income distribution becomes ever more equitable, the average tax rate for the elite is reduced, ultimately reaching a substantially flat tax at the far left-hand side of the graph where the difference between the high and low curve is slight.

---

* At MAJ8, there is only a pauper's share of income for the majority, a mere 8% of the income for 60% of the people.

You have already seen adaptive taxation in action. It was referred to as "equitable taxation" in graph-183 and subsequent graphs. Those graphs showed how adaptive taxation compared with our history of past taxation. It would have eliminated the egregious over-taxation of the rich in the 1970s and would have prevented the vast Stage IV under taxation.

#189

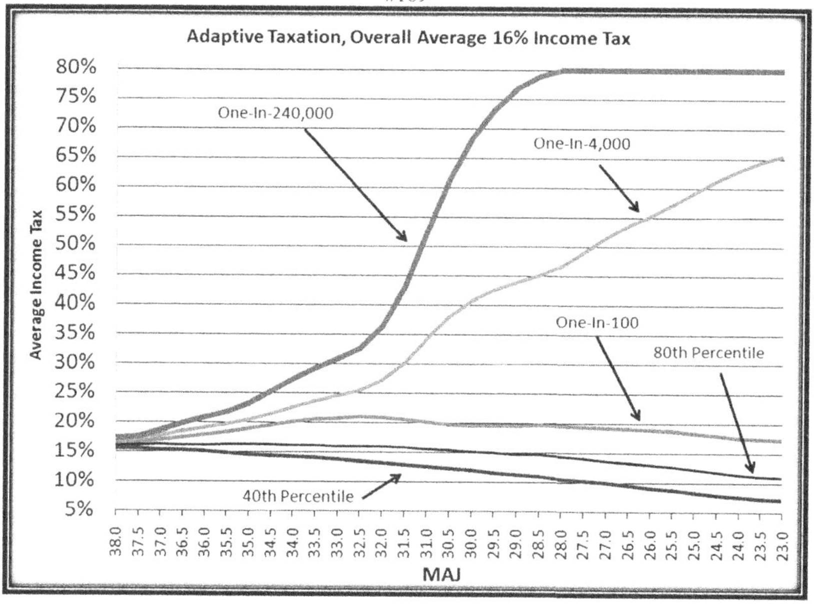

#189B

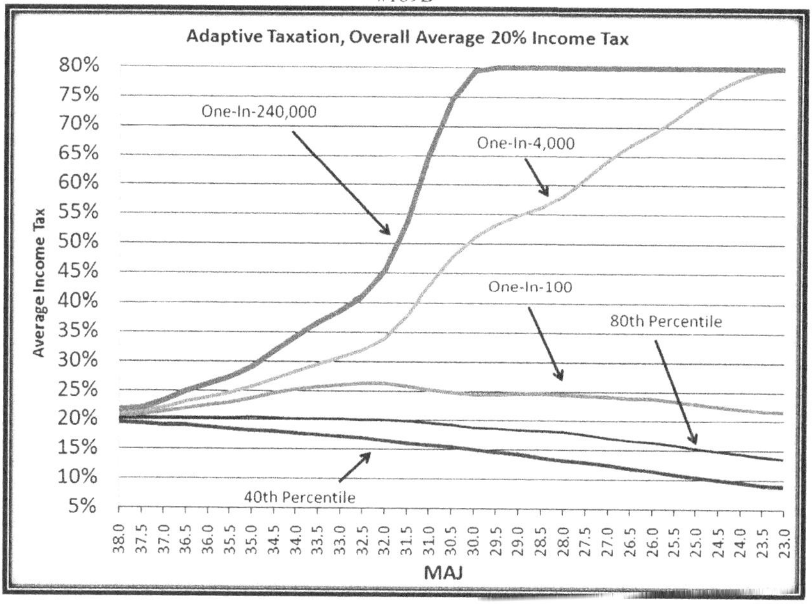

Adaptive taxation is the bridge that directly connects the elites to the wellbeing of the MAJ. Producing a prosperous MAJ cuts taxes for the Top1%.[124]

The remedy.

The plain point is that when a nation elects to have a maldistributed economy, it chooses to concentrate wealth and income in a few hands. Those beneath the teeter point who have neither much income or wealth become severely subordinated, directly or indirectly, to the wealthy. The wealthy benefit because they are holders of money that is lent. Those at the low end, having reduced income by way of maldistribution, are hard-pressed to pay those debts. Together, the interplay of income and wealth under such circumstances is precarious and subject to failure. Within these machinations, the financial sector disproportionately grows, sometimes dwarfing productive sectors. The financial sector not only concentrates wealth, its chief actors and minions profit from it.[125] It becomes a maldistribution between sectors and between people.

These observations are pragmatic. Long ago, in graph-57 and 58, we saw a sharp and ever-reducing share of wealth at the MAJ as income distribution worsened. When the 60% majority is a full player in the U.S. economy as it was in the 1950s-1970s, the relationship between income and wealth distribution creates a strong base for a market economy, for a capitalistic system, and for a democracy. That base has been chiseled apart by men who were not nearly as wise as they professed to be.

Just as Madison was concerned with elected officials and structure of government, we now must turn our attention to the modern elites who govern the private sphere of our nation. We need a structure that ensures that our private governing elites, too, are motivated to act in the national interest, not just for their exclusive self benefit. They must serve the tribe. They derive their strength from it and in turn must be motivated to return strength to it. That the 60% majority prosper and are full players is essential for this system that we call a democracy to work.

Adaptive taxation (graph-189 & 189B) meets Madison's objective for the "most exact impartiality." Its structure is plain. It derives its form from the lookup table curves. The base curve is MAJ39. Each curve for the

MAJs in graph-189 or 189B is divided by the base curve.* The outcome provides a predictable in-place adaptive schedule based on income share. The taxpayer, in advance, knows that the income tax that he or she pays will vary according to changes in income distribution and can look to the curves to see how much the changes will be.

The objective is for the economy over time to find its best functioning natural income distribution on its own. Adaptive taxation is intended to instill responsibility in all classes. As maldistribution becomes less intense, those at the low end have their taxes increase. They also receive larger incomes (higher MAJs) and are thus able to pay the taxes and still be net gainers. In short, they are full and responsible players as much as anyone else and not just organisms for receiving government largess.

Those at the high end are also held to a high standard, as they should be, because they make the decisions that determine how the rest of us fare. If their greed devolves primarily to their benefit alone without filtering advantages down to lower classes, then they must pay a burdensome tax. If they treat the MAJ fairly, their taxes are reduced. If a particular individual makes a hobby of amassing huge fortunes, whether it be for good or indifferent reasons, that person may do so. He or she just must pay a very high average tax not exceeding 80%. There is no need to vilify this person, for he or she is contributing mightily to the government treasury and thus is making a bona fide contribution to the nation's wellbeing.

Adaptive taxation delivers the message to the high reaches of the Upper½%: You may have your low taxes, but you may not impoverish 60% of the population and simultaneously have your low taxes. If you want low taxes, you must provide a fair income share for the 60% majority.

We have too long argued taxation and income distribution. It is time to give the noise a rest. A known adaptive taxation schedule provides the incentive in advance to avoid maldistribution. More positively, it provides

---

* The resulting array of ratios are the key. To illustrate how unbiased and uncomplicated the method is, the subroutine is called with this simple statement:
CALL GetAdaptiveTax(MAJ, OverallTaxRate, population, AdaptiveTax())
The key subroutine line for determining the resulting OverallTaxRate is:
sum=sum+(BASEadjust*Ratio(x)*CurrentDistributionCurve(x))
The BASEadjust is a constant designed to yield the particular OverallTaxRate (called the sum when it is being applied throughout the backbone).
When this condition is met: AdaptiveTaxAtEachPoint(x)=BASEadjust*Ratio(x)
Required adjustments are subsequently made at the top end, and the highest average tax is capped at 80%. If MAJ>39 then it is a flat tax = OverallTaxRate. The final array is then sorted..

the rich with an incentive to migrate toward income distributions that are wholesome for the MAJ, the nation, and the rich alike.

Outside the direct reach of taxes, the workings of adaptive taxation indirectly motivate the rich in their customary business practices to encourage more regular and more remunerative employment for the MAJ because a prosperous MAJ lowers their personal tax bill. As the historical record illustrates, a prospering MAJ carries with it a thriving economy. By such a combination of means, we all prosper, whether we are beneath or above the teeter point.

Thank you Madison. Thank you Smith.

Our nation and our economy are now vastly different from when Madison wrote the *Federalist Papers*. His focus was on government and creating a Constitutional design for it. Now government and the economy are so intertwined that even sufficient Constitutional measures are insufficient to ensure national success.

Taking the cue from Madison, adaptive taxation can offer the "most exact impartiality." It is so plainly simple that, if they elect to do so, the citizenry can amply monitor it, widely audit it, and appropriately implement it. By bringing many people into the process, the fractious impulses which Madison so greatly lamented and so greatly feared can be reduced.

Adaptive taxation takes a second cue from the same era. That cue comes from Adam Smith's observation that we benefit by addressing enlightened self-interest.

They said it all. It is now time for this author to stop.

ACKNOWLEDGEMENTS

To claim this work as mine alone would be an exaggeration. It has been transformed by others. Mary Geisenhoff, with each draft, gave it a thorough going over, cleaning up originalities in spelling, grammar, punctuation, and more. It was a stroke of fortune to have her reliable and helpful observations. Patricia Grenseman continued in that vein, adding in her linguistic abilities, organization, and (again) more. It was a great pleasure to have her hand in the pie. And the ever self-deprecating Aoife Herlihy who insists that she cannot be called a physicist (because she studied that too long ago), who's job title is quality engineer (not civil engineer), and who is completely Irish but now in London, who notwithstanding all of the foregoing made her well-aimed and indispensable contributions – exactly where they were needed. And Lorie DeWorken worked her magic on the ebook, notwithstanding formidable impediments. And to others who bask in privacy: Thanks all. Every person on this project went beyond the common call of duty. The contributions, all coming from vastly different perspectives, was a much needed bonus. Even with such energetic and able help, my wild pen managed to slip in a few items to drag it down to the low level that I am comfortable with. For all of it, I take full responsibility.

I am also indebted to a person who never knew this book was being written. Bob Zale wrote and has been the mainstay behind PowerBasic – the computer language I used for writing the computer programs that are the foundation on which this work rests.

There are billions of people in the world. My programs looked through substantially each of them, at times for hundreds of years, examining thousands of potential outcomes before arriving at the best fit for each year. To do this required programs at least as fast as C++ computer programs. The PowerBasic Console Compiler delivered this and more.[126] It has a deceptively plain screen, but what is under the hood is reliable and pure muscle. It can easily handle vast amounts of data. It is especially well suited for economic analysis and modeling.

This book is about fairness and virtues being rewarded. To the extent that I am familiar with the company, PowerBasic conforms to those precepts. For the customer, its business practices are those that I associate with integrity: fair pricing, fair updating, and providing the user with a fair shake – in my case for almost 20 years. The way I see it, in this instance, the little guy triumphed. Bob and those at PowerBasic did a better job than many software conglomerates.

Along these lines, it strikes me as fitting that they were at the heart of this work.*

* A necessary disclosure: Bob Zale does not know me from Adam. I do not have, nor will I have a financial intermingling or any compromising relationship with his company. However, I do expect to continue to be a customer, as I have been in the past.

APPENDIX 1. Lookup table

In Chapter 2, spreadsheet lookup-table data illustrated the consequences for the MAJ that occurred as a result of going from a one third income share to a one quarter income share. Lookup-table data lets you understand the approximate form that all income and wealth distributions take. This is not to say that the table is a rigid standard. It is to say it is a reasonable guide that seeks to illustrate central tendencies based on information now available, processed by my computer programs. About 2,500 income-distribution cases worldwide and a small number of wealth distribution cases were used.

When you download the lookup-table spreadsheet, its header row contains the following listed information in sequence. Excluding the columns with the headings, "MAJ, KeyRatio, Gini, Population, and Top/Bottom Ratio," all the data beneath the headings are in X$s. Regardless of what nation you live in or the currency you use, you can multiply the X$s by your GDP per capita to understand how incomes at all points from bottom to top influence your nation, depending on income distribution. Separately, if you know your nation's average net worth per capita, you can multiply it by the X$s in the lookup table. That will show how wealth tends to change from bottom to top as wealth distributions change.

Descriptors: MAJ, KeyRatio, Gini, Lower½%, Upper½%.

Backbone: Top1%, 1, 2, 3, 4, 5, 6, 7, 8, 9, 10, 11, 12, 13, 14, 15, 16, 17, 18, 19, 20, 21, 22, 23, 24, 25, 26, 27, 28, 29, 30, 31, 32, 33, 34, 35, 36, 37, 38, 39, 40, 41, 42, 43, 44, 45, 46, 47, 48, 49, 50, 51, 52, 53, 54, 55, 56, 57, 58, 59, 60, 61, 62, 63, 64, 65, 66, 67, 68, 69, 70, 71, 72, 73, 74, 75, 76, 77, 78, 79, 80, 81, 82, 83, 84, 85, 86, 87, 88, 89, 90, 91, 92, 93, 94, 95, 96, 97, 98, 99.

Scarcity levels within the Top1%: 100, 125, 200, 250, 500, 1,000, 2,000, 4,000, 8,000, 10,000, 15,000, 30,000, 60,000, 120,000, 240,000, 480,000, 1,000,000, 2,000,000, 4,000,000, 8,000,000, 15,000,000, 30,000,000, 60,000,000, 120,000,000, 240,000,000, 300,000,000, 480,000,000, 1,000,000,000, 7,000,000,000.

Top-end threshold categories: Top500, Top400, Top100, 10th, 3rd , 2nd, 1st

Details: Population, Top/Bottom Ratio.

A word of caution: The lookup table is calculated based on a population of 307 million. This closely approximates the United States. But for significantly different population sizes, you cannot use the Top-end threshold data (Top500 to 1st). All of these references are highly populations sensitive. For Top-end threshold data, you are best advised to consult spreadsheets pertaining to your nation or other nations of approximately the same population size.

The abridged lookup table is spread over the next 4 pages. In contrast to the complete downloadable lookup table, it is abridged to fit the space available and contains the following headings.

Descriptors: MAJ, Gini, Lower½%, Upper½%.
Backbone: Top1%, 1, 5, 10, 15, 20, 25, 30, 35, 40, 45, 50, 55, 60, 65, 70, 75, 80, 85, 90, 95.
Scarcity levels within the Top1%: 100, 200, 500, 1,000, 30,000, 120,000, 1,000,000.
Top-end threshold categories: Top400, Top100, 10th, 1st

The table starts with an excessively equitable MAJ49 income distribution and ends with an excessively inequitable wealth distribution (MAJ1.6). In the downloadable version at Dilives.com, the MAJ values are shown at 0.1 increments. Here they are shown at 0.25 increments (except for MAJ33.3 which was added to exactly match the base case so often referred to in the text).

To those of you who turned to the Appendix before reading the book, the MAJ refers to the percent of income (or wealth) received by the bottom 60% of the population. On page 198, the income MAJ range we have principally discussed (MAJ36 through MAJ25) is shown and the key rows are highlighted (MAJ36, MAJ33.3, MAJ25). On page 200, MAJs lower than 13.25 are shown. They pertain mainly to U.S. wealth distribution, which in recent years has ranged from about MAJ6 to MAJ4.

Once you have familiarized yourself with the lookup table by dividing a row into other rows to see how much changes in distribution influence conditions, and once you have summed various sections of the backbone to see the percent of income received in various segments, you will be the autodidact on the way to becoming a useful DIY economist. Print up your own degree. Hang it wherever you like. An appropriately sized mural of it is always nice.

Never forget. Only sum numbers within the backbone. (All of them together sum to 100.) If you sum other numbers (Lower½%, Upper½%, scarcity levels within the Top1%, or Top-end threshold categories), you are honor bound to tear up your degree and start over.

MAJ	Gini	Lower ½%	Upper ½%	Top1	1	5	10	15	20	25	30	35	40	45	50	55	60	65	70	75	80	85	90	95	100	200	500	1,000	30,000	120,000	1,000,000	Top400	Top100	10th	1st
49.00	16.1	2.1	2.7	2.4	0.47	0.61	0.67	0.71	0.75	0.79	0.83	0.88	0.92	0.94	0.95	0.97	0.98	1.02	1.06	1.11	1.17	1.26	1.37	1.56	2.0	2.3	2.6	2.9	4.9	6.1	8.5	8.1	10.1	14.0	21.0
48.75	16.4	2.2	3.0	2.6	0.46	0.60	0.66	0.71	0.75	0.79	0.83	0.87	0.91	0.93	0.95	0.96	0.98	1.02	1.06	1.11	1.18	1.26	1.38	1.58	2.0	2.3	2.9	3.5	6.3	8.1	11.9	11.4	14.5	22.0	33.0
48.50	16.7	2.2	3.2	2.7	0.45	0.59	0.66	0.71	0.75	0.79	0.83	0.87	0.91	0.93	0.94	0.96	0.98	1.02	1.06	1.12	1.18	1.27	1.39	1.59	2.0	2.4	3.1	3.9	7.6	10.0	15.2	14.4	19.0	30.0	47.0
48.25	17.0	2.2	3.3	2.7	0.44	0.59	0.65	0.70	0.75	0.78	0.82	0.86	0.90	0.92	0.94	0.96	0.99	1.02	1.07	1.12	1.19	1.28	1.40	1.60	2.0	2.4	3.1	3.9	7.7	10.1	15.3	14.5	19.1	30.0	47.0
48.00	17.3	2.2	3.3	2.7	0.44	0.58	0.65	0.70	0.74	0.78	0.82	0.85	0.89	0.92	0.94	0.96	0.99	1.02	1.07	1.13	1.19	1.28	1.40	1.61	2.0	2.4	3.1	3.9	7.7	10.1	15.4	14.6	19.2	30.0	48.0
47.75	17.5	2.2	3.3	2.8	0.43	0.57	0.65	0.70	0.74	0.78	0.81	0.85	0.88	0.91	0.93	0.96	0.99	1.03	1.08	1.13	1.20	1.29	1.41	1.62	2.0	2.4	3.2	4.0	7.8	10.3	15.7	14.9	19.7	31.0	49.0
47.50	17.8	2.2	3.3	2.8	0.42	0.57	0.64	0.70	0.75	0.78	0.81	0.84	0.87	0.90	0.93	0.96	0.99	1.04	1.08	1.14	1.21	1.30	1.42	1.62	2.0	2.4	3.2	4.0	7.8	10.3	15.8	14.9	19.7	31.0	49.0
47.25	18.1	2.2	3.4	2.8	0.41	0.56	0.63	0.69	0.74	0.78	0.81	0.83	0.86	0.89	0.92	0.96	1.00	1.04	1.09	1.15	1.22	1.30	1.42	1.62	2.0	2.4	3.2	4.0	8.0	10.6	16.3	15.5	20.5	32.5	52.0
47.00	18.3	2.2	3.4	2.8	0.40	0.55	0.63	0.69	0.74	0.78	0.80	0.83	0.85	0.88	0.92	0.96	1.01	1.05	1.10	1.16	1.23	1.31	1.43	1.62	2.0	2.4	3.2	4.1	8.1	10.8	16.6	15.7	20.8	33.0	53.0
46.75	18.7	2.2	3.4	2.8	0.39	0.54	0.62	0.68	0.73	0.77	0.80	0.83	0.85	0.89	0.93	0.97	1.01	1.06	1.11	1.16	1.23	1.32	1.43	1.62	2.0	2.4	3.3	4.1	8.3	11.0	17.0	16.1	21.3	34.0	54.5
46.50	19.1	2.2	3.5	2.8	0.38	0.53	0.61	0.67	0.72	0.76	0.79	0.82	0.85	0.89	0.93	0.97	1.01	1.06	1.11	1.17	1.24	1.33	1.45	1.65	2.0	2.4	3.3	4.2	8.5	11.3	17.6	16.7	22.2	36.0	58.0
46.25	19.5	2.2	3.5	2.9	0.37	0.52	0.60	0.66	0.72	0.76	0.79	0.82	0.85	0.89	0.93	0.97	1.01	1.06	1.11	1.17	1.24	1.33	1.45	1.66	2.1	2.5	3.4	4.3	8.7	11.6	18.0	17.1	22.8	37.0	59.5
46.00	19.8	2.2	3.6	2.9	0.36	0.51	0.59	0.65	0.71	0.75	0.79	0.82	0.85	0.89	0.93	0.97	1.02	1.07	1.12	1.18	1.25	1.34	1.46	1.65	2.1	2.5	3.4	4.3	8.7	11.7	18.2	17.2	23.1	37.0	61.0
45.75	20.2	2.3	3.6	2.9	0.35	0.50	0.58	0.65	0.70	0.75	0.78	0.82	0.85	0.89	0.93	0.97	1.01	1.06	1.11	1.18	1.25	1.34	1.47	1.68	2.1	2.5	3.5	4.4	9.0	12.1	18.9	17.8	24.0	39.0	63.5
45.50	20.5	2.3	3.7	3.0	0.34	0.50	0.58	0.64	0.70	0.74	0.78	0.81	0.85	0.88	0.92	0.97	1.01	1.06	1.12	1.18	1.26	1.35	1.48	1.69	2.1	2.5	3.5	4.4	9.1	12.3	19.3	18.3	24.6	40.0	66.0
45.25	20.9	2.3	3.7	3.0	0.33	0.49	0.57	0.63	0.69	0.73	0.77	0.81	0.85	0.88	0.92	0.97	1.01	1.06	1.12	1.18	1.26	1.35	1.49	1.71	2.1	2.6	3.6	4.5	9.5	12.8	20.3	19.2	25.9	43.0	70.5
45.00	21.2	2.3	3.9	3.1	0.32	0.48	0.57	0.63	0.68	0.73	0.77	0.80	0.84	0.88	0.92	0.96	1.01	1.06	1.12	1.18	1.26	1.36	1.50	1.72	2.1	2.6	3.7	4.7	10.0	13.7	21.9	20.7	28.2	47.0	79.0
44.75	21.6	2.4	4.0	3.2	0.31	0.47	0.56	0.62	0.68	0.72	0.76	0.80	0.84	0.88	0.92	0.96	1.01	1.06	1.12	1.19	1.27	1.37	1.50	1.73	2.1	2.7	3.9	5.0	10.9	15.0	24.4	23.0	31.6	53.5	91.5
44.50	22.0	2.4	4.2	3.3	0.31	0.47	0.55	0.61	0.67	0.72	0.76	0.80	0.84	0.88	0.92	0.96	1.01	1.06	1.12	1.19	1.27	1.37	1.51	1.74	2.2	2.7	4.1	5.2	11.6	16.1	26.6	25.0	34.8	60.0	104.0
44.25	22.4	2.4	4.4	3.4	0.30	0.46	0.55	0.61	0.66	0.71	0.75	0.79	0.84	0.88	0.92	0.96	1.01	1.06	1.12	1.19	1.27	1.37	1.51	1.74	2.2	2.8	4.3	5.4	12.4	17.4	29.1	27.3	38.3	67.0	117.5
44.00	22.7	2.4	4.4	3.4	0.29	0.46	0.54	0.60	0.66	0.71	0.75	0.79	0.83	0.87	0.91	0.96	1.01	1.06	1.12	1.19	1.28	1.38	1.52	1.75	2.2	2.8	4.3	5.5	12.7	17.8	30.1	28.2	39.6	70.0	123.0
43.75	23.0	2.5	4.5	3.5	0.29	0.45	0.53	0.60	0.66	0.70	0.74	0.78	0.82	0.87	0.91	0.96	1.01	1.06	1.12	1.20	1.28	1.38	1.52	1.76	2.3	2.9	4.4	5.6	13.0	18.4	31.1	29.1	41.1	73.0	129.5
43.50	23.4	2.6	4.6	3.6	0.28	0.44	0.53	0.60	0.65	0.70	0.74	0.78	0.82	0.86	0.91	0.96	1.01	1.06	1.13	1.20	1.29	1.39	1.53	1.76	2.3	2.9	4.5	5.7	13.3	18.9	32.2	30.1	42.7	76.0	136.0
43.25	23.8	2.6	4.8	3.7	0.27	0.44	0.52	0.59	0.64	0.69	0.74	0.78	0.82	0.86	0.91	0.95	1.00	1.06	1.12	1.20	1.29	1.39	1.53	1.77	2.4	3.1	4.7	5.8	13.9	19.7	33.9	31.7	45.1	81.5	146.0
43.00	24.2	2.7	4.9	3.8	0.27	0.43	0.52	0.58	0.64	0.69	0.73	0.78	0.82	0.86	0.90	0.95	1.00	1.05	1.12	1.19	1.29	1.39	1.53	1.78	2.4	3.1	4.8	6.0	14.4	20.6	35.6	33.2	47.6	86.0	157.0
42.75	24.6	2.7	5.0	3.9	0.26	0.43	0.51	0.57	0.63	0.68	0.72	0.77	0.82	0.86	0.90	0.95	0.99	1.05	1.12	1.19	1.29	1.39	1.54	1.80	2.5	3.2	4.9	6.1	14.8	21.1	36.8	34.3	49.3	89.5	163.5
42.50	24.9	2.8	5.1	3.9	0.26	0.42	0.51	0.57	0.62	0.67	0.72	0.77	0.82	0.86	0.90	0.94	0.99	1.05	1.12	1.20	1.29	1.40	1.55	1.82	2.5	3.2	5.0	6.1	15.0	21.5	37.6	35.1	50.4	92.0	169.0
42.25	25.2	2.8	5.1	4.0	0.25	0.42	0.50	0.57	0.62	0.67	0.72	0.76	0.81	0.85	0.90	0.94	0.99	1.05	1.12	1.20	1.29	1.41	1.56	1.83	2.5	3.2	5.1	6.2	15.3	22.0	38.5	35.9	51.8	95.5	175.0
42.00	25.5	2.9	5.3	4.1	0.24	0.41	0.50	0.56	0.62	0.67	0.71	0.76	0.81	0.85	0.89	0.94	0.98	1.04	1.11	1.20	1.30	1.41	1.57	1.84	2.6	3.3	5.2	6.3	15.6	22.6	39.8	37.1	53.6	99.0	183.0
41.75	25.9	2.9	5.3	4.1	0.24	0.41	0.50	0.56	0.61	0.66	0.71	0.76	0.80	0.85	0.89	0.93	0.98	1.04	1.11	1.20	1.30	1.41	1.58	1.86	2.6	3.4	5.3	6.4	16.0	23.2	41.0	38.1	55.4	102.5	190.5
41.50	26.2	2.9	5.4	4.2	0.23	0.40	0.49	0.55	0.61	0.66	0.70	0.75	0.80	0.84	0.88	0.93	0.98	1.04	1.11	1.20	1.30	1.42	1.59	1.87	2.6	3.4	5.4	6.5	16.2	23.6	41.9	39.0	56.7	106.0	197.0
41.25	26.5	3.0	5.5	4.2	0.22	0.40	0.48	0.55	0.60	0.65	0.70	0.75	0.79	0.84	0.88	0.93	0.98	1.04	1.12	1.20	1.31	1.42	1.59	1.88	2.6	3.4	5.4	6.6	16.5	24.1	42.9	39.9	58.1	108.5	203.5
41.00	26.9	3.0	5.5	4.3	0.22	0.39	0.47	0.54	0.59	0.65	0.69	0.74	0.79	0.84	0.88	0.93	0.98	1.05	1.12	1.21	1.31	1.43	1.60	1.88	2.7	3.5	5.5	6.6	16.8	24.5	43.8	40.7	59.5	112.0	210.0
40.75	27.3	3.0	5.6	4.3	0.21	0.38	0.47	0.53	0.59	0.64	0.69	0.74	0.79	0.84	0.88	0.93	0.98	1.05	1.12	1.21	1.31	1.43	1.60	1.89	2.7	3.5	5.6	6.7	17.1	25.1	44.9	41.8	61.1	115.0	217.0
40.50	27.6	3.1	5.7	4.4	0.21	0.38	0.46	0.53	0.58	0.63	0.68	0.74	0.79	0.84	0.88	0.93	0.98	1.04	1.12	1.21	1.32	1.44	1.61	1.90	2.8	3.6	5.6	6.8	17.5	25.7	46.2	42.9	63.1	119.0	226.0
40.25	28.0	3.1	5.8	4.5	0.20	0.37	0.46	0.52	0.58	0.63	0.68	0.73	0.79	0.83	0.88	0.92	0.98	1.04	1.12	1.21	1.32	1.44	1.62	1.92	2.8	3.7	5.7	6.9	17.9	26.3	47.6	44.2	65.1	124.0	236.0
40.00	28.4	3.2	5.9	4.6	0.20	0.37	0.45	0.52	0.57	0.62	0.68	0.73	0.78	0.83	0.87	0.92	0.97	1.04	1.12	1.21	1.32	1.45	1.62	1.93	2.8	3.7	5.8	7.0	18.2	27.0	49.0	45.5	67.2	128.0	246.0
39.75	28.7	3.3	6.0	4.6	0.19	0.36	0.45	0.51	0.57	0.62	0.67	0.72	0.78	0.82	0.87	0.92	0.97	1.04	1.12	1.21	1.32	1.45	1.63	1.93	2.9	3.8	5.8	7.1	18.7	27.7	50.6	47.0	69.6	134.0	257.5
39.50	29.0	3.3	6.1	4.7	0.19	0.36	0.45	0.51	0.56	0.62	0.67	0.72	0.77	0.82	0.86	0.91	0.97	1.04	1.12	1.21	1.33	1.45	1.63	1.94	2.9	3.9	5.9	7.2	19.1	28.4	52.1	48.3	71.7	139.0	268.0
39.25	29.4	3.4	6.2	4.8	0.18	0.35	0.44	0.50	0.56	0.61	0.66	0.71	0.77	0.81	0.86	0.91	0.97	1.03	1.12	1.21	1.33	1.45	1.63	1.95	3.0	3.9	6.0	7.4	19.6	29.2	53.8	49.8	74.4	144.5	280.5
39.00	29.7	3.4	6.4	4.9	0.18	0.35	0.44	0.50	0.56	0.61	0.66	0.71	0.76	0.81	0.86	0.91	0.96	1.03	1.12	1.21	1.33	1.46	1.64	1.95	3.1	4.0	6.1	7.5	20.0	30.0	55.5	51.4	77.0	150.0	294.0
38.75	30.1	3.5	6.4	4.9	0.17	0.34	0.43	0.49	0.55	0.60	0.65	0.71	0.76	0.81	0.85	0.91	0.96	1.03	1.12	1.21	1.34	1.46	1.65	1.97	3.1	4.1	6.2	7.6	20.4	30.6	56.9	52.6	78.9	154.5	304
38.50	30.4	3.5	6.5	5.0	0.17	0.33	0.42	0.49	0.55	0.60	0.65	0.70	0.76	0.80	0.85	0.91	0.96	1.03	1.12	1.22	1.34	1.46	1.65	1.96	3.1	4.1	6.2	7.6	20.8	31.2	58.3	53.9	81.0	160.0	314
38.25	30.8	3.6	6.6	5.1	0.16	0.32	0.42	0.48	0.54	0.60	0.65	0.70	0.75	0.80	0.85	0.90	0.96	1.03	1.12	1.22	1.34	1.47	1.65	1.97	3.2	4.2	6.3	7.7	21.0	31.7	59.2	54.8	82.5	162.5	322
38.00	31.2	3.6	6.7	5.1	0.15	0.32	0.41	0.47	0.53	0.59	0.64	0.70	0.75	0.80	0.85	0.90	0.96	1.04	1.12	1.22	1.35	1.48	1.66	1.98	3.2	4.2	6.3	7.8	21.3	32.2	60.4	55.9	84.3	167.0	331
37.75	31.5	3.6	6.7	5.2	0.15	0.31	0.40	0.46	0.52	0.58	0.63	0.69	0.75	0.80	0.85	0.91	0.96	1.04	1.12	1.23	1.35	1.48	1.67	1.99	3.2	4.3	6.4	7.8	21.5	32.5	61.1	56.5	85.4	169.0	336
37.50	31.8	3.6	6.8	5.2	0.14	0.30	0.39	0.46	0.52	0.57	0.63	0.69	0.75	0.80	0.85	0.90	0.97	1.04	1.13	1.23	1.36	1.49	1.67	2.00	3.2	4.3	6.4	7.9	21.8	33.0	62.2	57.5	87.0	173.0	345
37.25	2.1	3.7	6.8	5.3	0.14	0.30	0.39	0.46	0.52	0.57	0.63	0.68	0.74	0.79	0.84	0.90	0.97	1.04	1.13	1.24	1.37	1.49	1.68	2.00	3.3	4.3	6.5	7.9	22.0	33.3	62.9	58.2	88.1	176.0	350

MAJ	Gini	Lower ½%	Upper ½%	Top1	1	5	10	15	20	25	30	35	40	45	50	55	60
37.00	32.5	3.7	7.0	5.3	0.13	0.29	0.38	0.45	0.51	0.57	0.62	0.68	0.73	0.79	0.84	0.90	0.96
36.75	32.9	3.8	7.1	5.5	0.13	0.29	0.38	0.45	0.50	0.56	0.62	0.67	0.73	0.79	0.84	0.89	0.95
36.50	33.3	3.8	7.3	5.6	0.13	0.29	0.38	0.44	0.50	0.56	0.61	0.67	0.73	0.78	0.83	0.89	0.95
36.25	33.7	3.9	7.5	5.7	0.13	0.29	0.37	0.43	0.49	0.55	0.61	0.67	0.73	0.79	0.83	0.88	0.94
36.00	**34.1**	**4.0**	**7.6**	**5.8**	**0.13**	**0.28**	**0.37**	**0.43**	**0.48**	**0.54**	**0.60**	**0.67**	**0.73**	**0.78**	**0.83**	**0.88**	**0.93**
35.75	34.3	4.0	7.6	5.8	0.12	0.28	0.36	0.43	0.49	0.54	0.60	0.66	0.72	0.77	0.82	0.88	0.94
35.50	34.6	4.0	7.6	5.8	0.11	0.27	0.36	0.42	0.48	0.54	0.59	0.65	0.71	0.77	0.82	0.88	0.95
35.25	34.9	4.1	7.7	5.9	0.11	0.26	0.35	0.42	0.48	0.53	0.59	0.65	0.70	0.76	0.82	0.88	0.95
35.00	35.2	4.2	7.9	6.0	0.11	0.26	0.35	0.41	0.47	0.53	0.58	0.64	0.70	0.76	0.81	0.88	0.94
34.75	35.7	4.3	8.3	6.3	0.11	0.26	0.34	0.41	0.46	0.52	0.58	0.64	0.71	0.76	0.81	0.87	0.93
34.50	36.2	4.4	8.6	6.5	0.11	0.26	0.34	0.40	0.45	0.51	0.57	0.64	0.71	0.76	0.81	0.86	0.92
34.25	36.5	4.5	8.7	6.6	0.11	0.26	0.34	0.39	0.45	0.50	0.57	0.63	0.71	0.76	0.80	0.86	0.91
34.00	36.8	4.6	8.9	6.7	0.10	0.25	0.33	0.39	0.44	0.50	0.56	0.63	0.70	0.75	0.80	0.85	0.92
33.75	37.2	4.6	9.0	6.8	0.10	0.24	0.33	0.39	0.44	0.50	0.56	0.62	0.69	0.75	0.80	0.85	0.92
33.50	37.5	4.7	9.2	6.9	0.10	0.24	0.32	0.38	0.43	0.49	0.55	0.62	0.69	0.74	0.79	0.85	0.91
33.30	**37.8**	**4.7**	**9.3**	**7.0**	**0.09**	**0.24**	**0.32**	**0.38**	**0.43**	**0.49**	**0.55**	**0.62**	**0.69**	**0.74**	**0.79**	**0.84**	**0.91**
33.25	37.9	4.7	9.4	7.1	0.09	0.24	0.32	0.38	0.43	0.49	0.55	0.61	0.69	0.74	0.79	0.84	0.90
33.00	38.3	4.8	9.6	7.2	0.09	0.24	0.32	0.37	0.42	0.48	0.54	0.61	0.68	0.74	0.78	0.84	0.89
32.75	38.7	4.9	9.8	7.3	0.09	0.24	0.31	0.37	0.42	0.47	0.54	0.61	0.68	0.73	0.78	0.83	0.89
32.50	38.9	4.9	9.9	7.4	0.09	0.23	0.31	0.37	0.42	0.47	0.53	0.60	0.67	0.72	0.77	0.83	0.89
32.25	39.2	4.9	9.9	7.4	0.08	0.23	0.31	0.37	0.42	0.47	0.53	0.59	0.66	0.72	0.77	0.83	0.90
32.00	39.5	5.0	10.2	7.6	0.08	0.22	0.30	0.36	0.41	0.47	0.52	0.59	0.65	0.71	0.77	0.83	0.90
31.75	39.9	5.0	10.8	7.9	0.08	0.22	0.30	0.36	0.41	0.46	0.52	0.58	0.65	0.71	0.76	0.82	0.89
31.50	40.3	5.1	11.4	8.3	0.08	0.22	0.30	0.35	0.40	0.45	0.51	0.58	0.65	0.70	0.76	0.82	0.89
31.25	40.7	5.2	12.1	8.7	0.08	0.21	0.29	0.35	0.40	0.45	0.51	0.57	0.64	0.70	0.75	0.81	0.88
31.00	41.1	5.3	13.1	9.2	0.08	0.21	0.29	0.34	0.39	0.44	0.50	0.57	0.64	0.70	0.75	0.81	0.87
30.75	41.6	5.4	13.9	9.6	0.08	0.21	0.29	0.34	0.38	0.43	0.50	0.57	0.65	0.70	0.75	0.80	0.86
30.50	42.0	5.5	14.6	10.0	0.08	0.21	0.28	0.33	0.38	0.43	0.49	0.56	0.64	0.70	0.74	0.79	0.85
30.25	42.3	5.5	15.0	10.3	0.07	0.21	0.28	0.33	0.37	0.43	0.49	0.56	0.64	0.69	0.74	0.79	0.85
30.00	42.6	5.6	15.5	10.6	0.07	0.21	0.28	0.33	0.37	0.42	0.48	0.55	0.63	0.68	0.73	0.78	0.85
29.75	43.0	5.7	15.9	10.8	0.07	0.20	0.27	0.32	0.37	0.42	0.48	0.55	0.63	0.68	0.73	0.78	0.84
29.50	43.4	5.8	16.3	11.0	0.07	0.20	0.27	0.32	0.36	0.41	0.48	0.55	0.62	0.68	0.72	0.77	0.83
29.25	43.8	5.9	16.5	11.2	0.07	0.20	0.27	0.31	0.36	0.41	0.47	0.54	0.62	0.67	0.72	0.77	0.83
29.00	44.1	5.9	16.7	11.3	0.07	0.20	0.26	0.31	0.35	0.41	0.47	0.54	0.61	0.67	0.71	0.76	0.82
28.75	44.5	6.0	17.1	11.5	0.07	0.19	0.26	0.31	0.35	0.40	0.46	0.53	0.61	0.66	0.71	0.76	0.82
28.50	44.8	6.1	17.3	11.7	0.06	0.19	0.25	0.30	0.35	0.40	0.46	0.53	0.60	0.66	0.70	0.76	0.82
28.25	45.2	6.2	17.7	11.9	0.06	0.18	0.25	0.30	0.34	0.39	0.45	0.52	0.60	0.65	0.70	0.75	0.82
28.00	45.4	6.2	17.9	12.0	0.06	0.18	0.25	0.30	0.34	0.39	0.45	0.52	0.59	0.64	0.69	0.75	0.82
27.75	45.7	6.3	18.1	12.2	0.05	0.17	0.24	0.30	0.34	0.39	0.45	0.51	0.57	0.63	0.69	0.75	0.82
27.50	46.2	6.4	19.0	12.7	0.06	0.17	0.24	0.29	0.33	0.38	0.44	0.51	0.58	0.63	0.68	0.74	0.81
27.25	46.9	6.6	20.3	13.5	0.06	0.18	0.24	0.28	0.32	0.37	0.43	0.51	0.59	0.64	0.68	0.72	0.78
27.00	47.3	6.7	20.9	13.8	0.06	0.18	0.23	0.28	0.32	0.37	0.43	0.50	0.59	0.64	0.67	0.72	0.77
26.75	47.6	6.8	21.2	14.0	0.06	0.17	0.23	0.27	0.32	0.37	0.43	0.50	0.58	0.63	0.67	0.71	0.77
26.50	47.9	6.9	21.6	14.2	0.06	0.17	0.23	0.27	0.31	0.36	0.42	0.49	0.57	0.62	0.66	0.71	0.77
26.25	48.2	6.9	22.0	14.4	0.05	0.16	0.23	0.27	0.31	0.36	0.42	0.49	0.56	0.61	0.66	0.71	0.77
26.00	48.6	7.0	22.4	14.7	0.05	0.16	0.22	0.27	0.31	0.36	0.41	0.48	0.55	0.61	0.65	0.70	0.77
25.75	48.9	7.1	22.9	15.0	0.05	0.16	0.22	0.26	0.31	0.35	0.41	0.47	0.55	0.60	0.65	0.70	0.76
25.50	49.4	7.2	23.7	15.5	0.05	0.16	0.22	0.26	0.30	0.35	0.41	0.47	0.54	0.60	0.64	0.69	0.76
25.25	49.7	7.3	24.2	15.7	0.05	0.16	0.21	0.26	0.30	0.35	0.40	0.47	0.54	0.59	0.63	0.69	0.75
25.00	**50.2**	**7.4**	**25.4**	**16.4**	**0.05**	**0.16**	**0.21**	**0.25**	**0.29**	**0.34**	**0.40**	**0.46**	**0.54**	**0.59**	**0.63**	**0.68**	**0.74**

MAJ	65	70	75	80	85	90	95	100	200	500	1,000	30,000	120,000	1,000,000	Top400	Top100	10th	1st
37.00	1.04	1.13	1.24	1.37	1.50	1.69	2.01	3.3	4.4	6.5	8.1	22.6	34.3	65.2	60.2	91.5	183.0	368
36.75	1.03	1.12	1.23	1.36	1.50	1.70	2.04	3.3	4.5	6.7	8.3	23.5	35.8	68.5	63.2	96.6	195.5	395
36.50	1.03	1.12	1.23	1.36	1.50	1.71	2.06	3.4	4.6	6.8	8.5	24.2	37.2	71.6	66.0	101.3	206.0	421
36.25	1.01	1.11	1.22	1.36	1.50	1.72	2.10	3.4	4.7	7.0	8.7	25.0	38.6	74.8	68.9	106.2	213.0	448
36.00	**1.01**	**1.10**	**1.21**	**1.36**	**1.51**	**1.73**	**2.12**	**3.5**	**4.8**	**7.1**	**8.8**	**25.7**	**39.7**	**77.4**	**71.3**	**110.3**	**228.0**	**470**
35.75	1.02	1.11	1.23	1.37	1.51	1.73	2.10	3.5	4.8	7.1	8.8	25.7	39.8	77.5	71.3	110.3	227.5	470
35.50	1.03	1.12	1.24	1.38	1.52	1.72	2.08	3.5	4.8	7.1	8.8	25.7	39.7	77.4	71.2	110.2	227.0	469
35.25	1.03	1.13	1.24	1.39	1.52	1.72	2.08	3.6	4.9	7.2	8.9	26.1	40.5	79.1	72.7	112.8	233.5	484
35.00	1.03	1.13	1.24	1.39	1.52	1.73	2.08	3.6	5.0	7.3	9.1	27.0	42.1	83.0	76.3	118.9	248.0	519
34.75	1.01	1.11	1.23	1.38	1.52	1.73	2.10	3.8	5.2	7.6	9.5	28.9	45.3	90.5	83.0	130.4	276.0	585
34.50	1.00	1.10	1.22	1.37	1.52	1.73	2.12	3.9	5.3	7.8	9.8	30.4	48.1	97.0	88.8	140.6	301	646
34.25	1.00	1.10	1.22	1.37	1.52	1.74	2.13	3.9	5.4	8.0	10.1	31.3	49.6	100.7	92.2	146.5	316	682
34.00	1.00	1.10	1.23	1.38	1.52	1.74	2.12	4.0	5.5	8.1	10.2	31.9	50.8	103.6	94.8	151.0	327	709
33.75	1.00	1.10	1.23	1.39	1.53	1.74	2.13	4.0	5.6	8.2	10.4	32.6	52.1	106.6	97.5	155.7	339	738
33.50	1.00	1.10	1.23	1.39	1.53	1.75	2.14	4.0	5.7	8.3	10.5	33.6	53.8	110.9	101.3	162.5	356	780
33.30	**0.99**	**1.09**	**1.22**	**1.38**	**1.53**	**1.76**	**2.16**	**4.1**	**5.8**	**8.5**	**10.7**	**34.5**	**55.6**	**115.1**	**105.1**	**169.2**	**373**	**823**
33.25	0.99	1.09	1.22	1.38	1.53	1.76	2.16	4.1	5.8	8.5	10.8	34.7	56.0	116.1	106.0	170.8	377	833
33.00	0.98	1.09	1.22	1.38	1.54	1.77	2.19	4.1	5.9	8.7	11.0	36.0	58.2	121.7	111.0	179.7	400	890
32.75	0.97	1.08	1.21	1.38	1.54	1.78	2.21	4.1	6.0	8.9	11.3	37.1	60.3	126.7	115.5	187.7	421	943
32.50	0.98	1.09	1.22	1.39	1.55	1.78	2.20	4.2	6.1	8.9	11.3	37.4	60.8	128.0	116.6	189.8	426	956
32.25	0.99	1.10	1.23	1.40	1.55	1.78	2.19	4.2	6.1	8.9	11.3	37.5	61.0	128.6	117.2	190.7	429	963
32.00	0.99	1.10	1.23	1.40	1.55	1.78	2.19	4.2	6.2	9.1	11.7	39.0	63.9	135.8	123.6	202.3	459	1,040
31.75	0.98	1.09	1.23	1.40	1.55	1.78	2.20	4.2	6.5	9.6	12.4	42.7	70.7	153.0	138.9	230.1	532	1,231
31.50	0.98	1.09	1.23	1.40	1.55	1.78	2.20	4.2	6.7	10.1	13.1	46.6	78.1	172.1	156.0	261.5	617	1,454
31.25	0.97	1.08	1.22	1.40	1.55	1.78	2.20	4.1	7.0	10.7	13.9	50.9	86.3	193.5	174.9	296.7	714	1,717
31.00	0.96	1.08	1.22	1.40	1.55	1.78	2.20	4.1	7.3	11.4	15.0	56.8	97.8	224.3	202.2	348	858	2,116
30.75	0.95	1.06	1.21	1.39	1.54	1.78	2.21	4.1	7.7	12.1	15.9	62.3	108.5	253.8	228.3	398	1,001	2,520
30.50	0.94	1.06	1.20	1.39	1.54	1.78	2.22	4.1	8.0	12.6	16.7	66.6	117.1	277.6	249.3	438	1,120	2,860
30.25	0.94	1.06	1.20	1.39	1.54	1.78	2.21	4.1	8.2	13.0	17.2	69.8	123.6	295.9	265.3	470	1,212	3,129
30.00	0.94	1.06	1.20	1.39	1.54	1.77	2.20	4.1	8.4	13.3	17.7	73.2	130.3	315	282.20	503	1,311	3,420
29.75	0.93	1.05	1.20	1.39	1.54	1.78	2.21	4.1	8.6	13.7	18.2	76.1	136.1	332	296.70	531	1,398	3,677
29.50	0.93	1.04	1.19	1.39	1.54	1.78	2.23	4.2	8.8	13.8	18.6	78.2	140.6	345	308	554	1,466	3,882
29.25	0.92	1.04	1.19	1.39	1.55	1.79	2.24	4.2	9.0	14.1	18.9	80.0	144.3	355	318	572	1,523	4,054
29.00	0.92	1.04	1.19	1.39	1.55	1.79	2.25	4.2	9.1	14.2	19.1	81.6	147.4	365	326	589	1,573	4,204
28.75	0.92	1.04	1.19	1.39	1.55	1.79	2.25	4.3	9.4	14.4	19.4	83.8	151.9	378	337	611	1,644	4,419
28.50	0.91	1.04	1.19	1.39	1.55	1.80	2.26	4.3	9.5	14.6	19.7	85.7	155.8	389	347	632	1,707	4,613
28.25	0.91	1.04	1.19	1.40	1.55	1.80	2.25	4.3	9.7	14.9	20.1	88.2	161.0	404	360	658	1,790	4,867
28.00	0.92	1.04	1.20	1.40	1.56	1.80	2.24	4.3	9.8	15.0	20.3	89.5	163.8	413	368	673	1,837	5,013
27.75	0.92	1.05	1.21	1.41	1.56	1.79	2.23	4.4	10.0	15.2	20.6	91.0	166.8	422	376	689	1,887	5,167
27.50	0.90	1.03	1.19	1.40	1.55	1.79	2.24	4.4	10.4	15.8	21.5	97.7	180.9	464	413	764	2,126	5,917
27.25	0.87	1.00	1.16	1.38	1.54	1.79	2.26	4.5	11.0	16.8	23.1	108.2	203.2	532	472	885	2,524	7,185
27.00	0.87	1.00	1.16	1.38	1.53	1.78	2.26	4.5	11.2	17.2	23.7	112.6	212.5	561	497	939	2,695	7,741
26.75	0.87	1.00	1.16	1.38	1.54	1.78	2.25	4.5	11.4	17.5	24.1	115.0	217.7	578	511	968	2,793	8,060
26.50	0.87	1.00	1.17	1.38	1.54	1.78	2.24	4.5	11.5	17.7	24.4	117.7	223.5	596	527	1,001	2,905	8,428
26.25	0.87	1.00	1.17	1.39	1.54	1.78	2.24	4.6	11.7	18.0	24.8	120.8	230.2	617	546	1,039	3,033	8,848
26.00	0.87	1.00	1.17	1.39	1.54	1.77	2.23	4.6	11.8	18.3	25.3	124.1	237.3	640	565	1,081	3,173	9,314
25.75	0.86	0.99	1.16	1.39	1.54	1.77	2.23	4.6	12.1	18.7	25.8	128.0	245.7	667	589	1,130	3,340	9,871
25.50	0.86	0.99	1.16	1.39	1.53	1.75	2.20	4.7	12.4	19.2	26.7	134.8	260.6	714	630	1,218	3,642	10,889
25.25	0.85	0.98	1.16	1.38	1.53	1.76	2.21	4.7	12.6	19.6	27.3	138.9	269.7	744	656	1,273	3,832	11,534
25.00	**0.84**	**0.97**	**1.14**	**1.38**	**1.52**	**1.75**	**2.20**	**4.7**	**13.0**	**20.4**	**28.6**	**149.0**	**292.0**	**817**	**719**	**1,409**	**4,308**	**13,172**

MAJ	Gini	Lower ½%	Upper ½%	Top1	1	5	10	15	20	25	30	35	40	45	50	55	60	65	70	75	80	85	90	95	100	200	500	1,000	30,000	120,000	1,000,000	Top400	Top100	10th	1st
24.75	50.7	7.5	26.5	17.0	0.05	0.15	0.21	0.25	0.29	0.33	0.39	0.46	0.54	0.59	0.63	0.67	0.73	0.83	0.96	1.14	1.37	1.51	1.73	2.18	4.7	13.4	21.2	29.7	157.9	312	883	776	1,532	4,746	14,702
24.50	51.0	7.6	26.9	17.2	0.05	0.15	0.20	0.25	0.28	0.33	0.39	0.45	0.53	0.58	0.62	0.67	0.73	0.83	0.97	1.14	1.38	1.51	1.73	2.16	4.8	13.5	21.4	30.1	161.2	319	909	797	1,579	4,915	15,297
24.25	51.3	7.6	27.2	17.4	0.04	0.14	0.20	0.24	0.28	0.33	0.38	0.45	0.52	0.57	0.61	0.67	0.73	0.83	0.97	1.15	1.38	1.51	1.72	2.15	4.8	13.6	21.7	30.5	163.9	325	929	815	1,618	5,053	15,782
24.00	51.7	7.6	27.9	17.7	0.04	0.14	0.20	0.24	0.28	0.32	0.38	0.44	0.52	0.57	0.61	0.66	0.72	0.83	0.96	1.14	1.38	1.51	1.73	2.16	4.8	13.3	22.1	31.2	169.7	339	973	853	1,701	5,356	16,859
23.75	52.2	7.5	28.8	18.2	0.04	0.14	0.19	0.23	0.27	0.31	0.37	0.44	0.52	0.57	0.61	0.65	0.71	0.81	0.95	1.13	1.37	1.50	1.73	2.18	4.8	13.1	22.8	32.2	178.1	357	1,038	908	1,824	5,803	18,463
23.50	52.7	7.5	29.5	18.5	0.04	0.14	0.19	0.23	0.26	0.31	0.37	0.44	0.52	0.57	0.60	0.65	0.70	0.80	0.94	1.12	1.36	1.50	1.73	2.19	4.8	12.9	23.2	33.0	184.8	373	1,091	954	1,924	6,173	19,806
23.25	53.0	7.5	30.1	18.8	0.04	0.14	0.18	0.22	0.26	0.31	0.36	0.43	0.51	0.56	0.60	0.64	0.70	0.80	0.94	1.12	1.36	1.50	1.73	2.18	4.9	12.7	23.7	33.7	190.3	385	1,134	991	2,007	6,481	20,928
23.00	53.3	7.5	30.4	18.9	0.04	0.13	0.18	0.22	0.26	0.30	0.36	0.43	0.51	0.55	0.59	0.64	0.69	0.80	0.94	1.12	1.37	1.50	1.73	2.18	5.0	12.5	23.9	34.0	193.2	392	1,158	1,011	2,053	6,651	21,551
22.75	53.7	7.5	30.8	19.2	0.04	0.13	0.18	0.22	0.25	0.30	0.35	0.42	0.50	0.55	0.59	0.63	0.69	0.79	0.93	1.12	1.36	1.50	1.72	2.17	5.0	12.3	24.3	34.7	198.2	404	1,198	1,046	2,129	6,939	22,614
22.50	54.2	7.5	31.4	19.5	0.04	0.13	0.18	0.21	0.25	0.30	0.35	0.42	0.50	0.55	0.58	0.63	0.68	0.78	0.92	1.11	1.36	1.49	1.72	2.17	5.2	12.1	24.7	35.3	204.3	418	1,248	1,089	2,226	7,304	23,966
22.25	54.6	7.6	32.2	19.9	0.04	0.13	0.17	0.21	0.25	0.29	0.35	0.41	0.49	0.54	0.58	0.62	0.67	0.78	0.92	1.10	1.35	1.48	1.69	2.12	5.4	11.8	25.4	36.4	213.7	440	1,325	1,155	2,376	7,874	26,098
22.00	55.0	7.7	32.7	20.2	0.04	0.12	0.17	0.21	0.24	0.29	0.34	0.41	0.49	0.54	0.57	0.61	0.67	0.77	0.91	1.10	1.35	1.48	1.69	2.12	5.5	11.7	25.8	37.1	219.5	453	1,373	1,196	2,469	8,231	27,442
21.75	55.5	7.8	33.4	20.6	0.04	0.12	0.17	0.20	0.24	0.28	0.34	0.41	0.49	0.53	0.57	0.61	0.66	0.76	0.90	1.09	1.35	1.46	1.66	2.07	5.7	11.5	26.5	38.1	228.6	475	1,451	1 262	2,620	8,814	29,656
21.50	55.9	8.0	34.0	21.0	0.04	0.12	0.16	0.20	0.23	0.28	0.33	0.40	0.48	0.53	0.56	0.60	0.66	0.76	0.90	1.09	1.35	1.45	1.63	2.02	6.0	11.5	27.0	39.0	236.8	494	1,521	1,322	2,757	9,349	31,702
21.25	56.3	8.1	34.4	21.2	0.03	0.11	0.16	0.19	0.22	0.27	0.32	0.40	0.48	0.53	0.56	0.60	0.66	0.76	0.90	1.09	1.35	1.44	1.62	1.99	6.1	11.5	27.4	39.6	242.1	507	1,566	1,361	2,846	9,700	33,057
21.00	56.7	8.2	34.7	21.4	0.03	0.11	0.15	0.18	0.22	0.26	0.32	0.39	0.48	0.53	0.56	0.60	0.66	0.76	0.91	1.10	1.36	1.44	1.61	1.97	6.2	11.5	27.7	40.1	247.0	518	1,609	1,397	2,930	10,028	34,326
20.75	57.0	8.2	34.9	21.5	0.03	0.10	0.15	0.18	0.22	0.26	0.32	0.39	0.47	0.52	0.55	0.60	0.66	0.76	0.91	1.10	1.36	1.45	1.61	1.97	6.3	11.4	28.0	40.6	251.3	528	1,646	1,429	3,004	10,322	35,468
20.50	57.3	8.1	35.2	21.7	0.03	0.10	0.14	0.18	0.21	0.26	0.31	0.38	0.46	0.51	0.55	0.60	0.65	0.76	0.90	1.10	1.36	1.45	1.62	1.99	6.3	11.2	28.4	41.3	257.9	544	1,705	1,478	3,119	10,779	37,253
20.25	57.7	8.1	35.5	21.8	0.03	0.10	0.14	0.17	0.21	0.25	0.31	0.38	0.46	0.51	0.54	0.59	0.65	0.75	0.90	1.09	1.36	1.45	1.63	2.00	6.3	11.1	28.9	42.1	265.0	561	1,768	1,532	3,244	11,281	39,227
20.00	58.1	8.2	36.1	22.2	0.03	0.10	0.14	0.17	0.21	0.25	0.30	0.37	0.45	0.50	0.54	0.59	0.64	0.75	0.90	1.09	1.36	1.44	1.61	1.97	6.5	11.1	29.1	43.3	276.5	589	1,872	1,620	3,450	12,112	42,519
19.75	58.4	8.2	36.2	22.2	0.03	0.10	0.14	0.17	0.20	0.24	0.30	0.36	0.45	0.50	0.53	0.58	0.64	0.74	0.89	1.09	1.36	1.45	1.63	2.01	6.4	11.0	29.1	43.5	278.7	594	1,891	1,637	3,489	12,270	43,147
19.50	58.8	8.3	36.6	22.5	0.03	0.10	0.13	0.16	0.20	0.24	0.29	0.36	0.44	0.49	0.53	0.57	0.63	0.74	0.89	1.08	1.35	1.45	1.62	2.01	6.6	11.1	28.5	44.2	285.3	610	1,952	1,688	3,610	12,763	45,118
19.25	59.2	8.4	37.1	22.8	0.02	0.09	0.13	0.16	0.19	0.23	0.29	0.36	0.44	0.49	0.52	0.57	0.62	0.73	0.88	1.08	1.35	1.44	1.62	2.00	6.7	11.2	28.0	44.9	292.3	627	2,016	1,743	3,740	13,293	47,250
19.00	59.6	8.5	37.6	23.1	0.02	0.09	0.13	0.16	0.19	0.23	0.28	0.35	0.43	0.48	0.52	0.56	0.62	0.72	0.87	1.07	1.35	1.44	1.61	1.99	6.8	11.3	27.5	45.6	299.4	645	2,082	1,799	3,872	13,836	49,443
18.75	60.1	8.8	38.2	23.5	0.02	0.09	0.13	0.16	0.18	0.22	0.28	0.35	0.43	0.48	0.51	0.56	0.61	0.72	0.86	1.06	1.34	1.43	1.59	1.96	7.0	11.6	27.6	46.3	306	660	2,142	1,849	3,992	14,334	51,463
18.50	60.6	9.1	38.8	24.0	0.02	0.09	0.13	0.15	0.18	0.22	0.27	0.34	0.43	0.48	0.51	0.55	0.60	0.71	0.86	1.06	1.33	1.41	1.56	1.91	7.3	12.0	27.8	46.8	311	674	2,194	1,893	4,097	14,770	53,241
18.25	61.1	9.5	39.5	24.5	0.03	0.09	0.12	0.15	0.17	0.21	0.27	0.34	0.42	0.47	0.50	0.54	0.59	0.70	0.85	1.05	1.33	1.39	1.53	1.86	7.6	12.4	28.1	47.4	317	687	2,245	1,937	4,201	15,203	55,016
18.00	61.6	9.9	40.1	25.0	0.03	0.09	0.12	0.14	0.17	0.20	0.26	0.33	0.42	0.47	0.50	0.53	0.58	0.69	0.84	1.04	1.32	1.37	1.50	1.81	7.9	12.8	28.4	47.9	322	700	2,295	1,979	4,302	15,626	56,753
17.75	61.9	9.8	40.4	25.1	0.03	0.09	0.12	0.14	0.16	0.20	0.25	0.33	0.42	0.47	0.49	0.53	0.57	0.68	0.83	1.03	1.31	1.38	1.52	1.85	7.9	12.9	28.6	48.3	325	708	2,327	2,006	4,366	15,893	57,854
17.50	62.4	10.3	41.1	25.7	0.03	0.09	0.12	0.14	0.16	0.19	0.25	0.32	0.42	0.46	0.49	0.52	0.57	0.67	0.82	1.02	1.31	1.36	1.48	1.79	8.3	13.3	29.1	48.7	330	720	2,374	2,045	4,461	16,293	59,506
17.25	62.8	10.3	41.4	25.9	0.03	0.09	0.12	0.14	0.15	0.19	0.24	0.32	0.41	0.46	0.48	0.51	0.56	0.66	0.81	1.01	1.30	1.36	1.49	1.81	8.3	13.4	29.4	49.1	333	728	2,404	2,071	4,523	16,553	60,583
17.00	63.2	10.4	41.8	26.1	0.03	0.09	0.12	0.13	0.15	0.19	0.24	0.31	0.41	0.45	0.47	0.51	0.55	0.65	0.80	1.00	1.29	1.36	1.50	1.84	8.4	13.5	29.7	49.4	337	736	2,436	2,098	4,588	16,831	61,738
16.75	63.6	10.4	42.1	26.3	0.03	0.09	0.11	0.13	0.15	0.18	0.24	0.31	0.40	0.45	0.47	0.50	0.54	0.64	0.79	0.99	1.29	1.36	1.51	1.86	8.4	13.6	30.0	49.7	340	744	2,465	2,123	4,647	17,081	62,778
16.50	64.0	10.5	42.5	26.5	0.03	0.09	0.11	0.13	0.14	0.18	0.23	0.30	0.40	0.44	0.46	0.49	0.53	0.63	0.78	0.99	1.28	1.36	1.52	1.88	8.4	13.7	30.3	50.0	343	752	2,499	2,151	4,716	17,371	63,987
16.25	64.4	10.6	42.8	26.7	0.03	0.09	0.11	0.12	0.14	0.17	0.23	0.30	0.40	0.44	0.46	0.48	0.52	0.62	0.77	0.98	1.27	1.36	1.53	1.91	8.5	13.8	30.7	50.3	346	760	2,528	2,176	4,776	17,629	65,069
16.00	64.8	10.6	43.2	26.9	0.03	0.09	0.11	0.12	0.13	0.17	0.22	0.29	0.39	0.44	0.45	0.48	0.51	0.61	0.76	0.97	1.26	1.36	1.54	1.93	8.5	13.9	30.9	50.6	349	768	2,559	2,202	4,840	17,900	66,201
15.75	65.3	10.7	43.5	27.1	0.03	0.08	0.10	0.11	0.13	0.16	0.21	0.29	0.39	0.43	0.45	0.47	0.51	0.60	0.75	0.96	1.26	1.36	1.55	1.96	8.6	14.0	31.3	50.9	353	776	2,592	2,230	4,907	18,185	67,400
15.50	65.7	10.8	43.9	27.3	0.03	0.08	0.10	0.11	0.12	0.16	0.21	0.29	0.39	0.43	0.44	0.46	0.50	0.59	0.74	0.95	1.25	1.36	1.56	1.99	8.6	14.1	31.7	51.2	356	784	2,623	2,256	4,970	18,459	68,549
15.25	66.1	10.9	44.2	27.5	0.05	0.08	0.09	0.10	0.12	0.15	0.21	0.28	0.38	0.42	0.44	0.46	0.49	0.58	0.74	0.93	1.24	1.35	1.57	2.04	8.7	14.3	32.2	51.4	357	788	2,639	2,270	5,003	18,600	69,142
15.00	66.4	10.2	45.3	27.8	0.07	0.08	0.09	0.10	0.12	0.15	0.20	0.28	0.37	0.42	0.43	0.45	0.48	0.58	0.73	0.91	1.24	1.36	1.56	2.07	8.1	13.5	33.1	53.1	375	833	2,820	2,422	5,375	20,201	75,930
14.75	66.8	10.2	45.7	28.0	0.07	0.07	0.08	0.10	0.11	0.15	0.20	0.27	0.37	0.41	0.43	0.45	0.48	0.57	0.73	0.90	1.24	1.36	1.57	2.09	8.1	13.7	33.7	53.4	378	839	2,844	2,442	5,425	20,420	76,864
14.50	67.1	10.3	45.9	28.1	0.07	0.07	0.08	0.10	0.11	0.15	0.20	0.27	0.36	0.40	0.42	0.44	0.47	0.57	0.72	0.90	1.23	1.36	1.57	2.10	8.1	13.7	34.0	53.4	379	842	2,855	2,451	5,447	20,515	77,268
14.25	67.6	11.0	45.7	28.4	0.06	0.07	0.08	0.09	0.11	0.14	0.19	0.26	0.35	0.39	0.41	0.44	0.47	0.55	0.72	0.90	1.20	1.34	1.62	2.17	8.8	14.6	34.0	52.8	371	823	2,778	2,386	5,288	19,825	74,330
14.00	68.0	11.1	46.0	28.5	0.06	0.07	0.08	0.09	0.11	0.14	0.19	0.26	0.34	0.38	0.40	0.43	0.46	0.55	0.72	0.89	1.20	1.34	1.63	2.18	8.8	14.6	34.1	53.0	374	830	2,808	2,412	5,349	20,092	75,465
13.75	68.3	11.1	46.3	28.7	0.04	0.07	0.08	0.09	0.11	0.14	0.19	0.25	0.34	0.38	0.40	0.42	0.45	0.54	0.69	0.89	1.19	1.35	1.61	2.20	8.9	14.7	34.3	53.3	378	839	2,842	2,440	5,419	20,396	76,760
13.50	68.6	11.3	46.5	28.9	0.02	0.07	0.08	0.09	0.11	0.14	0.18	0.25	0.34	0.38	0.39	0.41	0.44	0.54	0.68	0.89	1.20	1.36	1.62	2.15	9.0	14.9	34.3	53.4	379	841	2,851	2,448	5,440	20,484	77,135

MAJ	Gini	Lower ½%	Upper ½%	Top1	1	5	10	15	20	25	30	35	40	45	50	55	60	65	70	75	80	85	90	95	100	200	500	1,000	30,000	120,000	1,000,000	Top400	Top100	10th	1st
13.25	69.0	11.0	47.1	29.0	0.04	0.07	0.08	0.09	0.11	0.13	0.18	0.24	0.33	0.37	0.38	0.41	0.44	0.54	0.69	0.88	1.21	1.36	1.61	2.18	8.7	14.6	34.8	54.4	389	866	2,953	2,534	5,649	21,397	81,050
13.00	69.3	10.6	47.8	29.2	0.06	0.06	0.07	0.09	0.10	0.13	0.18	0.24	0.31	0.35	0.38	0.40	0.44	0.53	0.69	0.86	1.21	1.36	1.61	2.22	8.4	14.2	35.4	55.3	399	892	3,055	2,620	5,861	22,324	85,036
12.75	69.6	10.7	48.0	29.4	0.05	0.06	0.07	0.08	0.10	0.13	0.17	0.23	0.31	0.35	0.37	0.40	0.43	0.53	0.68	0.86	1.20	1.36	1.61	2.23	8.4	14.4	35.8	55.5	401	897	3,075	2,637	5,903	22,511	85,842
12.50	70.0	11.3	47.7	29.5	0.05	0.06	0.07	0.08	0.10	0.13	0.17	0.23	0.30	0.34	0.36	0.39	0.43	0.52	0.68	0.86	1.21	1.35	1.62	2.22	9.0	15.0	35.6	54.6	392	874	2,986	2,561	5,717	21,694	82,322
12.25	70.3	11.7	47.7	29.7	0.03	0.06	0.07	0.08	0.10	0.13	0.17	0.22	0.29	0.33	0.35	0.39	0.42	0.51	0.67	0.87	1.20	1.35	1.64	2.23	9.3	15.4	35.7	54.3	388	865	2,948	2,530	5,639	21,355	80,864
12.00	70.6	11.7	47.9	29.8	0.01	0.05	0.07	0.08	0.10	0.13	0.16	0.22	0.29	0.33	0.35	0.38	0.42	0.51	0.66	0.88	1.19	1.36	1.64	2.21	9.3	15.5	36.0	54.5	390	871	2,970	2,548	5,685	21,552	81,709
11.75	71.0	11.8	48.1	30.0	0.01	0.05	0.07	0.08	0.10	0.12	0.16	0.21	0.28	0.32	0.34	0.37	0.41	0.51	0.66	0.87	1.19	1.36	1.65	2.22	9.4	15.6	36.3	54.7	392	875	2,987	2,563	5,720	21,708	82,381
11.50	71.3	11.9	48.4	30.1	0.01	0.05	0.07	0.08	0.10	0.12	0.16	0.21	0.27	0.31	0.33	0.37	0.41	0.51	0.66	0.87	1.19	1.36	1.65	2.23	9.4	15.7	36.6	54.8	394	879	3,006	2,578	5,759	21,878	83,111
11.25	71.6	11.9	48.6	30.2	0.01	0.05	0.06	0.08	0.10	0.12	0.15	0.20	0.26	0.30	0.32	0.36	0.41	0.51	0.65	0.87	1.19	1.36	1.66	2.24	9.5	15.8	36.8	55.0	396	884	3,025	2,595	5,799	22,056	83,877
11.00	71.9	12.0	48.8	30.4	0.01	0.04	0.06	0.08	0.10	0.12	0.15	0.20	0.26	0.29	0.32	0.35	0.40	0.50	0.65	0.87	1.19	1.37	1.66	2.26	9.5	15.8	36.9	55.2	398	890	3,049	2,615	5,848	22,268	84,796
10.75	72.3	12.0	49.1	30.6	0.01	0.04	0.06	0.07	0.09	0.12	0.15	0.19	0.25	0.28	0.31	0.35	0.40	0.50	0.65	0.86	1.19	1.37	1.67	2.27	9.5	15.9	37.1	55.5	400	896	3,072	2,634	5,897	22,483	85,722
10.50	72.6	12.1	49.4	30.7	0.01	0.04	0.06	0.07	0.09	0.11	0.14	0.19	0.24	0.28	0.31	0.34	0.40	0.50	0.65	0.86	1.19	1.37	1.67	2.28	9.6	16.0	37.2	55.6	402	902	3,095	2,653	5,944	22,690	86,619
10.25	73.0	12.1	49.6	30.9	0.01	0.04	0.05	0.07	0.09	0.11	0.14	0.18	0.23	0.27	0.30	0.34	0.39	0.49	0.64	0.86	1.18	1.37	1.68	2.29	9.6	16.1	37.3	55.9	405	907	3,118	2,673	5,991	22,900	87,528
10.00	73.3	12.2	49.9	31.0	0.01	0.03	0.05	0.07	0.09	0.11	0.14	0.18	0.23	0.26	0.29	0.33	0.39	0.49	0.64	0.86	1.18	1.37	1.68	2.31	9.7	16.2	37.4	56.1	407	913	3,142	2,693	6,042	23,125	88,504
9.75	73.6	12.3	50.2	31.2	0.01	0.03	0.05	0.07	0.08	0.11	0.13	0.17	0.22	0.25	0.29	0.33	0.38	0.48	0.63	0.85	1.18	1.37	1.69	2.32	9.7	16.3	37.6	56.4	410	920	3,172	2,718	6,103	23,394	89,669
9.50	74.0	12.3	50.4	31.4	0.01	0.03	0.05	0.06	0.08	0.10	0.13	0.16	0.21	0.25	0.28	0.32	0.38	0.48	0.63	0.85	1.18	1.37	1.69	2.33	9.8	16.4	37.7	56.6	413	928	3,201	2,743	6,165	23,666	90,853
9.25	74.3	12.4	50.7	31.5	0.01	0.03	0.05	0.06	0.08	0.10	0.12	0.16	0.21	0.24	0.27	0.32	0.37	0.48	0.63	0.85	1.18	1.37	1.70	2.34	9.8	16.4	37.9	56.9	415	935	3,230	2,767	6,225	23,933	92,016
9.00	74.7	12.5	51.0	31.8	0.00	0.03	0.04	0.06	0.08	0.10	0.12	0.15	0.20	0.23	0.27	0.31	0.37	0.47	0.62	0.84	1.17	1.37	1.70	2.34	9.9	16.6	38.1	57.2	419	944	3,267	2,798	6,303	24,279	93,525
8.75	75.0	12.5	51.3	31.9	0.00	0.03	0.04	0.06	0.08	0.10	0.12	0.15	0.19	0.22	0.26	0.30	0.36	0.47	0.62	0.84	1.17	1.37	1.70	2.36	9.9	16.6	38.3	57.5	422	952	3,300	2,826	6,371	24,583	94,853
8.50	75.3	12.6	51.6	32.1	0.00	0.02	0.04	0.06	0.08	0.09	0.12	0.14	0.18	0.21	0.25	0.30	0.36	0.46	0.61	0.83	1.17	1.37	1.71	2.37	10.0	16.7	38.5	57.8	426	962	3,340	2,859	6,454	24,952	96,471
8.25	75.7	12.7	52.0	32.3	0.00	0.02	0.04	0.06	0.07	0.09	0.11	0.14	0.17	0.21	0.24	0.29	0.35	0.46	0.61	0.83	1.16	1.37	1.71	2.38	10.1	16.8	38.7	58.2	430	971	3,380	2,893	6,537	25,325	98,106
8.00	76.0	12.8	52.3	32.5	0.00	0.02	0.04	0.05	0.07	0.09	0.11	0.13	0.16	0.20	0.23	0.28	0.35	0.45	0.60	0.83	1.16	1.37	1.71	2.39	10.1	16.9	38.9	58.5	434	981	3,421	2,927	6,624	25,711	99,805
7.75	76.4	12.8	52.6	32.7	0.00	0.02	0.04	0.05	0.07	0.09	0.11	0.13	0.16	0.19	0.22	0.28	0.34	0.45	0.60	0.82	1.16	1.37	1.72	2.40	10.2	16.9	39.1	58.9	438	992	3,466	2,965	6,717	26,130	101,647
7.50	76.7	12.8	52.9	32.9	0.00	0.02	0.04	0.05	0.07	0.09	0.10	0.12	0.15	0.18	0.22	0.27	0.34	0.44	0.59	0.82	1.15	1.37	1.72	2.42	10.2	16.9	38.7	59.3	443	1,005	3,518	3,009	6,827	26,624	103,830
7.25	77.0	12.9	53.2	33.0	0.00	0.02	0.03	0.05	0.07	0.09	0.10	0.12	0.14	0.17	0.21	0.26	0.33	0.44	0.59	0.81	1.15	1.37	1.73	2.44	10.3	16.9	38.4	59.7	448	1,017	3,569	3,052	6,935	27,111	105,984
7.00	77.4	12.9	53.5	33.2	0.00	0.02	0.03	0.05	0.07	0.08	0.10	0.11	0.14	0.16	0.20	0.25	0.33	0.43	0.58	0.81	1.14	1.37	1.74	2.46	10.3	17.0	38.0	60.2	453	1,030	3,622	3,096	7,046	27,610	108,201
6.75	77.8	13.0	54.1	33.5	0.00	0.01	0.03	0.05	0.07	0.08	0.09	0.11	0.13	0.16	0.19	0.25	0.32	0.43	0.58	0.80	1.14	1.37	1.74	2.46	10.3	17.1	38.4	60.8	460	1,048	3,699	3,161	7,208	28,346	111,475
6.50	78.1	12.9	54.8	33.9	0.00	0.01	0.03	0.04	0.07	0.08	0.09	0.10	0.12	0.15	0.19	0.24	0.31	0.42	0.57	0.79	1.13	1.37	1.75	2.49	10.2	17.1	39.6	61.4	466	1,065	3,769	3,219	7,354	29,012	114,448
6.25	78.5	12.9	55.7	34.3	0.00	0.01	0.03	0.04	0.06	0.08	0.09	0.10	0.11	0.14	0.18	0.23	0.31	0.41	0.56	0.79	1.13	1.37	1.75	2.50	10.2	17.2	41.0	62.1	473	1,084	3,848	3,285	7,522	29,775	117,866
6.00	78.9	12.9	56.7	34.8	0.00	0.01	0.02	0.04	0.06	0.08	0.08	0.09	0.11	0.13	0.17	0.23	0.30	0.40	0.55	0.78	1.12	1.36	1.75	2.51	10.1	17.4	41.4	62.7	482	1,105	3,936	3,359	7,708	30,630	121,708
5.75	79.3	12.9	57.9	35.4	0.00	0.01	0.02	0.04	0.06	0.07	0.08	0.09	0.10	0.13	0.16	0.22	0.29	0.39	0.54	0.77	1.11	1.36	1.75	2.53	10.0	17.6	41.9	63.6	491	1,130	4,044	3,449	7,937	31,679	126,444
5.50	79.8	12.8	58.8	35.8	0.00	0.01	0.02	0.04	0.06	0.07	0.08	0.09	0.10	0.12	0.16	0.21	0.28	0.38	0.53	0.75	1.10	1.35	1.75	2.55	10.0	17.4	42.8	65.0	508	1,173	4,226	3,601	8,323	33,465	134,558
5.25	80.2	12.8	59.6	36.2	0.00	0.01	0.02	0.03	0.06	0.07	0.07	0.08	0.09	0.11	0.15	0.20	0.27	0.37	0.52	0.74	1.09	1.34	1.75	2.56	10.1	17.2	42.0	66.7	527	1,225	4,446	3,785	8,793	35,656	144,588
5.00	80.6	12.8	60.4	36.6	0.00	0.01	0.02	0.03	0.05	0.06	0.07	0.08	0.09	0.11	0.14	0.19	0.26	0.36	0.51	0.73	1.07	1.33	1.75	2.58	10.1	17.0	39.6	68.5	549	1,281	4,689	3,988	9,314	38,103	155,885
4.75	81.1	12.8	61.2	37.0	0.00	0.01	0.02	0.03	0.05	0.06	0.07	0.07	0.08	0.10	0.13	0.18	0.26	0.35	0.50	0.72	1.06	1.33	1.75	2.59	10.2	16.9	38.0	70.1	569	1,334	4,918	4,179	9,806	40,436	166,749
4.50	81.5	12.7	62.2	37.5	0.00	0.01	0.02	0.03	0.05	0.06	0.06	0.07	0.07	0.09	0.13	0.18	0.25	0.35	0.49	0.71	1.05	1.32	1.75	2.60	10.2	16.7	36.1	72.7	600	1,417	5,281	4,481	10,591	44,196	184,428
4.25	82.0	12.6	63.9	38.2	0.00	0.01	0.01	0.03	0.05	0.06	0.06	0.06	0.07	0.09	0.12	0.17	0.24	0.33	0.47	0.69	1.03	1.30	1.74	2.61	10.1	16.4	34.2	68.5	653	1,562	5,924	5,016	11,994	51,021	217,048
4.00	82.5	12.4	65.6	39.0	0.00	0.00	0.01	0.03	0.04	0.05	0.06	0.06	0.06	0.08	0.11	0.16	0.23	0.32	0.46	0.67	1.02	1.29	1.74	2.62	10.0	16.2	32.7	62.1	714	1,728	6,674	5,638	13,643	59,197	256,860
3.75	83.0	12.3	67.3	39.8	0.00	0.00	0.01	0.02	0.04	0.05	0.05	0.06	0.06	0.08	0.11	0.15	0.22	0.31	0.44	0.66	1.00	1.28	1.73	2.63	9.9	16.0	31.6	57.8	783	1,919	7,558	6,370	15,607	69,145	306,340
3.50	83.4	12.1	67.6	39.8	0.00	0.00	0.01	0.02	0.04	0.05	0.05	0.05	0.05	0.07	0.10	0.14	0.21	0.29	0.43	0.64	0.98	1.28	1.77	2.76	9.7	15.7	31.2	57.2	799	1,963	7,762	6,539	16,063	71,474	318,041
3.25	84.0	12.2	69.6	40.9	0.00	0.00	0.01	0.02	0.04	0.05	0.05	0.05	0.05	0.06	0.09	0.13	0.19	0.28	0.41	0.62	0.96	1.25	1.74	2.70	9.8	15.8	30.7	53.8	891	2,221	8,980	7,543	18,804	85,731	390,362
3.00	84.4	12.2	70.2	41.2	0.00	0.00	0.01	0.02	0.04	0.04	0.04	0.04	0.05	0.06	0.08	0.12	0.18	0.27	0.39	0.60	0.93	1.24	1.75	2.78	9.8	15.7	30.5	53.0	922	2,308	9,397	7,887	19,751	90,729	416,787
2.75	84.9	12.2	70.8	41.5	0.00	0.00	0.01	0.02	0.03	0.04	0.04	0.04	0.04	0.05	0.08	0.11	0.17	0.25	0.38	0.58	0.91	1.23	1.77	2.86	9.8	15.7	30.4	52.4	954	2,401	9,847	8,257	20,773	96,173	445,252
2.50	85.4	12.1	71.4	41.8	0.00	0.00	0.01	0.02	0.03	0.04	0.04	0.04	0.04	0.05	0.07	0.10	0.16	0.24	0.36	0.55	0.88	1.22	1.79	2.94	9.7	15.7	30.3	51.8	990	2,503	10,340	8,662	21,901	102,224	477 134
2.25	85.9	12.1	72.1	42.1	0.00	0.00	0.01	0.01	0.03	0.03	0.03	0.03	0.03	0.04	0.06	0.09	0.15	0.22	0.34	0.53	0.85	1.20	1.80	3.04	9.7	15.7	30.3	51.7	1,014	2,571	10,673	8,936	22,664	106,346	499,003
2.00	86.4	12.1	72.8	42.4	0.00	0.00	0.00	0.01	0.02	0.03	0.03	0.03	0.03	0.04	0.05	0.08	0.13	0.20	0.32	0.50	0.82	1.19	1.82	3.14	9.7	15.7	30.3	51.7	1,029	2,616	10,895	9,118	23,174	109,113	513,745
1.75	87.0	12.0	73.5	42.8	0.00	0.00	0.00	0.01	0.02	0.02	0.02	0.02	0.03	0.03	0.05	0.07	0.12	0.19	0.29	0.47	0.78	1.16	1.84	3.27	9.6	15.6	30.2	51.8	1,047	2,666	11,142	9,321	23,743	112,212	530,316
1.60	87.3	12.0	74.0	43.0	0.00	0.00	0.00	0.01	0.02	0.02	0.02	0.02	0.02	0.03	0.04	0.07	0.11	0.18	0.28	0.45	0.76	1.15	1.85	3.35	9.6	15.6	30.2	51.8	1,058	2,700	11,311	9,459	24,132	114,334	541,701

APPENDIX 2.

THE USA: the fib, its danger, its correction

The great difficulty is that if one were cherry-picking data, or just randomly taking government data that came up in web searches, there is a high probability of being misled. You can see that there is a huge difference between minimum and maximum values in the following graph-201 and in each of the rows in the upcoming Table-203.

#201

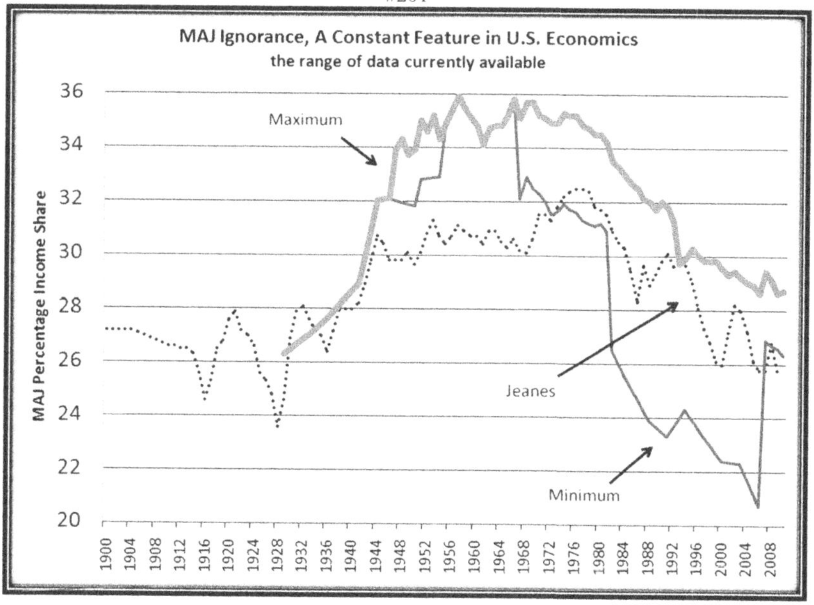

In many nations, there is a great incentive for governments (and politicians who want to preserve their electability) to understate the extent of maldistribution. Without diligent third party audits and careful data collection, we may never know precise distributions. Even in the USA with many studies making bona fide responsible analyses, we do not yet have adequate income-distribution data around which a consensus can be formed.

The Census Bureau's Current Population Survey (CPS) underreports high incomes.[127] Its highest listed survey category is vaguely stated as an income greater than $999,999. Roughly one in 659 people in 2011 were at a scarcity level sufficient to live in households with an income higher than this amount. This is precisely the group that the Census survey does not even look at. At this scarcity level, approximately 475,000 people were living in the USA at these high income levels. They slipped beneath the Census Bureau radar [475,314= 313,232,044/659]. This is the section of the population where the most dramatic maldistribution occurs. Census data misses it under the rubric of "top-coding." A top-coded dataset is one in which the upper bound is not reported, often to preserve the anonymity of people participating in the survey. The result: a huge amount of top income is missed. In truth, it cannot be claimed to be top-coding for the sake of preserving anonymity. With approximately 475,000 citizens at this level, anonymity is assured. Since anonymity is not the excuse, what is?

By not reporting the Top1% income share, the Census Bureau leaves the citizen completely without information about the most important maldistribution component. As Piketty and Saez explicitly state:

> ...the Census Bureau figures, based on data which cannot measure top 1% incomes, miss the extraordinary gains going to the top 1%, which is perhaps the most striking change in the U.S. income distribution in recent decades.[128]

The Census Bureau is not properly doing its income-distribution job. You can pick it up in the language they use and in the data they report. Take the term "income dispersion," a palatable term to express variance which has started to creep into their language, when what they are really talking about is increased concentration of income at the top and increased inequality. Call it what it is: inequality or concentration of income – not "income dispersion."

As for the Census data, look at the following Table-203.[129] You will see that the Congressional Budget Office (CBO) not only reports the Top1% (which the Census is silent on), but their data shows that in the period 1982-2006 Census failed to report a 6% average share that went to the Top5% [6.1%= 26.1-20.0%].[130] This is a large and serious omission that would significantly influence the shape of the entire distribution curve.

In 2003, the media took notice. Piketty and Saez's article "Income Inequality in the United States, 1913–1998" in the *Quarterly Journal of Economics* got traction. Census data received its shot over the bow. The public became increasingly aware that there was a huge high income problem that Census was not reporting. To take the metaphor to the next level, the aims with subsequent salvos have been lowered. Soon they should properly be low enough to blow the hull out of the water. We need good, responsibly-supported data. Not fiction.

#203 [*]

1982-2006 Income Shares According to Various Sources

	Min Other	Census Family	Census Household	Jeanes	Budget Office Congress	Saez, excluding capital gains	Wolff, Federal Reserve Study	Saez, including capital gains	Max Other
					Averages				
MAJ	23.5	30.8	28.3	28.5	28.6		23.5		30.8
Top5%	18.9	18.9	20.0	24.3	26.1	27.8	30.9	30.7	30.9
Top1%	13.3			12.0	13.6	13.3	16.5	16.2	16.5
					Medians				
MAJ	23.6	30.0	27.7	28.9	28.9		23.6		30.0
Top5%	20.1	20.1	21.0	23.6	25.4	27.9	30.3	29.5	30.3
Top1%	13.3			11.4	13.3	13.5	16.0	15.5	16.0

To their credit, as can be seen in Table-203, Census Household data and the Congressional Budget Office did have MAJs that were close. If you were to be a casual observer of data and saw Family or Household reports of income shares, you might initially expect them to be close. However the family unit (two or more people related by birth, marriage, or adoption), according to Census data, appears more stable at the low end, garnering a 30.8% share for the MAJ in contrast to the 28.3% for households (all people who occupy a housing unit regardless of relationship). In the previous graph-201, the maximum reported MAJ was customarily the Family (as opposed to Household) MAJ.

Family data is useful when studying family life alone. The spreadsheets (but not the charts here) show that prior to 1983, the family data had a MAJ that was an average 3.2 points higher than household data, consistent with the view that the family economic unit (by its binding of kinship) is stronger than a household unit of not necessarily related people. But that family advantage diminished to an average 2.4 points for the period after 1983.

---

[*] In the Table "Min Other" and "Max Other" refer to minimum and maximum for row data other than Jeanes. I emphasize in the tables and in the graphs the estimates and interpretations are mine alone and not necessarily those of the authors of the original studies. The Bureau of the Census, The Congressional Budget Office, The Federal Reserve Board, Thomas Piketty, Emmanuel Saez, and Edward N. Wolff provided source material and analysis of their own. They are not responsible for anything that appears here. Any errors here are my own. In some instances my position will conflict with the author's analysis, notwithstanding the merit of the original work.

The lowest MAJ came from Wolff's Federal Reserve work, which studied FED data since 1982. The Federal Reserve Board's (FED) Survey of Consumer Finances (SCF) tends to oversample the rich and is made available once every three years.[131] We see that Wolff's study of SCF (after my programs interpolated the data for absent years) tended to show a very low average MAJ23.5. But on the other hand, in the high range (Top5% and Top1%) his data was very close to Saez's income with capital gains. Saez's studies so far are of high income earners and do not provide MAJ data. But since Wolff and Saez are close at the top end, Wolff's study would seem to reflect a Saez-like MAJ, had Saez reported one.

I hope that this discussion reflects that data sampling favoring either the low end or the high end produces vastly different results. This is a key cause of the great differences between sources that we see in the graphs. The family-household difference is best put aside in favor of focusing on individual or household data when looking at national economics. The Jeanes data is individual (whole population) data and thus its scarcity levels will not correspond to the sampling used in Saez tax-based data.

#204

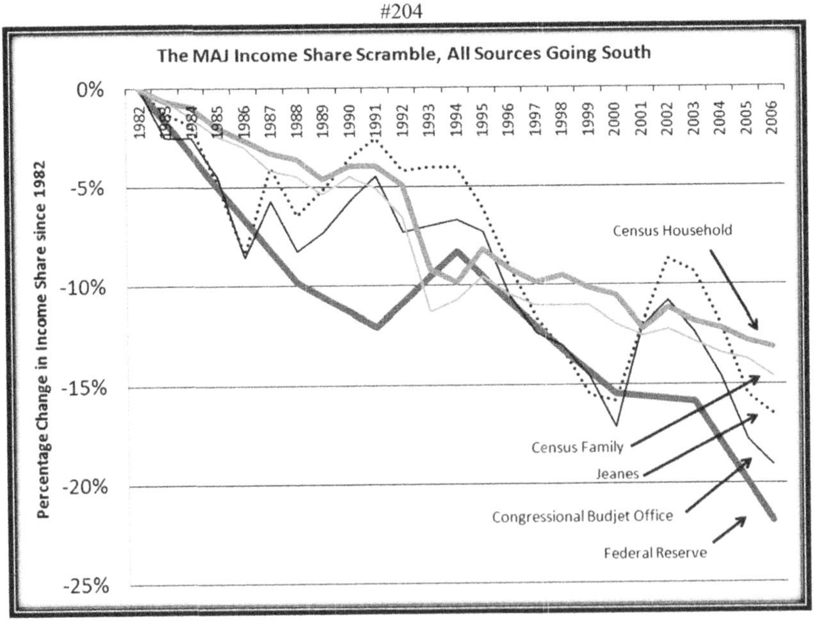

Notwithstanding the vast ranges of reported MAJs in the 1982-2006 period, there is no series that stands in opposition to the blindingly obvious reduction in MAJ share since 1982.* In the above graph-204, all sources saw MAJ income share declining, the degree of decline depending upon the source: Census Household, 13.1%; Census Family, 14.6%; Jeanes, 16.5%; Congressional Budget Office, 19.0%, and Wolff's Federal Reserve Study, 21.9%. The consensus is that there is a MAJ decline. The only debate is how great.

Congressional Budget Office. A nice balance.

My hunch is that the Congressional Budget Office (CBO) has struck a balanced position between Census Household data at the low end and Saez and Wolff's high-end data. I argue that Jeanes has set the floor. The MAJ decline is at least as great as Jeanes graph lines indicate.

#205

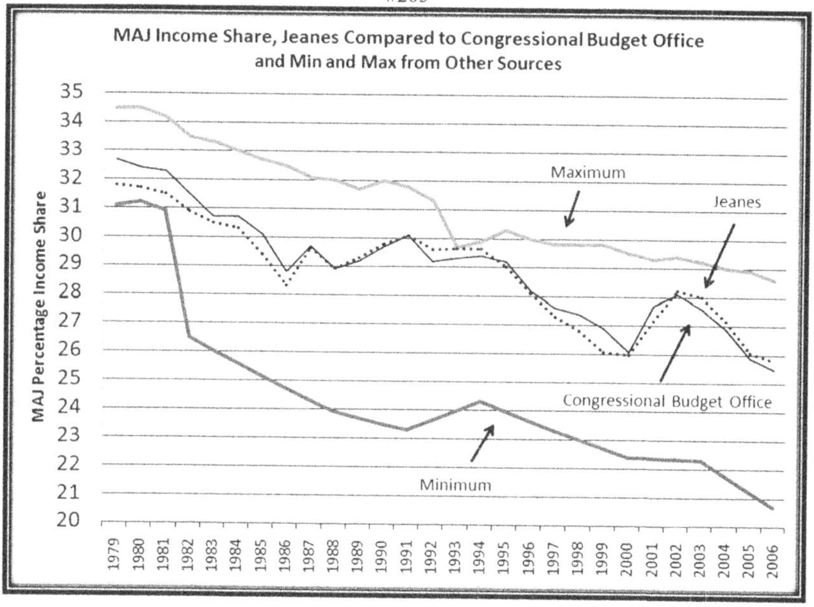

In the above graph-205, you see that my estimates of MAJ (Jeanes) are quite close to the CBO. The method I use provides a fortuitous way for estimating MAJ distributions without over sampling either high or low end data. Saez is the only source providing U.S. income-distribution data back to 1913, and there is no continuous data series from 1929 to the present other than his data. The continuous lines you see in the graphs using other data often required interpolation. At the start of my work years ago, I tried

*The starting year is 1982 because this is the first year that the Federal Reserve SCF and Wolff's data covered.

to stitch the wide variety of sources available with vastly different data to create a continuous series. The various outcomes were primitive and unreliable.

Then one day the light bulb flashed. My programs could dig into Saez data at a variety of scarcity levels to develop curves of the kind that you see in the lookup table. By this means, a continuous series of income-distribution data could be formed from 1913 to the present.[132] These curves tend to reflect the characteristics of the Congressional Budget Office MAJ data. Fortunately, the CBO provided data from 1979 to 2006. *Their MAJs ranged from 25.5-32.7, closely approximating the MAJ33 to MAJ25 transition on which the second chapter was based.* More importantly, this range was also sufficient to describe nearly all U.S. distributions since 1776, which in my estimates have ranged from 23.6-32.5.

If you find a MAJ estimate that, in your opinion, is more reliable than mine, you can readily adjust income data by methods we have already seen. Say a MAJ estimate is 32.5, but the believed true value is 33. This would require increasing estimated incomes in the MAJ by about 1.5% [1.5%= 33/32.5-1].

#206

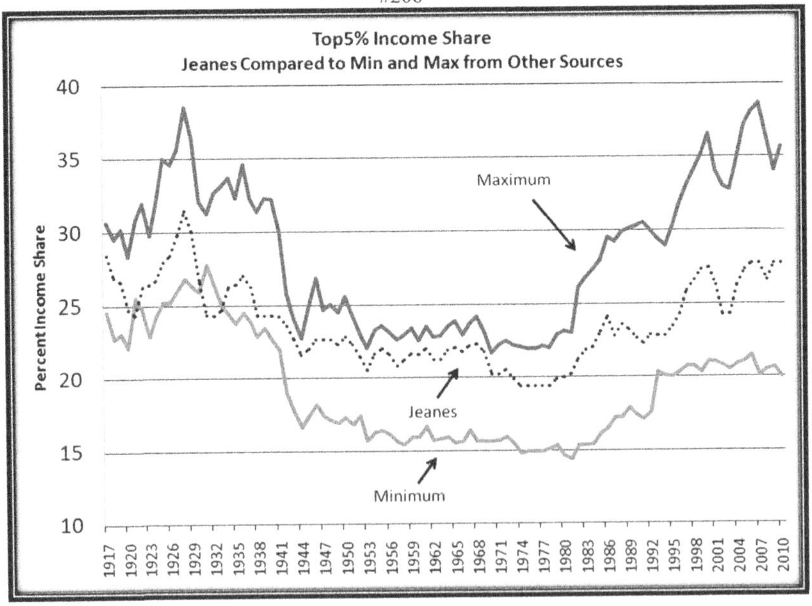

In the prior graph-206, we see that Jeanes' estimates for the Top5% income share were mainly between the minimum and maximum values from other sources back to 1917. However, unlike the close agreement between Jeanes and the Congressional Budget Office at the MAJ, Table-203 shows that at the Top5%, Jeanes' average Top5% was 24.3 while Congress showed 26.1. This 1.8% difference would result in Jeanes understating Top5% income by about 7% [1.8= 26.1-24.3; 7%= 26.1/24.3-1].

You will note that the Jeanes' MAJ estimates in the graph-201 are lower than Census data estimates, particularly from the mid 1940s to mid-1970s. But on the other hand, during the same period, Jeanes' estimates were close to maximum Top5% estimates during the same period shown in the above graph-206.

The following graph-207 of the Top1% drills deeper. Here we also see a long period where Jeanes' data is close to the maximum, but especially after the late 1980s, it is lower than all other reported data. During the 1982-2006 period, the Jeanes' Top1% was about 1.6% beneath the Congressional Budget office (Table-203). With that in mind, if you wanted to get Top1% data in the 1982-2012 period that tended to more closely conform to the Congressional Budget Office figures, you would be well advised to multiply Jeanes' Top1% incomes by 1.13 [1.6=13.6-12.0; 1.13= 13.6/12.0].

#207

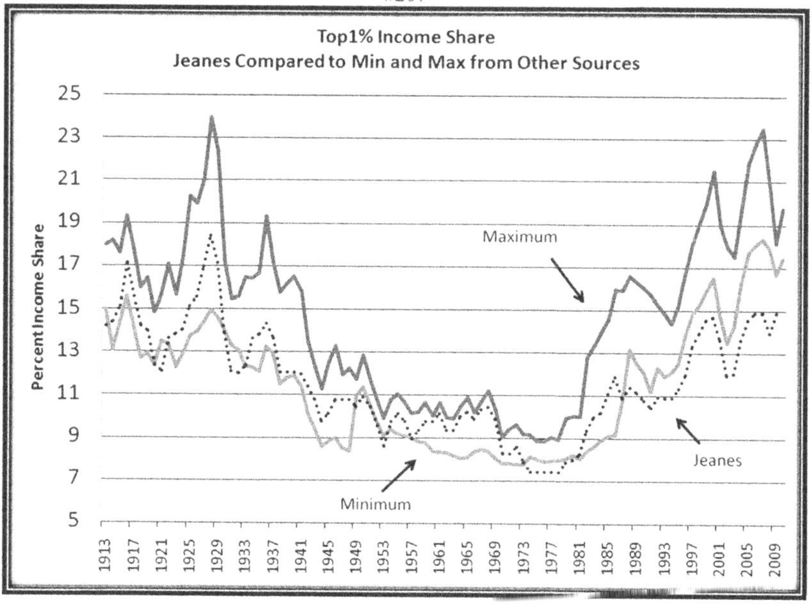

I submitted all the original data from the mentioned sources to my computer programs. They showed the following estimates for high-end incomes. The huge differences that you see in the table reflect the vast dispute that would exist if the published data were subjected to the test of rational analysis. We see that the estimates, based on Census data, would have produced a woefully low highest income (1st). It is not hard to cite a handful of CEOs who customarily earn far more than $80 million annually. And, that is before we consider the silent income that flows from vast wealth and capital appreciation. Census should have computer programs at least as good as mine. This should have been obvious to them.

#208

	Year 2006, USA	
	Top400	1st
Census Family	$6,952,228	$62,704,450
Census Household	$8,195,564	$79,516,867
Jeanes	$27,950,643	$467,228,794
Congressional Budget Office	$46,830,401	$984,357,233
Federal Reserve Based	$63,481,536	$1,527,046,409

Again, my preference is for the Congressional Budget Office data, which seems to do a credible job at the high and low end. The standard which should be met at the high end is that the threshold for the Top400 in the prior table must be accurately defined. The estimate for the highest position (1st) would of course vary from the highly variable real-world 1st.

The Jeanes' data, while it previously met the objective of satisfactorily defining the MAJ, had a low Top5% and Top1% in instances of acute maldistribution. When this portion of the backbone is understated, it greatly impacts top-end computer calculations. My programs require that the Top2% be stated with high accuracy, the Top1%, of course, having the dominant influence. Notwithstanding these observations, Jeanes and the Congressional Budget Office were nearly always within ±10% of each other prior to entering the Upper½%. You can see the degree of variation between them in the following graph-209: data from Wolff's Federal Reserve Study suggesting higher incomes than Jeanes and Congress, and Census being excessively low.

#209

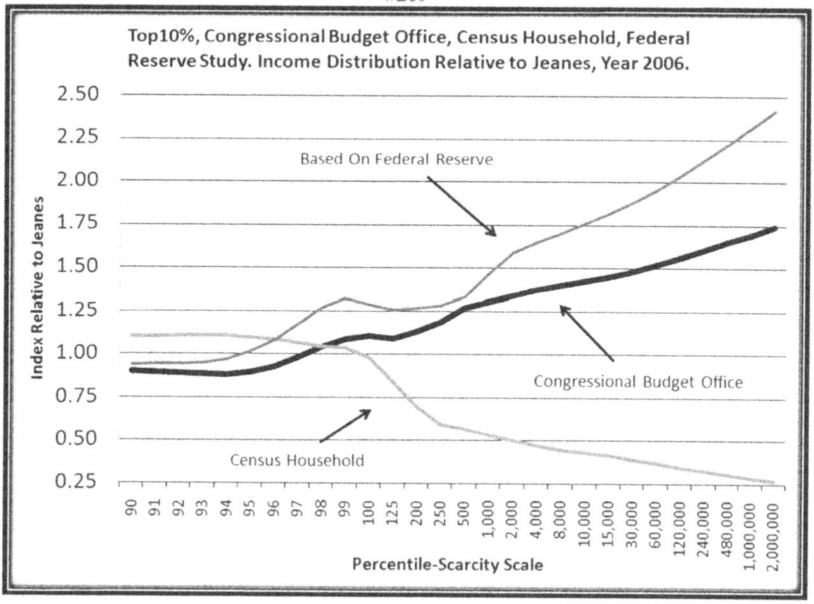

The comparison of different reports for the purpose of finding the most accurate is a risky business. Fortunately, we have an aid. The threshold wealth for the Forbes400 and Jeanes' estimated wealth for the Top400 are close. Also we know that GDP per capita adjusted for inflation grew an average 1.8% annually. And we know real inflation-adjusted bond yields because of TIPS bonds. If we look at the silent income expected from the vast fortunes in the Top400 wealth holders, we see that the estimated Top400 income/Top400 wealth would have produced the rates of return shown in the following table. The less reliable 1st position is also shown.

Average Required Inflation-Adjusted Return on Wealth Years 1982- 2006 in USA

	Top400	1st
Census Family	0.73%	0.15%
Census Household	0.88%	0.19%
Jeanes	2.57%	0.92%
Congressional Budget Office	3.28%	1.32%
Federal Reserve Based	4.81%	2.27%

As expected, Census is implausibly low. Jeanes, Congress, and Federal Reserve studies suggest rates of return higher than per capita GDP growth. Such silent income calculations combined with the list of known CEOs within the Top400 income rank may suggest to you which of the studies ultimately best define very high incomes. I do not have a definitive answer. Prior to entering the Upper½%, Jeanes and the Congressional Budget Office were nearly always within ±10% of each other. It is only after that point that substantial differences occurred.

In conclusion: If you are one of the Top1% wealthy, everything you have read so far disparaging maldistribution based on Jeanes data may have been candy-coated. The well-balanced Congressional Budget Office report seems to suggest that the Top1% is getting far higher incomes than has been shown in the previous pages. If this is so, the maldistribution problem is graver than represented within these pages.

The advantage of taking the lines of reasoning that this book has chosen is that it is operating on the safe side of the line of debate. You cannot sugar-coat an argument sufficiently to say that the rich have been unfairly treated here. To the contrary – the evidence is that within these pages, the rich have been too charitably treated.

Candy coating removed.

To be clear, the data you see here in the Appendix was not prepared by the CBO. Both Jeanes and Congressional Budget Office data were produced by my programs when given the available published public information. The difference between the two is a consequence of the initial data – not a difference in computer processing.

To the casual eye it would appear that for the bottom 99% in 2006 Jeanes and CBO were close in graph-211A. However, within the Top1% it becomes clear in graph-211B that Jeanes is significantly lower at the high end. For example, at the one-in-a-million level Jeanes shows an income 661 times larger than the average, but the CBO curve shows a much higher 1,121X$. The summary graph-212C shows the degree to which CBO and Jeanes differ throughout the range from the first percentile up through the one-in-60-million scarcity point. From the 5th to 32nd percentile and from the 51st to 97th percentile, Jeanes' estimate of income was higher than the CBO, but for all other points, especially within the Top1%, the CBO curve was usually considerably higher for the year 2006.

#211A

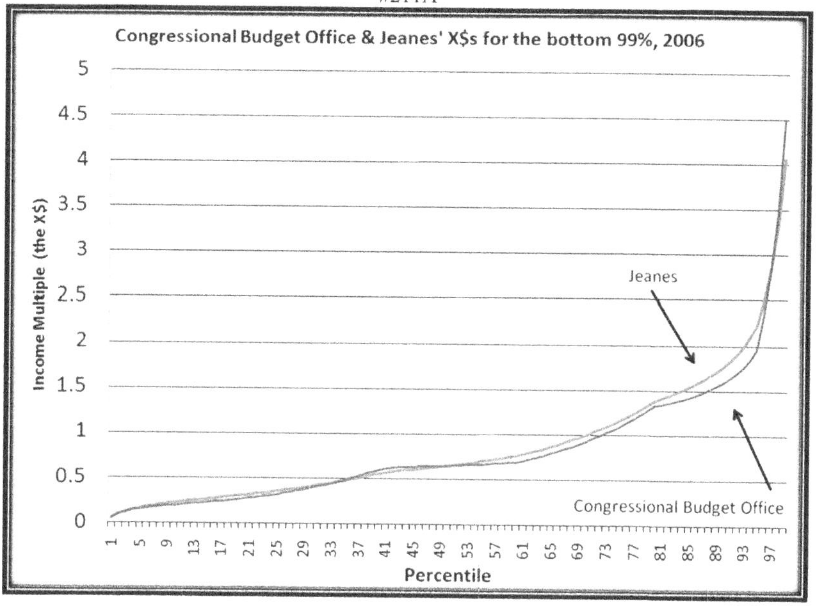
Congressional Budget Office & Jeanes' X$s for the bottom 99%, 2006
Income Multiple (the X$)
5
4.5
4
3.5
3
2.5
2
1.5
1
0.5
0
Jeanes
Congressional Budget Office
1
5
9
13
17
21
25
29
33
37
41
45
49
53
57
61
65
69
73
77
81
85
89
93
97
Percentile

#211B

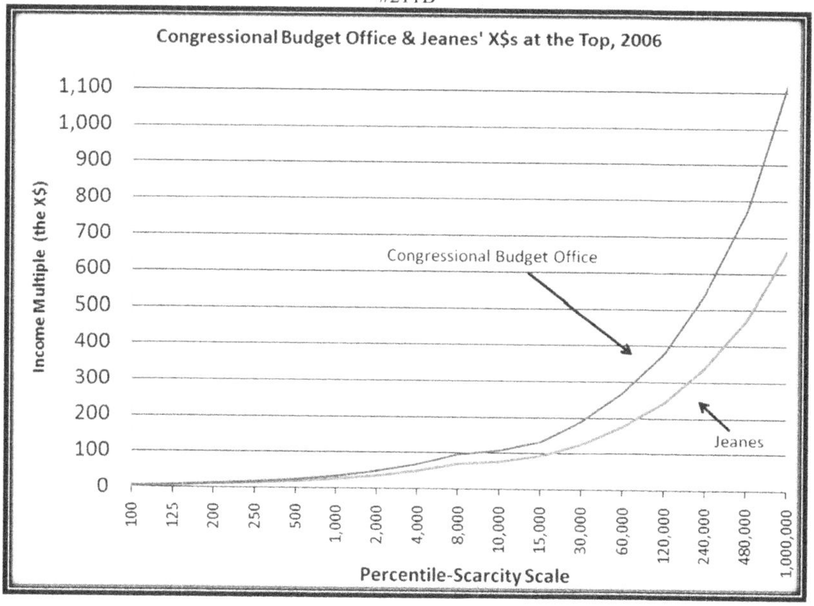
Congressional Budget Office & Jeanes' X$s at the Top, 2006
Income Multiple (the X$)
1,100
1,000
900
800
700
600
500
400
300
200
100
0
Congressional Budget Office
Jeanes
100
125
200
250
500
1,000
2,000
4,000
8,000
10,000
15,000
30,000
60,000
120,000
240,000
480,000
1,000,000
Percentile-Scarcity Scale

#212C

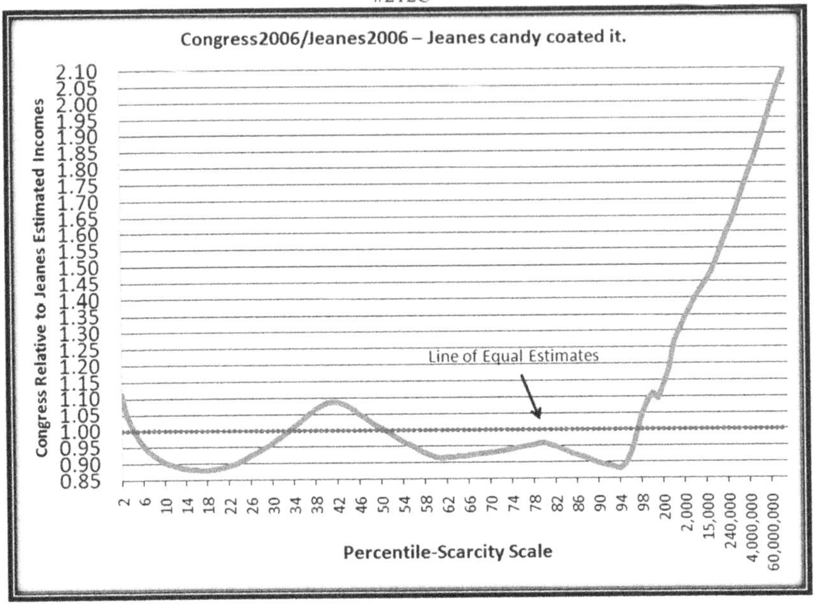

This book has been deeply concerned about the transitional impact of maldistribution. The 1979-2006 CBO data presents a more grim view than Jeanes has. While Jeanes showed a zone of indifference beneath the 92nd percentile teeter point, in graph-212A, the CBO graph line shows the teeter point at a higher point – the 96th percentile.

#212A

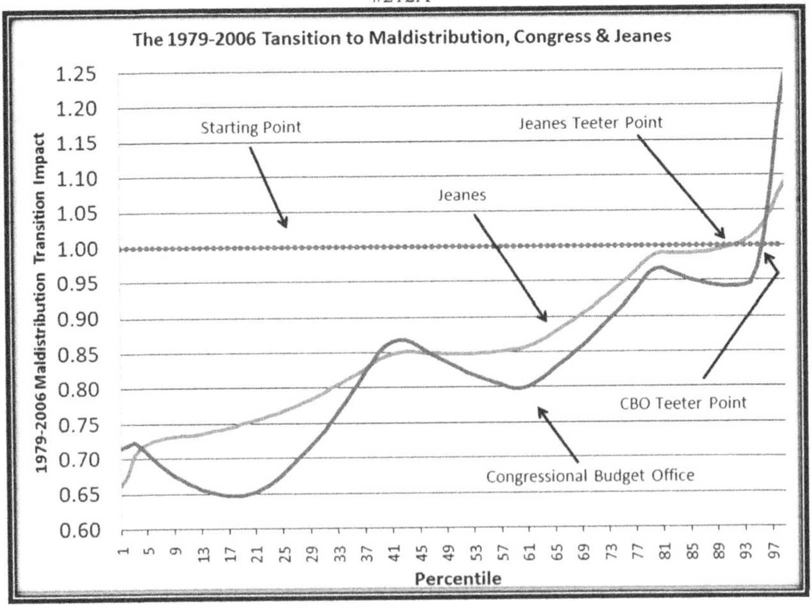

#213B

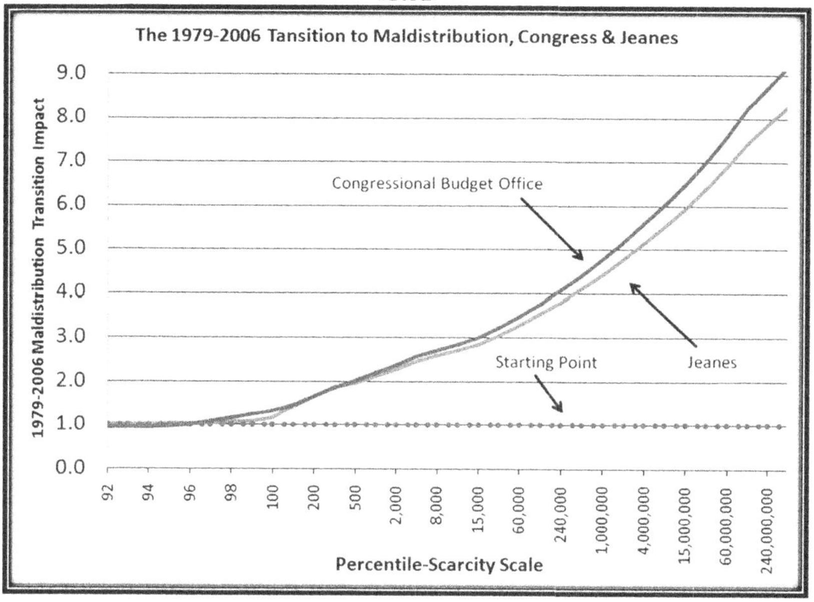

The point of flattening in the CBO graph line (comparable to the zone of indifference in Jeanes) occurs at a 5% reduction of income. To stress the point, in the CBO curve, the bottom 95% are definitive losers as a consequence of the maldistribution transition. Especially at the low end, which in better times benefited from a fair minimum wage, the maldistribution looses there were far sharper than Jeanes suggested.

At the other end of the scale: Within the Top1% in graph-213B the CBO gains at the one-in-a-million point were modestly higher than Jeanes (4.77 vs. 4.43). CBO indicates a more acute case than Jeanes, throughout the range from bottom to top. Together this suggests that reversing maldistribution is likely to be more beneficial than Jeanes suggested.

The worldwide numbers problem.

As for the Jeanes' discrepancies, they would have disappeared had the backbone been bent upward at the high end. However, the lookup table was designed to reflect income distributions worldwide, not just for the United States. The reported Top5% worldwide data available to me did not warrant further bending. The objective in the lookup table was to conform to median trend line conditions found in the worldwide historical record. The lookup table met that objective. If the curves had been further bent at the top to conform the U.S. Congressional Budget Office (CBO) data that I now have, they would have produced Ginis higher than those customarily suggested by worldwide reports. The CBO report was not available to me until October 29, 2011, after having spent years with other data sources.

My saga began with the UNU-WIDER World Income Inequality Database (WIID) which covers 159 countries, in some instances from 1960-2006.[133] When I started, I was a neophyte. I believed what I saw. A cursory computer-program examination of worldwide data revealed a few cases so implausible as to be obviously incompetently created, or to be outright fraudulent, but in the main, the data seemed ok, even after a few years of working with it. The chief objection that I have had (and continue to have) is that WIID data has not been updated since May 2008. The lethargy to update seems to reflect how low a priority nations and international institutions place on reporting income distribution and their disinterest in considering its import.

What you see before you now is a revelation that until a short while ago, I was lured like a fish, the angler being the master. I fell hard. Now I frequently suspect much income-distribution data is a lure: unpalatable and often best ignored rather than taken in a full bite. That Census so greatly misrepresented the case astounded me (and still does). Of the thousands of worldwide cases I have been studying, why should I expect other nations to be more reliable than Census has been?

Let me take yet another case in point. The most recent CIA World Factbook understated U.S. inequity. It reports a Gini of 45 for the year 2007. The Jeanes' USA Gini for 2007 is 48.9. As we have seen, the CBO provides sufficient data that my programs could construct complete curves based on its data and determine corresponding Ginis for them. In 2006, the Gini based on CBO data was 50.1. The CBO calculations I have suggest that the last time a USA Gini of 45 occurred was between 1995 and 1996 – sixteen years ago. This is for a major world power that should have ample and prompt income-distribution data available. How much more vulnerable are we to inaccurate reporting in less affluent or less able nations worldwide?

I hope you can appreciate the frustration a serious student of income distribution has. Major sources report implausible data. You start your work believing the data. Then you find it to be wrong. In such shifting sands, building a stable edifice is indeed challenging. My approach was to have my programs ride Saez stable tax-based data, but to do so in a way designed to generally reflect Congressional Budget Office MAJ reports. I believe that technique provides the best method for assessing distribution from bottom to top for a major swath of U.S. history.

There is a danger of my getting into excessive minutia. I am making the curves I developed from Census Family, Census Household, Jeanes, Congressional Budget Office, and Wolff's Federal Reserve data available in the spreadsheets so that you can consider them there.

I hope that people from a variety of disciplines will put income distribution under the microscope. There is no justification now for advancing a dogma – mine or anyone else's. Richard Feynman's principle comes to mind, "You must not fool yourself – and you are the easiest person to fool." Along the same lines, Jason Zweig nicely commented, "Remember that the smarter you are, the more easily you can fool yourself," and similarly, he points out that the more vehemently you ridicule a competing idea, the more likely you yourself are wrong.[134] If the subject comes under enough eyes, soon enough we should be able to be broadly confident that the prevailing data will be reliable.

Too little is now known. Too few methods have been tried. Being mindful of the great work done in high-end digital cameras, weather forecasting, medical technology, and in understanding and manipulating images, it seems that, in a wiki way, we can get to a better place than where we now are. With a new consensus, income-distribution analysis can become as easy and reliable as point-and-shoot photography. We all will be better off for it. Our economies will not function optimally otherwise.

Although it is quick and to the point, I can't tell you how weird it felt to use the third person ("Jeanes") in the above graphs and discussion. Try it yourself "Smith," "Jones," "Bernanke," or whatever name your parents or spouse saddled you with.

INDEX

B

C

D

E

F

G

H

I

N

O

P

Q

R

S

T

U

V

W

X

Y

Z

ENDNOTES

---

[1] For Colonial Economic History and distributions see: P. H. Lindert and J. G. Williamson, "America's Revolution: Economic Disaster, Development, and Equality," *VOX*. VoxEU, http://www.VoxEU.org/index.php?q=node/6751 .

[2] Spreadsheets are downloadable at Dilives: http://www.Dilives.com .

[3] This applies to the graphs. Tables may not be published without the publisher's consent. They are often in context with the text and subject to misinterpretation when that context is removed. Please note that the book is copyrighted. Making graphs available shall not be interpreted as reducing copyright protection.

[4] See USA spreadsheets at Dilives.com.

[5] Nations widely report GDP, thus it is a readily available standard that can be used as a base for X$ calculations. The calculations use GDP per capita, multiply it by the X$, and call the outcome income. More precisely, it is approximately the GDP contribution made at the point. And, in my view, that is the most important component. How much a person is able to contribute to the enterprise that we call the economy. To the extent that it is different from income received, the user can usually find a point on the curve that does match their current income and then view in the lookup table how that income changes as distributions changes. (An ancillary concern: How much those at the bottom receive on the dole is often a consequence of a dysfunctional economy that fails to integrate those at the bottom into the working economy.)

[6] A generation is the average time between a mother's first offspring and her daughter's first offspring – 30 years in Germany, 25 years in the U.S., and fewer years in most poor countries. This book will use 26 years as a standard when referring to a generation, with the understanding that different generational lengths exist. Indeed, lengths vary between the states in the U.S. and over time. The more backward states in the U.S. often show low generational years and only slight increases over time. See Wikipedia title "Generation" and its references.

[7] William Lazonick and Mary O'Sullivan, "Maximizing Shareholder Value: A New Ideology For Corporate Governance." *Economy and Society,* 29, no. 1 (2000), 29.

[8] For a lively view of maldistribution enthusiasts see Jacob S. Hacker, Paul Pierson, *Winner-Take-All Politics: How Washington Made the Rich Richer – And Turned Its Back on the Middle Class*, (New York: Simon & Schuster, 2010).

[9] "Vilfredo Pareto," Wikipedia, http://en.wikipedia.org/wiki/Vilfredo_Pareto ; "Pareto distribution," Wikipedia, http://en.wikipedia.org/wiki/Pareto_distribution .

[10] The Gini Index, as commonly used, is a theoretical number, which when divided by 100, ranges from zero to 1. It reflects the gradation between two outcomes: Zero is equivalent to everyone having equal incomes. A value of one indicates all the national income is going to a single person.

[11] Thomas Piketty and Emmanuel Saez, "Income Inequality in the United States, 1913–1998," *Quarterly Journal of Economics*, 118, no 1 (2003), 1-39; A. B. Atkinson and Francois Bourguignon, *Handbook of Income Distribution* Volume 1 (Amsterdam: Elsevier North Holland, 2007); Thomas Piketty and Emmanuel Saez, "Income and Wage Inequality in the United States 1913-2002" in A. B. Atkinson and T. Piketty, *Top Incomes over the Twentieth Century. A Contrast Between Continental European and English-Speaking Countries*, Chapter 5, (Oxford University Press, 2007); "The World Top Incomes Database," http://g-

mond.parisschoolofeconomics.eu/topincomes/ ; see additional material at Emmanuel Saez homepage: http://elsa.berkeley.edu/~saez/ .

[12] Daniel Kahneman and Angus Deaton, "High Income Improves Evaluation of Life but Not Emotional Well-being." *PNAS,* 107, no. 38 (2010).

[13] Christopher Hayes illustrated the transformation from meritocracy to oligarchy in *Twilight of the Elites.* He remarks on page 155, "[Extreme inequality] makes elites less accountable, more prone to corruption and self-dealing, more status-obsessed and less empathetic, more blinkered and removed from informational feedback crucial to effective decision-making. For this reason, extreme inequality produces elites who are less competent and more corrupt than those in a more egalitarian social order ..."

[14] *Scottsboro: An American Tragedy*, DVD, directed by Barak Goodman and Daniel Anker (PBS, 2005).

[15] *Naturalist E. O. Wilson - Lord of the Ants*, DVD, directed by David Dugan (PBS, 2008).

[16] "Gini coefficient," Wikipedia, http://en.wikipedia.org/wiki/Gini_coefficient .

[17] For a quick approximation within the MAJ33 to MAJ25 range, the following formula is often within a tenth of a MAJ value in the 400 case lookup table: Gini*-0.6687+58.506=MAJ.

[18] UNU-WIDER, WIID2C.xls Download, http://www.wider.unu.edu/research/Database/en_GB/wiid/ ; http://www.wider.unu.edu/research/Database/en_GB/wiid/_files/79789834673192984/default/WIID2C.xls .

[19] A pleasant exception is that the US Congressional Budget Office is now reporting the Top1%. It is reporting with greater accuracy than prior U.S. government reports. http://www.cbo.gov/publications/collections/tax .

[20] P. H. Lindert t and J. G. Williamson, "America's Revolution: Economic Disaster, Development, and Equality," *VOX.* VoxEU, http://www.VoxEU.org/index.php?q=node/6751 .

[21] Joseph E. Stiglitz, *The Price of Inequality,* (New York: W.W. Norton & Co., 2012), 126-127.

[22] P. H. Lindert, "Three Centuries of Inequality in Britain and America" , in *Handbook of Income Distribution*, ed. A. B. Atkinson and Francois Bourguignon, *Handbook of Income Distribution* Volume 1 (Amsterdam: Elsevier North Holland, 2007), 175.

[23] For wealth data, I rely mainly on four sources:
1) Table 1 and 2 in Working Paper No. 589 in Edward N. Wolff, "Recent Trends in Household Wealth in the United States: Rising Debt and the Middle-Class Squeeze— an Update to 2007" (March 2010). *Levy Economics Institute Working Papers Series No. 159.* SSRN.
2) Tables 1 and 3 in James B. Davies and others, "The World Distribution of Household Wealth," (November 2007). http://escholarship.org/uc/item/3jv048hx .
3) particularly Table 3 in *Handbook of Income Distribution*, ed. A. B. Atkinson and Francois Bourguignon, *Handbook of Income Distribution* Volume 1 (Amsterdam: Elsevier North Holland, 2007), 188.
4) "World Distribution of Wealth," Wikipedia, http://en.wikipedia.org/wiki/World_distribution_of_wealth .

[24] Technicians should note that great variability exists in the IncomeMAJ and Wealth-MAJ relationship. A somewhat tighter relationship exists at the Top1% income and wealth shares.

---

[25] Michael Kumhof and Romain Rancière, "Inequality, Leverage and Crises" , IMF Working Paper, WP/10/268, November 2010, www.imf.org/external/pubs/ft/wp/2010/wp10268.pdf .

[26] See Table 2 -- 3rd and "bottom" columns – in Working Paper No. 589 in Edward N. Wolff, "Recent Trends in Household Wealth in the United States: Rising Debt and the Middle-Class Squeeze — an Update to 2007" (March 2010). *Levy Economics Institute Working Papers Series No. 159.* SSRN.

[27] The seemingly irregular moves beneath the 40th percentile are, in part, a consequence of this group having so little wealth that any change has the capacity to produce unexpected results.

[28] The ratio can be derived by dividing "Net worth of households and nonprofit organizations" by GDP as given in the Federal Reserve Flow of Funds Accounts of the United States. The ratio should not be confused with the ratio of household net worth to disposable personal income reported by the US Bureau of Economic Analysis at: http://www.bea.gov/national/nipaweb/Nipa-Frb.asp .

[29] Robert J. Shiller, *Irrational Exuberance* (New York: Broadway Books, 2000 and 2005, updated). Home page: http://www.irrationalexuberance.com/
http://www.econ.yale.edu/~shiller/data/ie_data.xls (S&P500 data)
http://www.econ.yale.edu/~shiller/data/Fig2-1.xls (Housing market data)

[30] "Home Price and Income Ratio Chart," Seeking Alpha, http://seekingalpha.com/article/117085-home-price-and-income-ratio-chart .

[31] If liar's loans strike you as excessive, there were worse. Consider Christopher Hayes' report in *Twilight of the Elites*, p. 95: "As the housing bubble expanded, Countrywide maintained its competitive edge by pushing suicidally dangerous products like a mortgage that would – get this – allow borrowers to choose how much they would pay every month, adding the unpaid balance to their principal." As Hayes reports, the CEO got a $22.1 million compensation plus $121.5 million by exercising stock options; and (p.97) between 2001 and 2006 he received $470 million total compensation.

[32] Bill Moyers' Journal. *Watch & Listen*, PBS Apr 3, 2009 – William K. Black interview. Video (Liar's Loans): http://www.pbs.org/moyers/journal/04032009/watch.html ; YouTube also has numerous liar loan videos; see "Stated income loan," Wikipedia, http://en.wikipedia.org/wiki/Stated_income_loan . A leading rating agency even went so far as to have a state law prohibiting reckless and predatory mortgage failures overturned. See Stiglitz, *The Price of Inequality*, 192. Charles Ferguson, *Predator Nation: Corporate Criminals, Political Corruption, and the Hijacking of America*, (New York: Crown Business, 2012), 58-59.

[33] The graph is based on data from "World Distribution of Wealth" at http://en.wikipedia.org/wiki/World_distribution_of_wealth .

[34] Natalie Minnis, *Insight Guides: South America,* (London: Langenscheidt Publishing Group, 2003), 174.

[35] Michael Lewis, "Princeton Baccalaureate 2012 Michael Lewis," YouTube, http://www.youtube.com/watch?v=CiQ_T5C3hIM&list=UUcBYSgQTxc126-Ij_gdrO8Q&index=1&feature=plcp

[36] Stiglitz, *The Price of Inequality,* 243. Similarly, James Galbraith points out in *Inequality and Instability*, (Oxford University Press, 2012), 4: "In the classification system of the *Journal of Economic Literature* there was (and is) no category for work relating inequality to the financial system. In other words, both inequality and financial instability were large-

ly blank spots in dominant theory; neither concept was important to mainstream economics, and the relationship between them was not even thought of." And on page 5: "[The] study of inequality was divorced, entirely from the study of economic dynamics, and it therefore posed no challenge to the dominant doctrines."

[37] Internet searches: "FORTUNE 500 2007 Top Companies - Biggest Companies By Employees"; "Global 500 2008 Top Performers – Biggest Companies Employees"; "World's Largest Companies – World's Largest Companies by Employees"; "Blue Chip Largest Company List."

[38] Derived from: Tom Hertz, "Rags, Riches, and Race, The Intergenerational Economic Mobility of Black and White Families in the United States," in *Unequal Chances, Family Background and Economic Success* , ed. Samuel Bowles, Herbert Gintis, and Melissa Osborne Groves, (New Jersey: Princeton University Press, 2005), 186. Table 5.10 Decile Transition Matrix for the Pooled Income Distribution.

[39] Hertz, 186.

[40] See endnote #29.

[41] "Uncle Tom's Cabin," Wikipedia, http://en.wikipedia.org/wiki/Uncle_Tom%27s_Cabin . Simon Legree is the cruel slave owner character in *Uncle Tom's Cabin*.

[42] U.S. Department of Labor data normalized to 1977.

[43] "Elo rating system," Wikipedia, http://en.wikipedia.org/wiki/Elo_rating_system ; USCF Ratings Distribution Charts, http://archive.uschess.org/ratings/ratedist.php .

[44] Wikipedia's "Intelligence quotient" page is also a good reference.

[45] Christopher Hayes, "Why Elites Fail," *The Nation*, June 25, 2012, http://www.thenation.com/article/168265/why-elites ; Christopher Hayes, *Twilight of the Elites: America After Meritocracy*, (Crown, 2012).

[46] Nicholas Lemann, *The Big Test: The Secret History of the American Meritocracy*, (New York: Farrar, Straus and Giroux, 2000), 118.

[47] Michael Young, *The Rise of the Meritocracy*, (Transaction Publishers, 1999). 95.

[48] Young, 84.

[49] Judith Selvidge, "A Three-step Procedure for Assigning Probabilities to Rare Events," in *Utility, Probability, and Human Decision Making Vol. 11*, ed. Dirk Wendt and Charles Vlek, (Dordrecht: D. Reidel Publishing Company, 1975), 205.

[50] Albert Einstein, *Ideas and Opinions*, (New York: Crown Publishers, 1963), 4.

[51] Malcolm Gladwell, *Outliers*, (New York: Little, Brown and Co., 2008), 79.

[52] Jay L. Zagorsky, "Do You Have to Be Smart to Be Rich? The Impact of IQ on Wealth, Income and Financial Distress." *Intelligence* 35, no. 5 (2007), 489-501. Table 2, p. 495, with IQ 105 values removed, because of inconsistencies. Curves developed using interpolated IQ-income and IQ- wealth values mapped to known IQ percentile relationships. See Zagorsky's Fig. 1 and 2 scatter plots for income and net worth.

[53] A distribution close to the known points was located in the lookup table, MAJ49. For those points not available to me beneath the 6th percentile I employed points that were in the same fractional relationship with MAJ49 as was the last available data point. Then the adjustment at the top discussed in the previous paragraph was used.

[54] In a different context, Richard Lynn and Tatu Vanhanen, *IQ and Global Inequality*, (Augusta, Ga.: Washington Summit Publishers, 2006), 195-198, observe: "National IQ seems to explain quite well the relatively low level of income inequality in nearly all economically developed market economies and democracies."

---

[55] At the indicated page numbers in approximate sequence, all Kaiser references can be found in: Albert Heiner, *Henry J. Kaiser Western Colossus*, (San Francisco: Halo Books, 1991), 86, 128, 118, 152, 1, 135, 43, 203, 204, 77, 78, 82, 96.

[56] Please see above note for page numbers that apply to the foregoing quotations.

[57] Starting with "honor begets honor" are the words of Henry L. Stimson, *On Active Service in Peace and War*, (New York: Harper, 1948), 671-672. (paraphrased in some instances).

[58] Jared Diamond, *Collapse: How Societies Choose to Fail or Succeed*, (New York: Viking Penguin, 2005), 167-70.

[59] Long Island News, Homeless Science Whiz Gets a Home, ABC 7. Intel semifinalist; and Newsday, "Intel Semifinalist: Samantha Garvey of Brentwood High School," YouTube, http://www.youtube.com/watch?v=-UjX6OKWF2c .

[60] U.S. Bureau of Labor Statistics, Characteristics of Minimum Wage Workers: 2010; also Wage and Hour Division, History of Federal Minimum Wage Rates Under the Fair Labor Standards Act, 1938-2009.

[61] We have long known that de-unionization contributed to inequality, e.g., Sheldon Danziger and Peter Gottschalk, *Uneven Tides Rising Inequality in America*, (New York: Russell Sage Foundation, 1993),134

[62] "Poverty threshold," Wikipedia, http://en.wikipedia.org/wiki/Poverty_threshold . 15.1% of the population in 2010. 0.264 is the corresponding X$ in the accompanying USA spreadsheet.

[63] An aside: A pure transfer of 1.26% of the GDP to the damaged citizens at the low end at zero transaction costs would have erred on the side of excessive optimism. And an overestimate of the initial transfer (based on 0.3 of the average income, rather than the 0.264 poverty threshold) is offset by an underestimate of ancillary costs at the 0.3 threshold.

[64] Richard Wilkinson and Kate Pickett, *The Spirit Level: Why Equality is Better for Everyone,* (Penguin Books, 2010).

[65] Stiglitz, *The Price of Inequality*, 164.

[66] Robert D. Hare, *Without Conscience: The Disturbing World of the Psychopaths Among Us*, (New York: The Guilford Press, 1999). Jon Ronson, *The Psychopath Test: A Journey Through the Madness Industry,* (New York: Riverhead Books, 2011). Martha Stout, *The Sociopath Next Door,* (New York: Broadway Books, 2006). On page 6 and related endnote, she indicates that 4% of the USA population are sociopaths. More positively on page 136 and endnote, she shows a 0.03% to 0.14% rate for Taiwan; and relatively rare occurrences for certain East Asian nations, such as Japan and China. Paul J. Zak, *Moral Markets: The Critical Role of Values in the Economy*, (Princeton: Princeton University Press, 2008), 268. Oxytocin released in the brain influences moral behavior. Zak suggests that about 2% of subjects did not have a normal response and that this was roughly the proportion of sociopaths in the population.

[67] A deeper analysis of honesty can be found in Dan Ariely, "Why We Lie," *Wall Street Journal*, (May 26-27, 2012), C1.

[68] David Schwab and Elinor Ostrom, "The Vital Role of Norms and Rules in Maintaining Open Public and Private Economies"; Oliver Goodenough, "Values, Mechanism Design, and Fairness" in Paul Zak, *Moral Markets*, 204,247, 270. Schwab: Observe that in the former Soviet Union many policy analysts expected that rapid development would occur with

privatization and free market institutions. This did not happen. The influence norms were underestimated. Goodenough : High policing costs depress overall productivity.

[69] At 41 minutes 30 seconds into "The Corporation," DVD, directed by Mark Achbar and Jennifer Abbot (2003); Milton Friedman. http://hellocoolworld.com/files/TheCorporation/Friedman.pdf . Also see Stewart Lansley, *The Cost of Inequality: Why Economic Equality is Essential for Recovery*, p.32, Kindle location 522-31: Friedman, "Few trends could so thoroughly undermine the very foundations of our free society as the acceptance by corporate officials of a social responsibility other than to make as much money for their stockholders as possible."

[70] Paul Zak, *Moral Markets.* See Lynn A. Stout, "Taking Conscience Seriously" p157-172.

[71] Laura Feiveson, "Seven Questions about Income Inequality," *IMF Research Bulletin*, Volume 13, Number 2 June 2012, Figure 2: Trends in Income Inequality in OECD Countries, Mid-1980s to Mid-2000s, p.7, www.imf.org/researchbulletin , http://www.imf.org/External/Pubs/FT/irb/2012/02/index.pdf .

[72] Further, many nations are tempted to measure economic success by the number of billionaires that they produce. Yet, nations can ill afford to have many of them, because as we have seen MAJ income tends to stagnate or to move southerly when billionaires proliferate. A vastly wealthy elite also poses an often un recognized operational problem for nations. Their super rich have a propensity to move wealth "offshore" where it cannot be taxed -- taxation lost to often underfunded governments. "Offshore" activity is usually hidden and difficult to measure. In" Wealth doesn't trickle down – it just floods offshore, research reveals," guardian.co.uk, July 21, 2012, (http://www.guardian.co.uk/business/2012/jul/21/offshore-wealth-global-economy-tax-havens) , Heather Stewart reports: "The world's super-rich have taken advantage of lax tax rules to siphon off at least $21 trillion, and possibly as much as $32tn, from their home countries and hide it abroad – a sum larger than the entire American economy." Her report relies on James S. Henry, "The Price of Offshore Revisited," http://www.taxjustice.net/cms/upload/pdf/Price_of_Offshore_Revisited_120722.pdf .

[73] "America the Beautiful," Wikipedia, http://en.wikipedia.org/wiki/America_the_Beautiful .

[74] Jeffrey D. Sachs, Andrew D. Mellinger and John L. Gallup, "The Geography of Poverty and Wealth," *Scientific American*, March 2001, 73.

[75] National Oceanic and Atmospheric Administration, "Over half of the American population lives within 50 miles of the coast," http://oceanservice.noaa.gov/facts/population.html . As NOAA states, "The narrow fringe comprising 17 percent of the contiguous U.S. land area is home to more than half of the nation's population."

[76] "Parasitic worm," Wikipedia, http://en.wikipedia.org/wiki/Parasitic_worm .

[77] A small point: The first child is not always female. Instead of a generation being defined as the mother's age at birth of first offspring, if 26 years is defined as the mother's average age at the birth of the first female child, then this example holds.

[78] "List of countries by Failed States Index" Wikipedia, http://en.wikipedia.org/wiki/List_of_countries_by_Failed_States_Index . An informative interactive map is available at: http://www.foreignpolicy.com/failed_states_index_2012_interactive .

[79] The sort key for the table double weights present population growth and single weights trend-line expected population growth rates for 2030. The objective is not to pre-

dict a particular growth rate, but to illustrate the degree of movement that could occur if recent growth patterns are perpetuated.

[80] Leslie A. White, *The Evolution of Culture: The Development of Civilization to the Fall of Rome*, (New York: McGraw-Hill, 1959), 41.

[81] "Industrial Revolution" Wikipedia, http://en.wikipedia.org/wiki/First_Industrial_Revolution ; "Steam engine" Wikipedia, http://en.wikipedia.org/wiki/Steam_engine ; "Second Industrial Revolution" Wikipedia, http://en.wikipedia.org/wiki/Second_Industrial_Revolution ; "Watermill," Wikipedia, http://en.wikipedia.org/wiki/Watermill ; "Windmill" Wikipedia, http://en.wikipedia.org/wiki/Windmill .

[82] "White's Law," Wikipedia, http://en.wikipedia.org/wiki/White%27s_Law .

[83] "Olduvai theory" Wikipedia, http://en.wikipedia.org/wiki/Olduvai_theory ; Richard C. Duncan, "Peak Oil, Total Collapse, and the Road to the Olduvai," http://www.oilcrash.com/articles/arnett05.htm .

[84] "List of apologies by Pope John Paul II," Wikipedia, http://en.wikipedia.org/wiki/Apologies_by_pope_john_paul_ii .

[85] http://www.fundforpeace.org/global/library/cfsir1210-failedstatesindex2012-06p.pdf ;

http://www.foreignpolicy.com/failed_states_index_2012_interactive ;

http://www.fundforpeace.org/global/?q=fsi-grid2012 ;

http://www.fundforpeace.org/global/library/cfsis1201-fsi-spreadsheet177-public-06a.xls ;

http://www.fundforpeace.org/global/?q=cfsir1210 .

Note that I pared the list down from 179 nations to 151 matching nations in the Modernity Timeline. The key reason that the Modernity Timeline has fewer nations is because for some nations, income distribution data was unavailable.

[86] Note the points that are raised at about 11, 15, 17, and 21 minutes into the video. "Sir David Attenborough: People and Planet," http://www.youtube.com/watch?v=1sP291B7SCw .

[87] "America the Beautiful," Wikipedia, http://en.wikipedia.org/wiki/America_the_Beautiful .

[88] Matt McGrath, "Global weight gain more damaging than rising numbers," BBC, June 17, 2012.

[89] Sarah C Walpole, David Prieto-Merino, Phil Edwards, John Cleland, Gretchen Stevens, and Ian Roberts, "The weight of nations: an estimation of adult human biomass," *BMC Public Health* 2012, 12:439 doi:10.1186/1471-2458-12-439, June 18, 2012, http://www.biomedcentral.com/1471-2458/12/439 .

[90] Based on data in Jules Janick, "New Crops and the Search for New Food Resources," http://www.hort.purdue.edu/newcrop/proceedings1999/v4-104.html .

[91] "Cotton," Wikipedia, http://en.wikipedia.org/wiki/Cotton .

[92] An American football field is 100 yards long (goal line to goal line) and 53.33 yards wide. Observe that a yard is only slightly shorter than a meter and that a hectare is 100 x 100 meters. You can convert a hectare to square American football field by multiplying hectares by 0.836132404. By way of reference, a soccer field is 100 yards long and 60 yards wide.

[93] Jared Diamond, *Collapse*, 319-24.

[94] David Montgomery, *Dirt: The Erosion of Civilizations*, (University of California Press, 2007), 174, 182.

[95] Montgomery, 23.

[96] Tim De Chant, "Income inequality, as seen from space," May 24, 2012, http://persquaremile.com/2012/05/24/income-inequality-seen-from-space/ ; P. Zhu and Y. Zhang, "Demand for urban forests in United States cities" *Landscape and Urban Planning*, 84, No. 3-4, 2008, 293-300.

[97] Montgomery, 5.

[98] Montgomery, 119.

[99] Montgomery, 138.

[100] Based on http://data.worldbank.org/indicator/AG.LND.ARBL.HA.PC .

[101] Michael Wood, Iraq: The Cradle of Civilization (DVD, 1991), starting at the 10 minute point, http://www.youtube.com/watch?feature=player_embedded&v=NXohegE-lBY&list=PLFD498432C7808DF8# ; also see Montgomery, *Dirt*, 37-39 for Uruk's history of soil salinization and degradation.

[102] "Brown Bullion - What's Your Topsoil Worth?" http://www.mo.nrcs.usda.gov/news/pubs_download/brownbullion.html .

[103] Rigoberta Menchú, Nobel Peace Prize Laureate, 2 minutes into "When the Mountains Tremble," (Skylight Pictures, DVD, 1983).

[104] Wendell Berry's essay: "Conservation and Local Economy," 1991. Also see his YouTube appearances (e.g. YouTube - Wendell Berry a rare reading session), and start at 11 minutes: http://events.tvworldwide.com/Events/NEH2012JeffersonLecture.aspx?VID=events/neh/120423_NEH_Jefferson_Lecture_KennedyCtr.flv&Cap=events/neh/120423_NEH_Jefferson_Lecture_KennedyCtr.xml .

[105] Charles A.S. Hall, "Look What's Happening to Our Earth," *Bulletin of Atomic Scientists*, March 1975, 13. Also: J. F. Parr and S. B. Hornick, "Recent Developments in Alternative Agriculture in the United States," U.S Department of Agriculture, Agricultural Research Service, Beltsville, Maryland, http://www.infrc.or.jp/english/KNF_Data_Base_Web/PDF%20KNF%20Conf%20Data/C1-4-014.pdf .

[106] Dale Allen Pfeiffer, "Eating Fossil Fuels," http://www.fromthewilderness.com/free/ww3/100303_eating_oil.html

[107] Pfeiffer, "Eating Fossil Fuels," http://www.fromthewilderness.com/free/ww3/100303_eating_oil.html ; Mario Giampietro and David Pimentel, "The Tightening Conflict: Population, Energy Use, and the Ecology of Agriculture," (1994), http://www.dieoff.com/page69.htm ; Richard Manning, "The oil we eat: Following the food chain back to Iraq," http://www.harpers.org/archive/2004 .

[108] Montgomery, *Dirt*, 200.

[109] Michael Pollan, *Omnivore's Dilemma*, (New York, Penguin Books, 2006), 123-273.

[110] Montgomery, *Dirt*, 181.

[111] Montgomery, 41-3.

[112] Montgomery, 142-3, 242.

[113] Montgomery, 80.

[114] Montgomery, 222-3

[115] Montgomery, 179.

[116] Montgomery, 93.

---

[117] "Marginalism," Wikipedia, http://en.wikipedia.org/wiki/Marginalism ; "Neoclassical economics," Wikipedia, http://en.wikipedia.org/wiki/Neoclassical_economics ; "Alfred Marshall," Wikipedia, http://en.wikipedia.org/wiki/Alfred_Marshall.

[118] Yes, iniquity (not inequity) is intentional here. We are referring to wickedness, evil, injustice, et cetera.

[119] Explicitly a high marginal taxation did not prevent innovation or high income earners. David Halberstam's *The Fifties*, (New York: Villard Books, 1993), 116-179, gives a fun read of business movers and shakers.

[120] Thomas E. Mann and Norman J. Ornstein, "Let's just say it: The Republicans are the problem," *The Washington Post*, April 27, 2012, http://www.washingtonpost.com/opinions/lets-just-say-it-the-republicans-are-the-problem/2012/04/27/gIQAxCVUIT_story.html .

[121] James K. Galbraith, *Inequality and Instability: A Study of the World Economy Just Before the Great Crisis*, 147.

[122] James Madison, *The Federalist No. 10, The Utility of the Union as a Safeguard Against Domestic Faction and Insurrection (continued)*, Daily Advertiser, November 22, 1787, http://www.constitution.org/fed/federa10.htm .

[123] The original story by Dietrich Fischer goes like this:

A professor of management gave a lecture on time management. He filled a mason jar with a dozen fist-sized rocks, until no more would fit. He asked his students,

"Is this jar full?" and all shouted "Yes!"

Then he took some gravel from under the desk to fill the empty spaces and asked again, "Is it full now?"

Some said, "probably not."

He filled the space between the gravel with sand, and finally poured water into the jar to the brim.

"What is the lesson of this?" he asked.

A student answered, "No matter how full your schedule is, if you try really hard, you can always fit one more thing into it."

The professor replied, "No, the main lesson is that unless you put the big rocks in first, you'll never get them in at all."

What are the "big rocks" in our life?

[124] Just as this book was going to the printer, I saw this reference that may also interest students in the field: Leonard E. Burman, Robert J. Shiller, Gregory Leiserson, Jeffrey Rohaly, "The Rising Tide Tax System: Indexing the Tax System for Changes in Inequality." (March 8, 2007), http://newfinancialorder.com/burman-nyu-030807.pdf .

[125] Even in highly profitable times, the financial sector, under its own roof, provides few jobs and often cuts those they do have. For example, in the UK Lansley observes, "Despite its growing importance in the economy, financial services has hardly generated any net new jobs in the last thirty years. ... [Their employment] fell by 17,000 during the boom years of 2000 to 2007." Stewart Lansley, *The Cost of Inequality: Why Economic Equality is Essential for Recovery*, (Gibson Square, January 19, 2012). Chapter 3, Figure 3.5, p. 73, Kindle locations 1125-1152.

[126] Eric A. Lord, Alan Lindsay Mackay, and Srinivasa Ranganathan, *New Geometries For New Materials*, (Cambridge University Press, 2006) ("a very simple user interface ... speed and power of the underlying C++ ... runs extremely fast"); "PowerBASIC," Wikipedia, http://en.wikipedia.org/wiki/Powerbasic .

[127] Anthony B. Atkinson, Thomas Piketty, and Emmanuel Saez, "Top Incomes in the Long Run of History," *Journal of Economic Literature*, 49, No. 1 (2011), see pages 29-33 for Census CPS failure to account for Top1%, http:www.aeaweb.org/articles.php?doi=10.1257/jel.49.1.3 .

[128] "Response by Thomas Piketty and Emmanuel Saez to: The Top 1% . . . of What? By Alan Reynolds," http://elsa.berkeley.edu/~saez/answer-WSJreynolds.pdf .

[129] Table sources: 1) U.S. Census Bureau: "Table H-2. Share of Aggregate Income Received by Each Fifth and Top 5 Percent of Households, All Races: 1967 to 2010" http://www.census.gov/hhes/www/income/data/historical/household/2010/H02AR_2010.xls

2) "U.S. Census Bureau: Table F-2. Share of Aggregate Income Received by Each Fifth and Top 5 Percent of Families, All Races: 1947 to 2010" http://www.census.gov/hhes/www/income/data/historical/families/2010/F02AR_2010.xls ;

3) Edward N. Wolff, "Recent Trends in Household Wealth in the United States: Rising Debt and the Middle-Class Squeeze—an Update to 2007, Working Paper No. 589," March 2010, Levy Economics Institute of Bard College, based on Survey of Consumer Finances, conducted by the Federal Reserve Board (SCF), "Table 2. The Size Distribution of Wealth and Income, 1983–2007", http://www.levyinstitute.org/pubs/wp_589.pdf ;

4) The Piketty-Saez series are based on income tax statistics.

"Table A1: Top fractiles income shares (excluding capital gains) in the United States", "Table A3: Top fractiles income shares (including capital gains) in the United States;"

http://emlab.berkeley.edu/users/saez/piketty-saezOUP04US.pdf

http://elsa.berkeley.edu/~saez/TabFig2010.xls

5) Congressional Budget Office: Pre-Tax Income Shares All Households, by Household Income Category, 1979-2006, downloadable at the links in the following endnote.

[130] The Congressional Budget Office provides a well-balanced data that all serious students of United States income distribution need to be familiar with: http://www.cbo.gov/publications/collections/tax , Table: "Pre-Tax Income Shares All Households, by Household Income Category, 1979-2006" (downloaded 10/29/2011); http://www.cbo.gov/publications/collections/tax/2009 ; http://www.cbo.gov/publications/collections/taxdistribution.cfm .

[131] Atkinson, Piketty, and Saez, "Top Incomes in the Long Run of History," 29, footnote 18.

[132] The Jeanes income distribution data prior to 1913 was created from two trajectories: the trajectories from known wealth and income Top1% starting points in 1774 to their earliest available estimates during the early 1900s. Then the proportional variations about the wealth trajectory were applied to the Top1% income distribution trajectory. These were then, in each year, matched with lookup table distributions. During this period, the distribution transitions were mainly slow. There were several estimates of wealth distribution, but few of income. Thus, the piggybacking on wealth distribution characteristics seemed to form the most reliable income distribution estimates and, for lack of a better option, was necessary. Prior to the year 1900, I relied heavily on: Jeffery G. Williamson and Peter H. Lindert, "Long-Term Trends in American Wealth Inequality," Table 1.12, p. 53, in James D. Smith, *Modeling the Distribution and Intergenerational Transmission of Wealth*, (Chicago: The University of Chicago Press, 1980).

---

[133] The United Nations University's WIID2C.xls, not yet updated since May 2008, http://www.wider.unu.edu/research/Database/en_GB/wiid/ .

[134] Jason Zweig, "Polishing the Dimon Principle," *The Wall Street Journal*, May 12, 2012, B1.

Perhaps the humor may not appeal to you, but when we say "Endnotes" we mean notes at the "End." The Index can be found starting at page 216.

Made in the USA
Monee, IL
08 November 2026

67383081R00142